D1526444

MEMORIES OF
AN AFRICAN
HUNTER

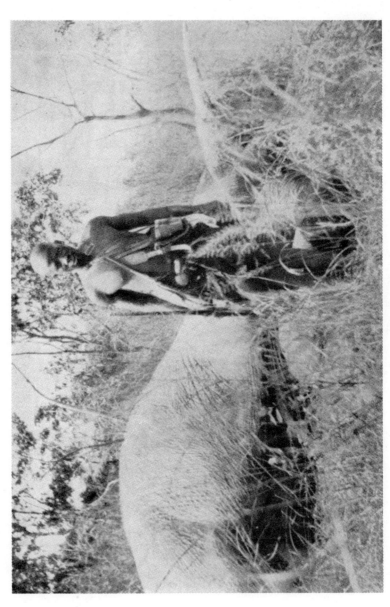

Frontispiece]

MY FIRST ELEPHANT.
Shot near Fort Manning, Nyasaland.

MEMORIES OF AN AFRICAN HUNTER

Denis D. Lyell

Peter Capstick, Series Editor

St. Martin's Press
New York

To the Reader:

The editors and publishers of the Peter Capstick Adventure Library faced significant responsibilities in the faithful reprinting of Africa's great hunting books of long ago. Essentially, they saw the need for each text to reflect to the letter the original work, nothing having been added or expunged, if it was to give the reader an authentic view of another age and another world.

In deciding that historical veracity and honesty were the first considerations, they realized that it meant retaining many distasteful racial and ethnic terms to be found in these old classics. The firm of St. Martin's Press, Inc., therefore wishes to make it very clear that it disassociates itself and its employees from the abhorrent racial-ethnic attitudes of the past which may be found in these books.

History is the often unpleasant record of the way things actually were, not the way they should have been. Despite the fact that we have no sympathy with the prejudices of decades past, we feel it better—and indeed, our collective responsibility—not to change the unfortunate facts that were.

—Peter Hathaway Capstick

MEMORIES OF AN AFRICAN HUNTER. Copyright © 1987 by Peter Hathaway Capstick. All rights reserved. Printed in the United States of America. No part of this book may be used or reproduced in any manner whatsoever without written permission except in the case of brief quotations embodied in critical articles or reviews. For information, address St. Martin's Press, 175 Fifth Avenue, New York, N.Y. 10010.

Library of Congress Cataloging-in-Publication Data

Lyell, Denis D.
    Memories of an African hunter.

    1. Hunting—Africa.   I. Title.
SK251.L829   1986   799.2'6'096   86-26260
ISBN 0-312-00155-X

First Edition

10 9 8 7 6 5 4 3 2 1

Editor's Note
to the Reprint Edition

To those sportsmen and adventurers starved for years of the truly fine antique Africana books, long out of print and commanding often incredible prices (if one is lucky enough to find first editions), this reprint of Denis David Lyell's *Memories of an African Hunter* must come as something of a godsend.

I have often pondered, if I knew I was about to be marooned, what fishing lure I would take for all situations. It would be a spinner. Given the same choice in African hunting literature, I believe I would select Lyell. If I were limited to one such book, it would most likely be this tome. Of course, I would be tempted by Stigand, Selous, Pease, and all the old shades of the world we used to know. Yet Lyell has the true gift of the anecdote, well mixed with a unique combination of humor and stark death. And in African hunting, especially early in this century, starkly was the only way that death was issued.

It was difficult to choose only one "best" Lyell book for this series, as Lyell wrote eight, including a joint effort—his first, in 1906—with the great Chauncey Hugh Stigand, one of whose works, *Hunting the Elephant in Africa*, is already part of this reprint series. Lyell, in *Memories of an African Hunter*, brings the reader the heat, fatigue, and adventure of African hunting, the smell of campfires long extinguished, the dust, the blood, the malaria, the sleeping sickness, the alcoholism, camaraderie and suicides, man-eating incidents and all those often harrowing condi-

tions of life in the British Central African bush of the day.
One had to be a survivor to tell the story, and well indeed
Lyell told it.

Denis David Lyell, a Scot, was born on February 6,
1871, in Calcutta, India. He was the eldest son of James
Carmichael Lyell and Kate Harriette Latham. Before
going to Africa in 1899, Lyell had been a tea planter in
East India, spending much time in Assam. (This book
gives some detail of Lyell's early experiences in India,
where he also hunted.) Recurring bouts of severe fever
and the desire to experience African hunting eventually
saw Lyell return to Britain for a while before going out to
Southern Rhodesia. It was not long before he was back in
India, but when the Boer War broke out in South Africa,
Lyell returned there to fight. He very nearly died of enteric fever before being nursed back to health in the brac-
ing Cape climate. The adventurous Lyell then decided to
set sail for Durban and Chinde, a seaport on the Portuguese East African coast and the only navigable mouth
of the mighty Zambezi River. This, as you are about to
discover, was the mere beginning of Lyell's African adventures.

But let him tell you in his own words—quoted from
his fine book, *Hunting Trips in Northern Rhodesia* (1910)—
what it was that drew him to Central Africa:

The reason that brought me to Central Africa was
the chance of getting some big game shooting, for
ever since I could read I had taken the greatest interest in accounts of shooting and travel in foreign
countries. I read and re-read the works of Harris,
Gordon Cumming, Baldwin, Baker, Selous, and
others who have written on African sport. . . . My
greatest ambition was to shoot an elephant, lion, and
rhinoceros, and as many more animals of different
species as I could, and to experience the life of a

hunter's excitements so well portrayed in the works I have mentioned. . . . Once a man has taken to a wandering life in the wilds of Africa, or in any other new country, he seems unable to leave it, or if he does he will surely return again. It seems to cast a spell on him. . . .

Lyell's father, who died in 1922, obviously shared his son's interest in such books and collected Africana and similar memorabilia. In fact, it was he who gave his son the much prized fifth edition of Harris' *The Wild Sports of Southern Africa*, which could only have fed the young man's African ambitions, as it did those of so many other people. Lyell's splendid and rare book, *The African Elephant and Its Hunters* (1924), is dedicated to his father. It is a diamond in my Lyell collection.

Upon arriving in Nyasaland, (now the Republic of Malawi), Lyell was fortunate to be welcomed by the officers of the 1st King's African Rifles in Zomba, where he not only found temporary employment but met Captain Stigand, who would become a great friend and literary collaborator. A gentleman and keen observer, Lyell developed an abiding love of Nyasaland and nearby Northern Rhodesia, both of which feature prominently in *Memories of an African Hunter*. The book also touches on South Africa, Southern Rhodesia, and Portuguese East Africa. Other words of his—*Nyasaland for the Hunter and Settler* (1912) and *Wild Life in Central Africa* (1913)—sustain this love of that part of Africa, as do his contributions to the Lonsdale Library, Volume XIV (1932), concerning big game shooting in Africa, and *The Hunting and Spoor of Central African Game* (1929).

If a man is to be reckoned by the company he keeps, then Lyell had few peers among African hunters. In his last book, *African Adventure* (1935), he relates in often fascinating detail his correspondence and association with people such as Selous, Stigand, Sir Alfred Pease, Steven-son-Hamilton, A. Blayney Percival, J. A. Hunter, Mil-lais, Norman Bayley Smith (to whom the book is dedicated), Abel Chapman, Karamojo Bell, and Leslie Tarlton. Through his writings and correspondence, Lyell might during his time have been called the lynchpin of African hunting, so esteemed was he by those who prac-ticed the same profession . . . possibly the most dan-gerous of all. Many fine and accomplished hunters have known Africa, but relatively few have written of their experiences, and written well. That is what enhances the value of Lyell's books.

I hunt, and I read, write, and research hunting in Af-rica. I have done so for many years. Yet never once have I heard Lyell's name besmirched. A man who believed and practiced the concept of "fair chase," he wrote (in *African Adventure*) that "A true sporting instinct and a full sense of fair play towards man or beast is largely inherited and is often the result of a decent upbringing. . . .

The present reprint has a special appeal for me, as it speaks of parts of Africa I know well, such as the Luangwa Valley. One of the most absorbing sections is contained in Chapter IX, *"Some Strange Incidents and Con-trasts,"* where Lyell tells of some of the unusual men who lived the African hunting experience, who also pros-pected and poached and who helped create legends in between bouts of sickness and various sorts of disaster. It is terrific reading.

Apart from rather minor preferences concerning cal-ibers for dangerous game, in all Lyell's work I can find only two instances in which I believe he was incorrect. The first is the matter of the death of his friend Stigand, killed by the Aliab Dinka in what Lyell said was Novem-ber 1919. He was in fact killed just after 7:15 A.M. on December 8 of that year, as borne out by the letter re-printed in this series for Stigand's *Hunting the Elephant in Africa*. The letter was to Stigand's widow from the officer who was commanding the Equatorial Battalion at the time. But it is reasonable to suppose that such details might not have been generally known to Stigand's friends in the deep African bush, even some years after his death.

The second concerns Lyell's statement as to the ages the Indian (Asian) and African elephants attain. He refers to records of an Indian elephant reaching "well over 100 years" and subsequently concludes that ". . . a wild African elephant probably sometimes reaches the age of one hundred and fifty years."

This was the theory at the time that *Memories of an African Hunter* was published, but more recent scientific research (especially that involving dental development) shows that the African elephant (*Loxodonta africana*) that ever sees sixty years of age is as rare as a chicken with fangs. But this does nothing to impair Lyell's reputation as a thoroughly reliable writer on the African hunting world, a man of integrity who had the talent and discipline to record what he lived of the now-diminishing world of adventure.

Lyell, as you will shortly determine, was a great fan of the .318 Axite caliber, although he killed much game with a variety of rifles, especially the British service caliber .303. In this book, packed as it is with memories of his years in Africa, Lyell takes the reader on hunts for the big five and a host of other game, interlacing the text with that fine gift for the anecdote I mentioned earlier. And, in so doing, he fills the reader with the inimitable aroma of Africa.

Lyell married late in life, in 1914. His wife, Marion, was also Scottish and the eldest daughter of a Dundee family named Brown. This particular book is dedicated to his wife, of whom he speaks with affection. If there were children, they are not mentioned anywhere. Considering that Lyell was in his forty-fourth year and that his roots were in Africa, the marriage was somewhat unusual for those days. . . .

Apart from his time in the Boer War, Lyell also served with the French Red Cross in the First World War, seeing considerable action at the front. That he was not a combatant was undoubtedly because of his advanced age. A formidable foe he would have been, though. Lyell received medals for his wartime activities.

He lived in Peebles, Scotland, in later life, dying on September 23, 1946. I believe that one of the most characteristic and evocative statements of this fine writer, hunter, and outstanding African personality—and a passage of which I am most fond—comes from the book you are about to read:

> But at home one is bound with petty regulations and irksome restraints. Instead of being a free wild man of the woods, one has become a herd animal. One's individualism is less apparent because there is less scope for it. People do not understand that a wanderer returned views things from a different standpoint, as his life has been spent away in the vast spaces where simplicity is the rule, and not complexity. He feels lost even in great crowds, for nothing and no one seem in sympathy. The people he knows may be good fellows, but they do not understand him, and he does not understand them. Environment (a favourite word with parsons) is at fault, because it has become foreign to him, and he longs to get back to the bush, the hills, and the plains, where he spent some of the happiest days of his life, for there he felt an exaltation that no civilized land can possibly supply.

—PETER HATHAWAY CAPSTICK

PREFACE

THE following pages contain my memories of many years spent in the African bush, where I did little else than hunt game and study their habits and tracks.

In 1906 my friend the late Major (then Captain) C. H. Stigand and myself brought out *Central African Game and its Spoor*, and then we both wrote further volumes on the game independently. I doubted whether I had enough material for another volume, but on looking up my diaries I found that there was quite a lot I had left unsaid.

The first chapter deals with some of my experiences when tea-planting in Eastern India, but I had so little opportunity there to get really good sport that I think it best here to mainly confine my attention to Africa, where I had a glorious time.

Eastern India is so jungly that without the use of trained elephants it is impossible for a man to do much with the rifle. On the other hand, Central Africa is a country where anyone can get (or perhaps I should say could get) as much shooting as he wants if he is a good walker and able to rough it in a bad climate ; for it is not a health resort.

Naturally a hunter's life in tropical Africa is not " roses all the way," although there are wonderful compensations for the hardships and fevers.

As to the dangers of hunting elephants, buffaloes, and other game, I would infinitely prefer such risks to crossing Piccadilly Circus at the busiest hour of the day. A ramping bull elephant will certainly not

7

make a greater mess of a human body than will a moderate-sized motor vehicle.

Many people say shooting is cruel, and so it is ; but not nearly so brutal as the atrocities perpetrated in dispatching domesticated stock for human consumption. A hunted animal, when fairly stalked and killed, suffers infinitely less than an ox or sheep led to its death through the blood-reek of an abattoir, therefore those who decry what they call " blood sports " are canters so long as they continue to practise carnivorous habits.

I have again to acknowledge the kindness of my friend George Garden, of Mlanje, Nyasaland, for permission to use some of his fine photographs of game, and his generosity in this way is much appreciated. The photograph of an elephant with a malformed tusk was given to me some years ago by my friend the late Captain Martin Ryan. At the time he told me I could use it for a book if I wished, and I now do so as it is an interesting example of a malformation. The other pictures were taken by myself with a film " Kodak," but are not very good as the damp and heat affect the films.

In conclusion I express my thanks to my publishers.

D. D. L.

EASTWOOD,
  BROUGHTY FERRY, N.B.
    April 10, 1923.

CONTENTS

CHAPTER I

CHAPTER VIII

LIST OF ILLUSTRATIONS

11

LIST OF ILLUSTRATIONS

MEMORIES OF
AN AFRICAN HUNTER

Chapter I   TEA-PLANTING LIFE IN EASTERN INDIA

MY first experience of the tropics was on the 6th of February 1871, when I was born in Calcutta, but these early experiences are quite hidden in the mists of infancy, and my recollections do not carry me quite so far back.

I always remember taking an extreme interest in reading books of travel, and when such volumes included stories of hunting big and dangerous game I was quite thrilled and wished I was older and able to go and do likewise.

Fortunately, there were a good many travel books in my home and plenty to be got in a good subscription library in Dundee, so I read profusely on Africa, India, and America.

I soon got to know the works of Gordon Cumming, Selous, Baker, Forsyth, Kinloch, Roosevelt, and many others almost by heart, and could have passed an examination early in life on the type of weapons used by the various hunters of big game.

Rifles with their projectiles, and shotguns and their charges, have always been hobbies, and I am afraid if I had been to-day what I was in the eighties of last century I would have been prosecuted by the Society for Prevention of Cruelty to Animals for killing cats with small rifles.

Lions and tigers being absent, I had to do the best I could on marauding cats, and after all I did not

13

see (and still cannot perceive) why it is more cruel for a human to kill a cat than for the cat to maul and torture pretty small birds. However, cat-hunting is not a wholesome subject, although I could tell quite an amusing story of one which I bagged, after many vigils, which had a blue ribbon round its neck. This animal had just mutilated a young thrush, in fact it was killed in the act.

I made a hut in a clump of fir-trees, and there I used to roast young blackbirds and think I was living a hunter's and trapper's life in the wilderness of Canada, for *Ungava* had quite fascinated me.

" Penny-dreadfuls," too, were at one time an absorbing passion, and although such literature was perhaps not the best reading for youngsters, I am sure it was manlier stuff than the melodramatic and undesirable matter shown in the cinemas of the present day.

In 1893 I went to Ceylon in the s.s. *Clan Macarthur* and spent a few months there. The voyage was very rough, especially in the Bay of Biscay, when we ran into a fierce storm. This was the gale which wrecked the old pier at Brighton, and to me the great seas and driving spray were most fascinating.

While two other men and myself were watching the ship put her bow into the large rollers we saw two seamen making for the fo'c'sle-head to fix something which had come adrift. Just as they got there the vessel plunged into a huge wave and the two men were enveloped completely. One landed on the deck below us, and the other came down on part of a winch, smashing his face horribly. The well deck was a seething mass of rushing water, so it took some time for the people who had seen the accident to get a hold of them. The one who hit the winch was unconscious, and the other, who was not so badly hurt, was also dazed considerably. The ship's doctor was

14

summoned, and in coming on to the wet deck he slipped and nearly dislocated a hip-joint, so he had to be carried back to a couch, where he lay for some time in great pain. In half an hour he was able to attend to the injured. They both recovered, though one was badly marked for life.

Later I was in another severe storm in the Indian Ocean. The P. & O. *Aden* had left Colombo about an hour before the P. & O. *Sumatra* from Calcutta, in which I was a passenger. In this storm the *Aden* was wrecked on Socotra Island, and we nearly went ashore ourselves, as the haze caused by the driving rain prevented any adequate look-out being kept. We did not know at the time that the *Aden* had gone ashore and that many of the passengers and crew had lost their lives, but we heard it at Suez when we got there.

I remember how the *Sumatra* rolled and pitched, and the state of her funnel and upper fittings when we got home. Her funnel was coated with a sheet of salt, quite a quarter of an inch thick, which had crystallized through the salt spray being dashed against it. The *Sumatra* was a steamer that did her 300-odd miles a day, but in the worst of the storm, when steaming at full speed ahead, she did less than forty for two days. The skipper was on the bridge for three days and nights, and the passengers presented him with a testimonial on reaching England. He deserved it.

In 1894 I went to a billet on Cossipore Tea Estate, Cachar, thinking that a tea-garden life probably offered me my best chance of getting some good shooting. I found that small game, such as jungle-fowl, snipe, and duck, were plentiful, but it was difficult getting shots at big game owing to the thickness of the jungles, which are mostly quite impenetrable without the help of elephants, and a poor assistant on a tea-garden was quite unable to afford such luxuries.

There were a good many tigers and leopards about, and the villagers were constantly losing cattle by carelessly leaving them out at nights. I used to sit up over kills, and twice got a shot at a tiger, missing one and hitting the other, which, however, escaped, to be found dead some time afterwards.

While at Cossipore I had two exciting experiences with two tigers—though they may have been the same tiger for all I know. One dark night the manager and I were making up some returns to send to the head office in Calcutta, when we found that a necessary book had not been brought up from the office, which was situated on the lower ground, near the factory. So the manager asked me to take a hurricane lantern and go down to get the volume.

There were two paths to the place, one a sort of native track through the tea-bushes, and the other from the front of the bungalow, by a broad avenue. I took the track and was going along, when at a sharp bend I met a fine tiger face to face, the distance certainly not being more than 6 feet. I will not pretend that I was not scared, for I was, not being accustomed to meeting tigers in the dark. I shook the lamp in his face until he must have thought there was something wrong. I can still remember the tap-tap of his tail as he swung it from side to side, touching the tea-bushes with the movement. It felt like a long period of time, although I suppose it was not more than twenty seconds, that we looked at each other. Then he gave a "wough-wough" and rushed off in the direction of the avenue.

By this time I had got over half the journey to the office, and I did not like to return and tell the manager that a tiger had frightened me home; and knowing he was rather a sarcastic fellow and would keep up

16

the joke for some time, I went for the book. When I got inside the office I shut the door and spent a few minutes in what a parson might call deep and contemplative thought, but it did not seem to do much good. Then I wondered whether the track or the wider avenue, towards which the tiger had gone, was the more healthy route homewards, and decided that as the tiger (which I have no reason to suppose was a man-eater) had missed the first chance of an easy dinner, he might not be so keen for a second opportunity, so I returned by the narrow path.

I got back all right, and admit the place looked more comfortable than it did before, notwithstanding the presence of the manager, who guffawed at the story, more particularly as he had lost no tigers himself and never went to look for any. Whether it was the same tiger which gave me a second fright I shall never know, but he, also, was not a bad sort of tiger.

A friend of mine, named Stoddard, was the assistant on the Arcuttipore Estate, which adjoined Cossipore. His bungalow was about three miles from mine, and the path led through a mass of thick jungle, intersected here and there by reed swamps. One evening I had been to dinner with him, and left for home about 11 p.m. There was no moon, but it was a clear, starry night.

I was riding the old garden pony, a nice quiet beast who had been along this path many times in his career. Having dined well, I was rather sleepy, so I gave the pony a loose rein and let him go his own pace, which was a fast walk. Suddenly, without the slightest warning, he threw up his head, which struck me in the face. Then he began to tremble all over. I knew he had winded something that did not meet with his approval, as he did not often have this kind of fit, having reached years of discretion. I gave him a crack with the cane I had and shoved my

17

spurless heels into his sides and got him to move on, still quivering with excitement. Then I heard something moving to my right and felt sure it was a tiger, and the beast was certainly keeping pace with us, for the faster the pony went the faster came the tiger, though he kept about thirty yards off in the jungle and not on the path.

I was only half-way home and quite out of hearing from both gardens, so I decided to give several piercing yells, which I did. Immediately the following sounds ceased, and I got home safely. Next day, after work was over, I rode the same pony back to the place and found the spoor (or " pugs " they say in India) clearly marked in the damp soil. When I had yelled the tiger had shot his claws out and stopped instantly, and then gone off fast. He had evidently not smelt us, but had heard the pony's feet on the hard path and had followed by sound, not scent. Had the tiger worked by scent, he would have smelt me as well as the pony, and not being a man-eater, this would have put him off. Only hearing the pony, he thought it was alone.

About a year before this a district doctor had been knocked off his pony near the same spot by a tiger and had spent the remainder of the night in a tree, listening to the demolition of his mount, so it is probable the animal which followed my pony was the same.

It was easy to tell from a " kill " whether a tiger or leopard had been responsible, as the bites of the tiger on a bullock's or cow's neck were always above, and the leopard's teeth-marks in the throttle or windpipe. While I was at Cossipore I saw quite thirty carcasses of cattle and goats killed by tigers and leopards.

During a night in the rains I was staying with the assistant on the out-garden of Felixstowe. I had intended to return that evening, but a violent thunderstorm came on, so he asked me to stay the night, which I was glad to do. Just before dark we noticed a domesticated buffalo feeding in a swamp about a mile away, and remarked what a fine chance it was for a tiger, if one was about. The natives were extremely careless, as I have said, in leaving their stock out instead of putting them in shelter and safety, especially as they knew that cattle were constantly being killed.

After dinner, at the height of the storm, we heard the bellowing of a buffalo and the growling of a tiger, and it was apparent that the struggle was intense considering the time the fight progressed. The rumbling and crashing of the thunder, the painful bellowings of the mutilated and dying buffalo, and the deep, menacing grunts of the ravening tiger were the notes of Nature at her wildest, and this was a night to be remembered.

The idealist who believes that Nature is all kindliness and peace would have been disillusioned had he been here and listened to that combat of rough strength against tooth and claw. His convictions would have suffered a change when he realized that Nature is an inexorable struggle for existence where the battle is to the strong. Darwin was right when he named it " the survival of the fittest." Civilization, with its false policy of nurturing the diseased and unfit, upsets for a time the balance of Nature, but Nature has a way of bringing the scales level again.

Mr. (now Lord) Balfour, in his *The Foundations of Belief*, says : " We survey the past and see that its history is of blood and tears, of helpless blundering, of wild revolt, of stupid acquiescence, of empty aspirations. We sound the future, and learn that after a period, long compared with the individual life, but short indeed compared with the divisions of time open to our investigation, the energies of our system will decay, the glory of the sun will be dimmed, and the earth, tideless and inert, will no longer tolerate the race which has for a moment disturbed its solitude. Man will go down to the pit, and all his thoughts will perish."

This is fine writing, but whether it is true neither the author, nor the last man who will be left toasting his frozen toes at a scanty camp fire, can know. Of one thing we may be certain, and that is that man's true God [1] is the beneficent sun, for without his warming rays we would all perish, and without him life would be absent from the face of our world.

It is a sad fact that man's knowledge is so limited, and that sooner or later the finest brains amongst us come up against that impenetrable rock which bars a further knowledge of man's true destiny in the scheme of the infinite. It is life's supreme problem.

To get back to Cachar and my early experiences on a tea-garden. Unfortunately, soon after I arrived I got badly bitten by malarial mosquitoes and for several months was very unfit. Being tormented one night, I foolishly took a clothes-brush to scrub the bites, and got a type of blood-poisoning which, with the fever, kept me seedy for some time, but I gradually became better.

At the time I reached the garden there was a spell of great heat, and for about a week the temperature hardly got below 100° at night. This was exceptional but unpleasant.

There was a nice old planter named Edgar who had previously owned the Cossipore estate and sold it to a firm in Calcutta. He had got the charge of a smaller garden near Cossipore. He was one of the old type of planters who had an open house for everyone,

[1] This remark is intended to be taken in the pantheistic sense.—AUTHOR.

20

A THUNDERSTORM AT MLANJE, NYASALAND.
Photograph by George Garden.

THE AUTHOR'S BUNGALOW ON COSSIPORE TEA ESTATE, CACHAR.

and he considered it almost an insult for a person riding past to omit to visit him. Many people who partook of his generous hospitality when he was well off were mean enough to forsake him when he lost most of his money, but he could well spare such blood-suckers, and he had plenty of friends left.

In the earlier days he had owned a steam-launch on the Barak River, which flowed past the garden, and sold it to the Government. The Bishop of Calcutta with his curate had gone farther north on a tour of inspection, and Edgar had been asked to ride out to a place (the name of which I have now forgotten) to bring the launch to Silchar, as he knew the Barak River so well. Passing Cossipore, he stopped for a drink, and hearing I had been seedy, he suggested to his friend the manager that I should go with him, as he thought the change would do me good. My manager agreed, so after lunch we started, each of us having a revolver, as we had to ride through some wild Naga villages to get to the place from where the launch and Bishop were to leave.

After we had gone some miles we nearly met with a disaster while crossing a stream. Edgar was riding rather a heavy Waler, and I was on the old garden pony. When crossing this stream, which was soft and muddy, I felt the pony's legs sinking, but he managed to recover and get out. Edgar, whose weight was greater with his heavier mount, got bogged in a quicksand. The pony sank to the girths, so I rode off to a village near to get some villagers with a rope. About twenty of them returned with me and soon hauled the animal clear. While I had been away, Edgar had managed to insert some broken branches under the beast's belly, which prevented it going under altogether, but it was a near shave for the pony, which got a bad fright and trembled vigor-ously.

Giving the villagers a tip, we went on and came to a Naga village where we heard the screams of a pig, evidently in agony. Passing through, we saw that the Nagas had bound a pig to a bamboo frame and were holding some kind of festival round the poor animal, which they were torturing in a way I shall not describe; but it was a horrible sight, especially to a youngster as I was at that time. I said to Edgar: "Let us stop them"; but he knew better than I did, I suppose, for he said: "Come on; we'll get out of this." Of course we might have had to use force to prevent the natives proceeding with their murder, and after all we could not stay long, so they would have resumed their operations as soon as we had left the place.

These Nagas are a cruel, wild lot who wear hardly any clothing and are treacherous to a degree. In wildest Africa I never saw a more primitive lot of savages. When they come in on trading expeditions to Silchar and other places, the police have to make them cover their nakedness before allowing them into the stations where there are white women about.

As we proceeded, Edgar told me that some of that tribe were mixed up with the murder of Horne, whose bungalow we passed in less than an hour from the village. Horne was murdered about a month before this date, with two *chowkidars* (watchmen) and a native woman, by a gang of scoundrels one dark night. Horne, I believe, slept with a revolver on a table near his bed. Hearing someone tapping at the door, he foolishly, being sleepy, I suppose, went to see who was there without his revolver. On looking out he was at once cut down with a sharp *dhao* (native billhook); and after the stroke he leaned against the white wall, which we saw was covered with blood. His jugular vein had been severed, and the blood had squirted some way along the whitewashed wall.

Afterwards the bodies of the two watchmen were found at the front and rear of the house, and the miscreants had also killed a native woman, near the same place, whom they had met. I forget what happened to the murderers, but I believe it was never known for certain if the police managed to get hold of the right men. This garden was one of the most outlying in Cachar, being surrounded on all sides by primeval jungle and very primitive men.

In the evening we reached the place where the launch was waiting in charge of two natives, and slept the night in the small cabin. Under the settees were capacious lockers containing food and several bottles of whisky and soda-water. These fluids led to an amusing episode next day, as I shall relate.

Next morning, soon after we had had breakfast, the Bishop with his curate arrived, so, as we wished to get to Silchar station by evening, we cast off and were soon buzzing down the river, which was very beautiful with palms, feathery bamboos, and other tropical vegetation on both sides. Bird life was also plentiful and interesting. It was very hot and muggy, so after lunch the Bishop and the curate were fixed up with pillows on the couches in the cabin, and Edgar, who was steering, and I sat under a small awning in the stern.

Edgar's only fault was a fondness for " pegs," and it was about 3 p.m. that a bottle of whisky had delivered up its last drop and he was thirsty for more. He asked me to go and get a bottle of " Scotch " and some bottles of soda from the locker, over which the Bishop was enjoying his siesta, so I told Edgar to go and get them himself. He demurred, as he said he had to steer the beastly launch, so without thinking he would do it, I said : " Run her on that sandbank." He had had several pegs since dewy morn, and he at once put over the helm and steered straight for the

23

sandbank. We were going pretty fast, but the bank was shelving, and as we hit it the launch lay over on her side and then stopped. The curate was thrown off his couch and came running to the tiny door, shouting: "What is wrong? Are we wrecked?" His face was chubby and very red and he was a typical curate, the type so much beloved of withered spinsters, but not so popular in the wild and woolly tea country.

The old Bishop, who was a fine, manly fellow, followed more sedately, and as soon as he appeared on deck Edgar dodged in and got his poison from the locker, saying: " I think this is the time a drink will do us all good."

The Bishop was not loath, as he was hot and thirsty, but his curate said: " A little soda, please; no spirits."

The launch was fast in the sand, so we hailed some natives and promised *backsheesh* for help, and it took quite two score of them to back off the launch. Nothing more of great interest happened, and we all reached Silchar in the evening, having spent quite an enjoyable day.

I think my old friend Edgar has now passed on, but I still remember his kindly, jolly face and his heart of gold. He was no saint, but, as the Scotch say, " he was nane the waur o' that," and I think his prospects of immortality were quite as good as the simple curate's.

Cachar was a wilder place in those days than I expect it is to-day, and the planters had a more glorious time. As competition became greater and business methods more detailed, the wild type gave place to tamer specimens of humanity—a change for the worse, I think.

Although I got an occasional hog-deer, there was no big-game shooting worth much, so I paid more atten-

24

tion to snipe and jungle-fowl, of which there were
fair numbers about.

A hockey (or polo) club was started, and we used
to have exciting games, especially on practice days,
when Shave, the assistant on Felixstowe, the out-
garden, and myself played with the Manipuris who
lived in the district. A brother (or, perhaps, he was
a cousin ?) of the Rajah of Manipur lived near Cossipore with some of his clan who had had to leave
Manipur for dynastic reasons. He was a man of note,
and when he rode on to the polo-ground the Manipuris would dismount, go up and make a deep bow,
going on their knees before him.

As the Manipuris have no rules at hockey on ponies,
there is much crossing, whacking of sticks, and col-
lisions which always bring much laughter, even
when a man gets a dangerous purler on the sun-baked
ground.

I had two accidents there which I will describe.
The first was due to a collision, when both parties
were unhorsed. Coming to the polo-ground with
Shave, we noticed that a bamboo bridge the garden
coolies had been repairing had been left unfinished,
with the sharp ends of the large 4-inch bamboos left
exposed, instead of being covered with earth or turf
to prevent humans and cattle from cutting their feet.
We remarked how dangerous it was, so I decided to
talk to the overseer next morning at muster-time, as
they all knew that work should not be left in this
state.

When I hit the ground my foot had turned over in
the iron and I was fast. My pony was excited and
she began to run over the ground, making for the
direction of the road which led over the bridge.
Luckily for me, Shave saw me, and having crossed the
bridge not long before, he remembered its dangerous
condition. He was riding a fast pony, so he rode

hard for the bridge, putting his spurs in and going for all he was worth. This rather excited my beast and she accelerated too, but was obstructed by my weight. She kept kicking up her legs, catching me several nasty bumps on the thighs and letting me down hard every time on the brick-like soil. Fortunately, Shave won the race, and when my pony reached his, standing across the path, she stopped and Shave got hold of the loose rein. Others came up, and the stirrup leather was pulled out of its catch and I was released, feeling very sore all over, but with all my bones intact. What remained of my shirt and singlet underneath was simply a handful of torn rags, and my back and legs were discoloured for some time afterwards.

The second accident was as follows : I was leaning far out to take a ball when the right stirrup leather and iron came away and I landed on my right shoulder on the hard ground. I felt something give and was rather sick. Shave and some Manipuris carried me to the bungalow and sent a man off for the District doctor. The time was about 5 p.m., and I waited until ten before the medico arrived, and he was rather frisky as he had been dining out. With the help of Shave he soon put in my dislocated shoulder, singing a dirge meanwhile about " Maxwelltown's braes are bonnie, etc." A peculiar thing about a bad dislocation is that it has a down-drag effect on the body and I could not lie comfortably on a bed, so they put a mattress on the floor for me, which was easier.

Just before I arrived in Cachar a planter named McDonald came to a violent end one dark night. He had been out dining with a friend, and to get there had passed through a long bamboo avenue, the sticks being on an average quite 4 inches thick. Returning fast in the dark, his pony arrived home without him, with blood on the saddle and rump. His servants set out with lamps to find him, and in the avenue found his body impaled by a bamboo, which had gone almost right through him.

What had happened was this. After he had first passed through the avenue a native had come along, and wanting a bamboo, had cut one. To cut one of these poles one bends it earthwards, and then with a *dhao*, or billhook, has to cut at a slant as bamboos cannot be cut directly across except with a saw. The slanting cut leaves a sharp point and edge very dangerous if struck hard. Poor McDonald, riding fast in the dark, had, of course, not seen the projection, and was hit just under the ribs and probably died quickly from his ghastly injuries.

It is impossible to live long in wild countries without seeing a good deal of death, and I was soon to witness too much of it.

Leaving Cossipore, and while in Calcutta, I saw an advertisement in the papers for an assistant to open out a new garden in Sylhet. I applied and got the billet, and I sometimes wished afterwards that I hadn't, for it was probably one of the hardest jobs going at that time. The place was called Ekaruni, a piece of swampy jungle belonging to the Etah Tea Estate. It was a veritable death-trap. For a few weeks I lived at Etah, going over by pony every day to superintend the work of opening out *nullahs* in the swamp called Ekaruni, and seeing to the building of a bungalow on a rise surrounded on three sides by fetid mud, and on the other by undulating ground, with forests of trees and bamboos.

While at Etah I got my head poisoned and was ill for a month or so with blood-poisoning, which made my face like a rotten turnip. My cheeks were swollen so much that both eyes disappeared to form only slits. The doctor used to come three times a week to squeeze

27

my head out, which relieved the burning pain that gave me agonies at times, especially at night, when I could not sleep at all.

Time either kills or cures, and I got better, and soon went off with my kit to take up my abode in the new bungalow. A description of tea-garden work is not particularly interesting, and during the seven years I was engaged in tea-planting my work was nearly all outside. Engineers on large estates are usually kept for running the factory where the leaf develops into the tea known to commerce. Work in the factory is even hotter than it is outside, and I preferred the latter.

Three enormous drains were made right through Ekaruni, two of them being nearly 20 feet broad and very deep. Into these channels sectional ditches, or *nullahs*, were cut to drain the intervening ground. Then the tangled jungle had to be cut down and many large roots removed from the soil if it was to be of any use for tea. Nurseries for the young plants had to be made, and these were much beloved of monkeys, which come for the tea-seed, which they like to eat. I had to shoot some of them and hang the carcasses up as a warning. I did not like killing monkeys, particularly after an incident of finding a shrivelled youngster in some long grass, evidently the offspring of one of my victims. I heard its dolorous cries and found it, a poor, shivering mortal. In revenge for its mother, or more likely in defence, when I picked it up it bit me in the thumb. I took it home and kept it for some time, but like most captive monkeys, it got a chill and died after I had got fond of it. Being starved in its babyhood, it always remained a stunted creature, and no amount of feeding seemed to make the slightest difference in its length or waist measurement, although until it got its final sickness it had an excellent appetite and was quite frisky.

28

I have two vivid remembrances of Ekaruni, one being an attempted robbery, and the other when I received a stab in the head from a native who thought it was better that I should go.

Before leaving Calcutta for Sylhet an aunt, Mrs. George Lyell, had given me a nice little fox-terrier dog called " Blackie," and it was doubtless through him that I am able to write these notes to-day.

Having about 300 coolies to pay every month, I used to get several thousand rupees sent me monthly, which I kept in a small steel safe in the dining-room of my bungalow. It was a small bungalow with a front verandah, a dining-room, and a bedroom, with a small room at the back used as a bathroom. The outside walls and the partitions between the rooms were made of reeds plastered over with mud, so were not very strong. The only weapon I had at the time was a 12-bore shotgun which fired spherical bullets fairly well. This weapon was usually in a corner of the dining-room, with a few ball and shot cartridges handy on a shelf above it.

There had been several robberies of money on the roads previously, and the matter got so bad that one or two men were usually sent as escort, armed with either old muzzle-loaders or Snider rifles. Two days before I had got in 2,000 rupees in silver to pay the labour, and it was shut up in the safe.

I was asleep, with Blackie curled up in a corner and a hurricane lantern turned low in the bathroom, divided from the bedroom by a curtain. Suddenly I was awakened by Blackie barking furiously, so I sat up and listened. Everything was quiet for a few moments except Blackie's barks and growls, but I knew something was wrong. Then I heard a sawing sound through the wall of the dining-room, and close to the safe, and I knew the rupees were the reason for my midnight visitors. At that time I was not so old,

29

experienced, and quick as I would be to-day if the same thing were to happen, so when I got my gun and had inserted two ball cartridges, instead of blazing through the wall, I shouted : " Who is there ?   What do you want ? " The *dhao* had been withdrawn by this time, but I saw a hole in the wall, about 18 inches long, by the light of the lantern.   I also heard a subdued chattering on the verandah, so shouted again : " I will shoot." They may have heard the click of the hammers going up, or thought that now I was awake their adventure was useless ; anyhow they cleared out, but this was not quite the last of them. The noise awakened my cook and bearer, and they came up from their huts to the bungalow and I let them in.

When we were standing on the front verandah, looking round in the darkness, we saw what looked like a falling meteorite go over the bungalow.   I said : " What is that?" but could not understand Hindustani very well and did not quite make out the cook's reply. Then another light came and it landed on the roof of the bungalow, so the cook went up on a bamboo ladder which I had for repairing the thatch, and recovered an arrow with some oily tow fixed to its point.   Luckily the grass was damp with recent rain, and it is doubtful whether it would have caught fire had it been left.   I now sent a ball into the jungle and the robbers cleared out, for we were no more troubled by them.   Blackie, who had been such a help, met his end about two years afterwards when in the care of a friend.   Either a jackal or pariah bit him in the neck, and he was brought to me with the wound septic and rotten, and although I tried my best, I could not save my little friend.

The other incident was peculiar in some respects. One leave-day the natives had started a quarrel among themselves in the native lines about three-quarters of

ROAN ANTELOPE BULL SHOT IN NORTH-EASTERN RHODESIA.

CHAMELEON ON PLANT, NYASALAND.
Photograph by George Garden.

a mile from my bungalow. The sounds of the row became so stringent that I decided, although feeling rather seedy with fever, to walk over to try to quell the disturbance, only taking a walking-stick with me. On getting to the huts I saw a confused mob of men trying to break each other's heads with *latees* (sticks), and it was just like what one can picture as a Donnybrook Fair, except that one wild Irishman would probably equal three Indian coolies when on the rampage.

Going up to the man who seemed to be taking a prominent part in the proceedings, I had just told him to keep quiet when, without the slightest warning, I went to sleep. When my senses began to recover there was a strange smell of iodoform in the air, and I found my back was being supported by the garden doctor *babu*, who was inquiring tenderly how I felt. On looking round there was hardly a native to be seen. They had all bolted. One or two men, who were evidently not mixed up in the affair, helped the doctor *babu* get me along to my bungalow, where a peg of whisky made me feel better. On making inquiries, I found that when I was talking to one of the ringleaders, his son had jumped on my back and struck me with a pruning-knife on the top of my skull. A pruning-knife has, fortunately, a well-rounded point, so it did not penetrate deeply, only the point went in, and though it bled profusely for a time, I was not much the worse.

The youth who was out for blood, his father, and some others were eventually caught and punished for their parts in the disturbance. As a matter of fact, I believe they had either been smoking *bhang* (hemp) or drugging themselves with opium, and did not know exactly what they were doing.

Ekaruni was a frightful place for deaths, and many of the coolies died of fever, ulcers, and cholera, the

31

latter disease being very bad in the surrounding districts at the time.

An old coolie who lived by himself was taken ill with smallpox, so I told the doctor *babu* to segregate him in a hut some way from the lines. We could get no one to carry him, so the doctor, who was a small, weak man, and myself, put him on a stretcher of bamboo and reeds and carried him to the hut. His face, body, arms, and legs were a mass of septic sores, and while carrying the head of the stretcher one of his hands, which he had put under his head, slipped and glanced over my right hand, leaving a smear of matter on it. After depositing him in his new quarters I went off and had a good wash and put some carbolic oil on my hand. Not having an abrasion, I did not suffer, though carrying and handling a smallpox patient is not pleasant.

In a few days the old man died and went to join many others in the patch of jungle near the lines, where numerous mounds of earth were all that was left of many human creatures.

Ekaruni was a very wet place in the rainy season, as it got about 450 inches in a year. It was not far from Cherra-Punji, in the Khasia Hills, which has an average of 600 inches per annum.

Before the bubonic plague devastated much of the population in parts of India, cholera was the worst scourge. I remember travelling on a river-steamer up the Bramaputra, with a lot of garden labour, bound for the Assam tea-gardens. Between Goalundo and Dibrugarh we threw fourteen bodies of men and women overboard, all of whom died within a few hours of being seized by the cholera germ. I have seen a strong man taken ill and be dead in half an hour with this horrible disease.

After spending about a year at Ekaruni (the European name for the place among the planters in the

32

district was " The Coffin "), I left for Assam, where I spent some time. I was obliged to leave Ekaruni owing to the bad state of my health, for I was full of fever. While living there the mosquitoes were so thick that I had to live and have all my meals under a large net. I also got my blood in a bad state by the bites of leeches, which often developed into deep ulcers, very difficult to cure. The leeches existed in myriads, and it was impossible to prevent them getting on one while superintending the work in the jungle. These small wire leeches are very thin before they have fed and can penetrate almost anywhere. I have seen one going through an eyelet-hole in my boot, and they transfer themselves instantly from a leaf to one's clothes. On an occasion I remember I pulled over fifty of them off my skin and clothes and dropped some salt on them, which immediately makes them vomit or dispel the blood. When I noticed the amount that came from them, I no longer wondered why I had dropped from ten to a little over seven stone in the year I was at Ekaruni. The natives suffered badly on account of their carelessness in pulling the things off after they had got their suction grip. If forcibly removed the leech takes a tiny bit of skin with it, which will likely develop into a sore and ulcer if not treated. I used to carry a small bottle of salt and put a pinch on the leech, which made it sick and release its hold immediately. Another plan is to use a sharp knife and get the blade between the sucker and flesh, but the fine salt is the best treatment.

Assam was very like Cachar and Sylhet, or the Terai Dooars, where I once spent a few months; they are all very hot and muggy and fever is rampant. Some people get the remittent and others the intermittent type. With the latter it is wonderful the regularity displayed by the attacks. I knew a man who on the same day every fortnight prepared for his attack, and

33

he was seldom disappointed, for they were usually as regular as clockwork. Doctors possibly may doubt this, but it is a fact nevertheless, at least it was so in the case of the individual of whom I write.

While in Assam I met Needham, who was well known in that part as a fine *shikari*. He was a magistrate and police officer at Sadiya on the frontier, and had shot many buffaloes and other game on foot. He told me, when I got leave, that if I cared to come to Sadiya he would give me a guide to the buffalo country, so when the time came I wrote to him and started off for Sadiya.

It was in May 1897 that I left Sealkottie, the garden I had been working on. After reaching a place called Talup, I found a bullock *gharrie* awaiting me, so I got my baggage on it and tramped in the hot sun to Saikam rest-house. When I had swallowed several cups of tea, I took my rifle and went out to try to find a deer, but saw nothing except a few jungle-fowl. For dinner I had a fowl recently killed and then got to bed. I was in bed and dozing when there was a knock at the door, so I got up and found that it was a man with a note from Needham saying he had sent me a boat and some men. A hurried *chota hazri* next morning, and I was off to Sadiya, which place we reached in three hours, as the current was against us.

Sadiya was at that time the farthest outpost on the north-eastern frontier of India, and there were some Gurkha troops there, under Needham. Their duties are mainly those of police unless there is a rising or trouble among the wild inhabitants of this part of India. The principal tribes are Abors, Mishmis, Miris, and Khamtis, all primitive races and needing a strong hand to control them. Needham, besides being such a noted *shikari*, was known throughout Assam as a most able frontier officer who always kept

34

good order in his district. His bungalow was built
on piles, and underneath it were many skulls and horns
of wild buffalo. In his house he showed me the
horns of that rare animal the takin, and also specimens of Eld's deer, which is also a localized species.
After dinner he gave me an account of the last Abor
expedition in which he took a prominent part, and
showed me a pack of cards given to him by Prince
Henri d'Orléans which he used with his companions in
their adventurous journey from China. It was here,
after many days, that he first came into contact with
a white man in the person of Needham.

Next morning, after the native *shikaris* had arrived,
I made a start. My destination was the Khampti
village of Sanpoora, about forty miles up the river
from Sadiya, and the two *shikaris* were to walk along
the bank and meet me there next day. Needham
gave me a letter to the headman of the place to act
as a kind of passport. Soon after leaving I began to
see tracks of game in the sand along the river, there
being numerous footprints of buffalo and deer, and
in one place those of wild elephants.

It seemed to me that I had now got to the land of
my dreams—a hunter's paradise—and I looked forward
eagerly to the next few days, when I might be able to
try my prentice hand on something big and dangerous. At that time high-velocity nitro rifles were
in their infancy, so I had a ·500 black-powder express
by Holland & Holland, shooting 5 drams of black
powder and heavy 440-grain lead bullets, quite a
powerful weapon and strong enough for anything, if
it were held straight.

By evening I had got three-quarters of the way to
Sanpoora, so, the men having done a good day's work,
we tied up to a sandbank and I took my rifle and went
off for a walk ashore, as I was rather stiff with sitting
in the canoe for so long. The place was littered with

35

tracks of buffalo and deer, and there were also marks of numerous pigs all over the place. I put up three large deer which were either *sambhur* or swamp deer, and had a snapshot, which missed. The jungle on the flats near the river was fearfully heavy and thick, the reedy grass being quite 12 feet high and almost impenetrable.

As it was getting dark, I returned to the boat and found my cook Kali was preparing dinner. I soon fed and got to bed, but was disturbed in the night by the grunts of a tiger not far off. I had not pitched the tent Needham had lent me, and was lying on a waterproof sheet which I had spread on the sand near where my men were sleeping. About midnight my men woke me with their chattering. On asking what was wrong, they said that a herd of buffalo had just passed the camp on their way to the river to drink. I had just got to sleep again when I was awakened by rain falling on my face and the rug which covered me. After that I could not sleep, so sat by the fire and smoked, at 2 a.m. making a cup of cocoa to warm me as the rain made it rather cold.

Just after dawn I took my rifle and had a walk, and found close to our camp a spot where a herd of buffalo had been lying down in the night. The place had a strong aromatic smell, and the grass where they had been lying was warm, so they must have just gone.

Since leaving Sadiya I had the most lovely views of the snows in the vast chain of the Himalayas which stretched along the horizon to the north. I wished I had been an artist, able to paint the charms of such views, but I did not have even a camera with me. The worst point of river travel is the fierce glare which comes off the water, at times almost blinding, and really necessitating the use of tinted glasses. I believe that eye-strain is often a cause of

36

fever; at least I have often felt feverish after my eyes have suffered glare from a hot sun, and of course such exposure often causes severe headaches.

Just before reaching Sanpoora, when rounding a bend in the river, I saw a herd of eight buffalo making for the jungle, about 300 yards away. I got my men to row to the bank as quickly as possible, and then jumped up and ran to try to intercept them. I got a shot at the last animal, I think the bull of the herd, and at my shot he stumbled and almost fell, but recovered himself and went on with the others. I followed him for some way, finding a few spots of blood, but the heavy reeds were so thick and the sun so strong that I had to give it up. As long as blood had showed I followed him, but the tracks got mixed up with many others and it was quite hopeless.

On reaching Sanpoora, about half an hour after seeing the buffalo, I was met by the headman, whose name was Sonirang, a tall, thin man, old and toothless. I gave him the letter Needham had given me for him. Many of his villagers who had collected to see the white man were badly marked with what seemed smallpox, in fact on some the sores were in a festering condition. Others had in the neck the swellings of goitre, probably caused by drinking the snow-water in the hill streams.

The old chief seemed affable and pleased to see me, but neither of us, of course, understood each other, and I had to use those of my men who understood his language to interpret what I said.

Saying good-bye to Sonirang, we pushed off for a distance of about ten miles up-stream, when we camped, pitching the tent near the water. Having slept well, I woke up and called up the *shikaris*, as I was having my morning tea. Needham told me that the man he wanted to get me was unable to come owing to an injured leg, and he did not think too much of the men he had engaged for me. One was certainly a poor *shikari*, as he was wearing a white *pugaree*, and no experienced hunter would do this. I got him to cover it with a rag so dirty that it passed for grey, and we started off. These men could not speak Hindustani, so it was impossible for us to understand each other—a bad beginning.

On coming to fresh buffalo tracks I told the hunters to follow them, but they were unable to do so for long, so I decided to walk about on chance of seeing something, keeping, of course, up-wind. After progressing through horrible country, we saw a herd of buffalo entering some thick jungle. When we got to the place the men did not fancy the job and practically refused to leave the open. It seemed rather hopeless, and, of course, my inexperience of the country and ignorance of the language were against me. I tried following alone, telling the men to wait for me, but the jungle was so thick and the reeds so sharp that I got my arms badly scratched. Foolishly I was going about with my sleeves rolled up. There must have been some irritant poison in the reeds, for soon my arms became inflamed and painful. The sun all the time was blazing down and it was terribly hot for this kind of work, and the fever in my system began to assert itself.

By the time I got back to the tent I was very bad, so had to lie down after drinking some tea Kali, my cook, had prepared for me. I now got a bad attack of fever, being burning hot and very cold in turn, and my arms were throbbing worse than ever, and so painful that I could not sleep.

Next morning I knew I was useless, for it became impossible for me to lift or use my arms, as they were festering badly with sympathetic swellings in both armpits. I had sense enough to see that the sooner I got to medical help the better. I had foolishly come away without any medicines except some quinine and phenacetin, neither of any use for festering arms. The two hunters (so-called) were to come a certain distance and then go overland to Sadiya, so I managed, with great difficulty as my fingers were numb and swollen, to write a note to Needham explaining my circumstances. I promised a present to the boatmen if they got to Saikam in the evening, and they worked splendidly all day, getting six times the pace out of the canoe with the current that they did coming up-stream.

As I was pretty bad I passed a very uncomfortable day lying on the bottom of the canoe on a waterproof sheet, and had no food until we got to Saikam, which we reached as the sun was sinking in the west. Kali prepared some tea, and, eating a few biscuits, I turned in on a shaky bed in the *dak* bungalow, arranging for a bullock *gharrie* to take the baggage and myself to Talup next day.

Eventually I reached Sealkottie, and with the doctor's help got better in a few weeks. He told me, if I had not come back when I did, I might have never recovered, as I was full of poison.

Although this shooting trip was not a success, it was a good lesson in many ways, and up to the time I had got ill I enjoyed it immensely. Compared with the African days ahead it was a fiasco. The lovely scenery and the abundance of game were all most interesting, but I made a mistake in starting at the break of the rains when the weather was uncertain.

Assam, in its more northerly parts, was a very wild country at that time and teemed with game. It was, however, a rough country to shoot in, as a man on foot was quite unable to get through most of it, and elephants were necessary to get about the place. In the morning one would hear the loud cries of the

Hooluk monkeys when they woke up and began to move about. Monkeys in a country like this have to be wary, as the leopard is fond of their flesh and lies in wait for them when they come to drink in the evenings.

When in Cachar I knew a planter named Bradford who had only one arm, having lost the other in a gun accident when a boy. He had a partially tame Hooluk which used to sit up in the roof of his verandah on some cross-poles. Bradford had a favourite joke which he always put into action with new-comers who had not heard of his monkey. Getting one nicely placed under the ape, he would offer a banana, and if one took it, the monkey had been taught to drop down on one's head and shoulders and grab the fruit. It gave one a start to be enveloped by a large, hairy thing such as a Hooluk, and on one occasion he made an enemy for life of a magistrate's wife he had played the joke on, as the quadruped sent her into a faint and ruined a nice London hat she had recently got from home.

Besides the monkey, Bradford kept a fighting ram in a paddock in front of his bungalow. He would offer one a plank of wood about 3 feet long, and bet 5 rupees that you would not stand the rush of the ram when he charged. The conditions were that one must stand up to the animal and not jump aside. Most people took the bet, and on the impact, which was exceedingly heavy, they got a good purler, much to the amusement of those who were watching the show.

The proper procedure for the occasion was to grip the plank firmly with both hands at the top, using one foot to jam the bottom of it. Then it was possible to stand the shock of impact, though one almost reeled back with the hard blow and vibration. Before an Indian ram charges, he steps backwards first of all

40

and then comes on with a swift rush. My first attempt saw me describe a somersault, with the ram doing his backward step a few feet away, so I got over the fence with my knees rather stiff. Then Bradford gave me the tip, and I had another go, which was more successful this time.

Bradford, notwithstanding his single arm, was an excellent shot at snipe and other small stuff. He was a nice fellow, but, like all the old planters, was rather fond of refreshers, a habit which, carried to excess, usually means a short life and a merry one. A good plan is to make a point of not drinking until sundown and then going slow. Advice is cheaper than whisky!

While at Cossipore I heard that a planter named Crozier had shot a leopard with snipe-shot, after it had got into a fowl-house. Owing to the darkness he missed it with his first barrel, but laid it out with the second shot, and I saw the skin afterwards, and noticed that the shot had gone in like a ball.

I had rather an exciting evening sitting up for a tiger which had killed a cow amongst the tea-bushes, close to a patch of jungle. A large clump of bamboos was within 20 yards of the kill, so I had a *machan* made in them, about 12 feet from the ground.

The moon was not due to rise until about 8.30 p.m., and it got dark before seven o'clock, so I was in my place by then. I had told the natives not to come near unless they heard a shot, so as not to be disturbed. The mosquitoes were a great nuisance, and so were the ants, and I noticed that a *machan* in a clump of bamboos was not very satisfactory, as the slightest movement caused the stems to rub and make creaks and squeaks. There were two small *nullahs* in front with a raised path between, beyond that a stretch of tea, and farther off the jungle.

When it got so dark that I could hardly see the kill, I heard the tiger coming from the jungle in

41

front, as he made quite a noise breaking sticks and rustling the vegetation. Foolishly, I was facing the kill, as I thought he would come from another direction, and I ought, when there was time, to have changed my position. Suddenly I heard him jump the *nullah* in front, and get on the path, so I tried to move round to get a shot, but the bamboos creaked so loudly that I had to desist. He evidently heard the noise, for instead of coming to the kill, he went into the jungle behind the *machan* and then came right under the *machan*, where he lay down. I heard him licking himself and give several low sighs of what sounded like contentment. My legs got so numb and the mosquitoes were biting so hard that I simply had to move. When I did so he left at once, as I heard him go off quietly. Of course it was dark and the tiger was quite hidden in the thick grass, and I could see nothing when looking down. It was a sickening experience, for the tiger did not return; so by not facing in the right direction to start with, I lost a grand chance.

When after a rogue elephant later in Assam, I lost a leopard I fired at, and a short account may be of interest. Coming back one day from chasing the elephant through some horrible jungle and swamp, we saw a small cowherd running towards us. He said a *chota-bagh* (leopard or panther) had just killed a cow in some thick grass to which he pointed. We went there and found the cow, so I got my men to fix up a platform in a tree near, which they did very quickly. Telling them to talk loudly when leaving, I had only sat about ten minutes when I saw the leopard lying close to the kill. How he got there without my seeing him I can't say, but I did not see him come. I fired at him immediately, using a black-powder Rigby ·500 I had bought from Manton's in Calcutta, for the elephant hunt. The black-powder smoke hung like a grey blanket in front. Suddenly I saw the leopard's head and paws come through the smoke as he came for my feet, which were hanging down. I pulled them up and nearly fell backwards out of the tree, as the platform was open behind. The leopard failed to secure a hold and fell down the trunk, making a loud scratching sound with his claws, and bounded off into the grass. The natives arrived and we followed him without success.

Soon after that I got very ill with fever and had to go to the Calcutta hospital for treatment. Through the attentions of Dr. Pilgrim and his nurses I soon recovered, and soon after that went to South Africa, which shall be the subject of my next chapter.

I am afraid my accounts of Indian sport are poor, but I promise my reader more interesting material when I come to write on the African bush, which offers much better shooting than the thick and impenetrable jungles of Eastern India, where one can do little without the help of elephants.

IN 1899, having suffered a good deal from fever in Assam, I came home, and my father kindly made it possible for me to visit Mashonaland.

The journey from Cape Town to Bulawayo was by train, so as the railway at that time found its terminus in the latter place, I set about finding a transport rider to take me on to Salisbury. At last I was introduced to a fine old Boer named W. Vanzyl, who was shortly starting with three wagons for Salisbury, so I came to an arrangement with him to take me and my baggage for £5. The mule coach which ran between the two places charged considerably more and only 30 lb. of baggage could be taken.

My chief object was to try to get some shooting, and I had brought with me a double ·500 black-powder " Express " rifle by Holland & Holland given to me by my father, and one of the new magazine ·303 rifles kindly presented to me by a friend in Scotland. I wished to experience some of the trekking I had read so much about in books on Africa, and what made me particularly interested was that old Vanzyl had known Selous when he hunted so much in Mashonaland, and had been an elephant hunter himself for a time. He could only speak broken English, and of course I could not speak Dutch, but we managed to understand each other in our long talks over the camp-fire in the evening. His wife, who knew not a word of English, and five wild children were with him, and at night all slept in the half-tented wagon

44

of the splendid black span of oxen. He had three spans, one all black, another all red, and the last of mixed colours. The first wagon he drove himself with a small Mashona boy as a leader, and there was a driver and leader for both the other spans.

At first, when we made the bargain, he promised to rig up a tent over one of the wagons for me to sleep under, but he never did so, so I slept under a wagon every night and was often very cold, especially the hour or two preceding dawn, always the coldest part of the night.

Each wagon was loaded with 10,000 lb. of goods, which I noticed consisted of tinned provisions with a very good proportion of whisky—called " Scotch " in Africa. As Vanzyl was getting 17s. 6d. per 100 lb. for his transport, he was making quite a lot of money, and I believe he owned an excellent farm in the Transvaal where he bred the fine trek oxen he had with him.

The Boer children used to amuse me with their fights, particularly when a fowl was to be killed, as the two eldest would quarrel for the honour of being executioner, and the matter invariably ended in their pulling the head off the body. Mrs. Vanzyl used to bake very good bread in an anthill, and never did so without presenting me with a small loaf or large chunk, and it was very good, as I had only brought biscuits, some tea, sugar, and tinned provisions. One of the wagon drivers was a Basuto boy named Abram, with whom I came to an arrangement to clean my utensils and cook at times. He was an obliging native and a hard worker.

Most of the trekking was done early in the morning and late in the afternoon, often until late at night. During the day the cattle were sent off into the bush for water and to feed and rest, the leaders of the teams acting as cattle-herds.

45

The month, being July, was the dry season in that country, with cool nights, but the days were very hot, so Vanzyl and I used to go about in a shirt, only wearing a coat late in the evenings and early in the mornings. I got some shooting after tramping for many miles during the time the cattle were feeding and resting, and was successful in shooting a fine kudu bull and also a good waterbuck bull, the heads of which I still possess.

We passed many spots well known in the history of Southern Rhodesia, and some of the forts used by the colonists in the native rebellion were just as they had been left, and a few graves of men who had fallen could be seen in places.

Once, when far in the bush, I nearly fell down a deep hole made by a gold prospector. Luckily I managed to get hold of a cross-pole and drag myself clear, but it wobbled badly. If I had fallen in, I certainly could not have got out without help, as it was too wide to grip with back and feet. Being quite eight miles from the wagon, there would have been another bush tragedy for someone else to relate had I gone to the bottom.

After a trek of five weeks we reached Salisbury, and I said good-bye to Vanzyl and his family. When here I heard of an appointment on a tea-garden in India, so decided to return there, and travelled to Beira via Umtali with two other men who wished to catch the s.s. *Umkuzi* for India. Our train broke down, but fortunately a goods train was just leaving the place where we stuck, so we transferred ourselves and baggage to an empty open truck and were showered with sparks from the wood burned by the engine, getting our clothes and baggage damaged considerably.

On the way to Umtali the passenger train caught fire twice with the wood sparks which settled on the roof of a carriage, and the fires were put out with

46

KUDU BULL.

Shot and photographed by George Garden.

46]

water-bottles. We ran into a cloud of locusts which made the rails so greasy that the train nearly had an accident on a down-grade, but all that happened was that two carriages left the metals. The driver, stoker, guard, and some of the passengers helped jack the carriages back again.

Another most amusing incident was when the train suddenly stopped. On looking out, the driver and stoker were seen to be having lunch under a large shady tree close to the line. After twenty minutes they started the train off again, until something smashed in the engine and, as I have mentioned, three of us left in a goods train and just managed to catch the steamer at Beira, a sandy place with a bad climate.

When I was in the Dooars (Terai) the South African War broke out, so I left my billet to go to Calcutta to join Lumsden's Horse, but got a bad attack of fever and could not manage to leave with them. After getting better I left for home, and after ten days started off for South Africa, and when I reached the Cape joined the Western Province Mounted Rifles. I had really no wish to shoot Boers or be shot by one of them, but craved for excitement.

As so much has been written about the Boer War, I need not say much here except that in three months I got a bad attack of enteric fever, and was carried for ten days among the baggage in a Cape cart and left at the small hotel owned by an old Scotchman named Macgregor, who had married a Dutch woman by whom he had a large family. I got a complication called pericarditis, and had bad bed-sores and vile toothache a great part of the time.

At last I got better and went to Ceres, and then spent some months in Cape Town, which was too civilized for me. Then the opportunity came for my getting to Nyasaland, so I booked a passage in the *Kildonan Castle*, and was not sorry to see Table

Mountain, Devil's Peak, and Lion's Head fade into the far distance, for I felt that adventures were ahead.

Reaching Durban on the 3rd of March 1903, a passenger named Pellatt and myself went to a boarding-house in the suburbs situated near Durban Bay, which looked pretty with small yachts and boats sailing about when the tide was in. Pellatt had fought in the war as an officer of the Rand Rifles, and was an old colonist who had many interesting tales to tell of the early days in South Africa, especially about the diamond fields and gold diggings. One of his stories was about a snake-stone which he said belonged to a farmer named Jones, whose farm was called Reitpoort, near Zeerust. Pellatt's description was a little vague, as he said it was not really a stone, but a horny substance which grows out over the eyes of an uncommon kind of snake, which he could not name. I could hardly credit this, and asked him if he was joking, but he assured me that he was quite serious, and I believe he was.

Selous mentions a snake-stone in his excellent book *Travel and Adventure in South-East Africa,* and describes it as being " of a very light and porous substance, round and flattish, an inch or so in diameter, and about one-third of an inch in thickness. Its upper surface was smooth and polished, with blackish and greyish mottlings, its underside being rough and unpolished." Selous also states how the stone he so fully describes was the means of saving the life of a white girl who had been bitten by a deadly snake. This stone belonged to a farmer named de Lange, and Selous wrote his description some time after seeing it.

Pellatt described the action of the stone which belonged to Jones as follows. On being placed on a wound, it adhered to the spot and was allowed to rest there for some minutes, when it was taken off and placed in some ammonia, or urine, when the poison came away like a white thread. This account exactly tallied with the one Selous mentioned. All the same, in the case of snake-bite I would rather depend on a gash made across the bite and rub in some permanganate of potassium crystals which I always carried with me for snake-bites and wounds. On two occasions I used it on a native with good results, except that in both cases the native had to be held down for the operation. Natives make horrible wounds on their feet by hitting stumps, and often a whole nail is removed, but they only grin. Yet if one wishes to make a slight cut, they run like hares to get away, which is rather amusing.

A small steamer, the *Induna*, having arrived from Chinde, I went down to the docks and met a man named Keyte, who told me a lot about Nyasaland, as he had just come from there.

I bought in Durban a magazine ·303 Lee-Enfield, as I could not think of going to a game country without a rifle. With this weapon I shot quite a lot of game later on.

At the boarding-house (Fernvilla) I met a man named Wolhuter from Umtali, who was a brother of the Transvaal game-ranger who, when he was knocked off his pony by a lion, killed it with a sheath-knife. The full story of this incident is given by Major J. Stevenson-Hamilton in his interesting book *Animal Life in Africa* (published by Heinemann) and is quite true, although I have heard some people doubt the story.[1]

At last I got away in the s.s. *Induna*, one of the oldest boats on the coast. She harboured many enormous cockroaches, and some of the fiercest mosquitoes I had yet met. There were a good many passengers

[1] Sir Alfred Pease, Bt., in *The Book of the Lion*, gives an interesting chapter on this incident which is well worth reading.—AUTHOR.

49

on board, most of them booked for Beira. The officers of the ship were pleasant men, the first, named de Pass, being a particularly nice fellow. We reached Beira on the 10th of May.

A passenger named Ford was to go on by the *Nyasaland*, a steamer belonging to the company which employed him, as he wished to get to Blantyre quickly, so he asked me if I would care to come with him ; so we got our kit transhipped from the *Induna* and said good-bye. There was little room on this vessel, which was hardly more than a tug, and her cockroaches beat the *Induna's* easily for size, and her mosquitoes were just as voracious. I slept on deck, and passed a comfortable night notwithstanding the perambulations of many rats, which seemed to spend most of the night in investigating the queer bundle which had invaded their domain.

A German East African liner which was anchored near us had a brass band on board, the raucous sound carrying very far. How these Teutons like to make a noise—it seems to refresh them and stimulate their love of beer ! At this time the Germans were getting a lot of the East Coast trade into their hands, and they never did a worse thing for themselves than when they forced a war on the world, as it will take them generations to recover what they have lost.

On the 13th of May 1903 we reached the Chinde bar, where all large vessels have to anchor to drop their passengers, who are put aboard a tug called the *Kadett*, belonging to the German East Africa Line. They have another tug called the *Adjutant* which is similarly used. A large basket is filled with passengers, taking about half a dozen, and then hoisted with a winch and dropped on the deck of the tug, sometimes landing with a big bump when there is a sea on. The baggage is put into a large net, and put aboard the tug, and I once saw a passenger's

DAR-ES-SALAAM, IN EAST AFRICA.

ROAD TO MLANJE PLATEAU, NYASALAND.
Photograph by George Garden.

box slip off and fall into the sea, much to his indignation, which was natural. It is wonderful how amusing such an incident is to the people who do not own the baggage!

After all, the *Induna* came up to the bar before we were able to get over it, so our change at Beira was trouble wasted.

As soon as the tide rose high enough we went on, and soon got over (taking a bump or two) and into the Zambezi River opposite the British concession. Chinde belongs to the Portuguese, but they rented a concession to the British, as nearly all the trade for Nyasa-land and Northern Rhodesia is in British hands and passes through without duty, I believe.

Chinde is an extraordinary spot, being built on sand, quite a foot deep in places when it is dry. It is beastly stuff to walk in, as it slips under one's feet. Beira is much the same in a lesser degree. This mouth of the Zambezi (it has several mouths) is constantly changing, necessitating the shifting of the buildings and stores. The African Lakes Corporation, Ltd. (called " Mandala " all over the country) and the British Central Africa Company (called " Kubula "), as well as other concerns, have large offices and stores here and in other places, from which one can buy all kinds of goods.

I took my passage in the river-steamer *Scorpion*, one of the oldest boats on the river. We had dinner on the little upper deck with the skipper, Deans, who was quite a character, closely resembling that erratic personality in fiction the gallant Captain Kettle. If the artist who drew the pictures for Cutcliffe Hyne's stories had not seen Deans, he certainly depicted his features exactly in Captain Kettle.

The *Scorpion* was only expected to get as far as Chiromo, as the water in the Zambezi was rather low.

At last I had reached Central Africa, which had

51

been the land of my dreams for a long time, and it gave me a welcome in a most lovely sunset that evening, colouring the river and mangroves beautifully.

There were three passengers on the steamer who were going to the Universities Mission—two ladies, Miss Matthew and Miss Bulley, and a man named Swinnerton.

Next day, the 15th of May, we left Chinde with two barges fixed on either side of the steamer. An hour after starting I saw a hippo rise to the surface, but when we got close he went under. Later I was to shoot many hippos in the Zambezi and other rivers, but I never thought of firing at this animal from the swaying deck of a steamer. Many of the unfortunate animals are fired at by thoughtless people and are wounded, for it is absolutely impossible to put in a vital shot under these circumstances unless it is a palpable fluke. From the bank one can get a steady shot, and I think that shooting at the animals from a steamer should be prohibited. When in a small boat, or dugout, it is occasionally necessary to put a shot into a hippo, as they sometimes attack and sink small boats. Many a native has been drowned in Central Africa by such an attack, and often it is the animals wounded from steamers which cause the mishap, as they are naturally morose and bad-tempered after receiving a painful wound with a rifle bullet.

As darkness came on it was interesting watching the shower of sparks from the funnel of the steamer, due, of course, to the wood fuel used in the furnaces. The steamer forged ahead in the darkness, so the native pilots must be very expert to pick their course under such circumstances with no lights to guide them. About 11 p.m. we anchored for the night and then went to bed. Next day the steamer started very early, and just after I got out of my cabin I saw a lot of ducks and some geese, also two hippos rising not far off. It is splendid seeing such animals from a modern steamer, but I am afraid not many years will elapse before such a sight will become very rare. The morning air was very chilly, and a warm tweed coat was a comfort. Africa can often be bitterly cold at night.

The scenery reminded me strongly of the Bramaputra River in Eastern India, though there the river-steamers are much more palatial than the steamers on the Zambezi at that time. The river-banks, too, were not unlike those one sees on an Indian river, with palms, native huts, and the young children who run along with the steamer and fight for empty bottles, biscuits, and anything that is thrown ashore. Parts of the banks, of course, are wild, and the villages only occur here and there. Many large patches of reeds are seen, into which the hippo often retire to escape notice, and to rest in solitude. It is wonderful how wild life gets accustomed to the sounds and sights of civilization, for on the Uganda Railway one can see great numbers of the different species feeding close to the train as it passes them, rumbling and whistling. It would be the same here with the hippos were they not molested so much by the more ignorant and heartless among the whites.

The two barges were very heavy, as they were taking a lot of sleepers for the new Nyasaland Railway, and I was glad that I was able to say that I had reached that country before a beastly railway was made. On the barges was also carried a quantity of firewood for the steamer, which prevented us stopping to pick it up at the wooding-stations we sometimes passed on the banks. The wood soon goes, however, and the following day we had to stop and take some on, so the passengers made a fire to warm themselves on the bank and sat and smoked for an hour or two. There were the remains of a hippo here, as strips of the skin were hung up to stretch and dry. The skull was not very large. After starting we nearly got aground, but the steamer managed to scrape over the sandbank.

A spark from the funnel burnt a large hole in a good double " Terai " hat I had on—which is a common event on steamer travel, so the skipper told me. I was amused at seeing the joy of another passenger, who thought it a great joke, while all the time a larger hole was being burnt in his own hat without his knowing it!

Double " Terai " hats do not grow on every bush in Nyasaland, but one or two stores keep them in Blantyre, Zomba, and Fort Jameson.

When we had passed Shupanga Mission-station (now gone, I believe) we went on for half a mile and then stopped, so some of us went ashore to see Mrs. Livingstone's grave. She was, of course, the wife of the famous missionary explorer, and before her marriage was Miss Moffat, the daughter of Dr. Moffat, also a fine old missionary. She died here in 1862, and the stone is in a fair state of preservation. There is a flat stone over the grave and an erect stone at the head, with the inscription on it. The dried skull of a fair-sized crocodile was lying on the flat stone, so I picked it up to throw it away, but on second thoughts kept it to send home, and it is now amongst my trophies.

Dr. Livingstone, as most people know, died at Chitambo's village, North-Eastern Rhodesia, in 1873, and his " boys " (native servants) buried his heart under a tree and carried the body to the coast, where they were met by a search-party. The remains were taken home and rest in Westminster Abbey. Some years afterwards, about the late eighties of last century, the tree was showing signs of decay, and the inscription, which the thoughtful natives had cut, was getting grown over by the bark and suffering from the weather. The tree was cut down, and the base with the inscription sent to the Geographical Society in London.

When in Fort Jameson in 1904 I saw some branches of a tree in a store, and asked the storekeeper why he kept firewood there. He told me the branches came from the Livingstone tree, so I asked permission (as did a friend with me) to cut off a few segments with a saw. I took two pieces, one of which I gave to the Scottish Geographical Society in Edinburgh, as they had not a piece. The Secretary, in thanking me, said it would be put in a glass case with a full description of its authenticity. I kept the other piece, and though I have given a few bits to friends, it is still an interesting memento of a great man and explorer.

After the tree at Chitambo's village was cut down, a monument was raised in its place with a full description of the historical event.

Dr. Livingstone was an indomitable man, calm and patient, and just the type of explorer suitable for what he did. He was helped greatly in his earlier days by that splendid hunter, William Cotton Oswell, who spent five years hunting in the game districts of South Africa when animals teemed there. It was really Oswell's expedition that discovered Lake Ngami, when Dr. Livingstone and Mr. Murray were his companions. Dr. Livingstone usually gets the credit of the discovery of this lake, but it was really Oswell's expedition, as he was paying the expenses of the trip.

There were two other graves near Mrs. Livingstone's at Shupanga—one of a Portuguese, and the other of Catherine Cameron, of the Blantyre Mission, who died in 1887. She must have been among the first of the women missionaries to Central Africa. One could not help admiring the courage of a woman who had left her home in Scotland and come here to die for the cause she had taken up, for then, as well as now, this is a rough country for British women to live in.

A strange thing about the inscription on Mrs. Livingstone's memorial was that it was given in Portuguese, not English.

After leaving the graves, we called on the French missionaries in the large house they have, surrounded by gardens. Then the steamer went on and we came to a place named Lacedonia, which struck me as a peculiar name to find in this country. The country to the south is covered with forest, known as the Shupanga Forest, a favoured haunt of elephants and buffaloes, which still exist there. The Morambala Mountains now came in view, and they break the monotonous line of the flat country all round them.

A river trip is always interesting with the bird life, which is, however, not nearly so plentiful here as what I have seen on the large Indian rivers. We saw a few crocodiles every day, sleepy-looking beasts as they lie basking in the sun on a sandbank.

We passed the steamer *Herald* on the 18th bound for Chinde. The *Herald* was an old river gunboat and so was the *Mosquito*, which I saw in Chinde. All the river-steamers on the Zambezi at that time had stern paddles, and not side ones like the larger Indian river-steamers. We then entered the Shire River, a name I knew well from reading books on this country.

That evening we stopped at a place called Villa Bocage. We took a walk ashore to stretch our legs, and late in the evening walked along a bush path and I saw a large, light-coloured animal cross from one side to the other. I think it was a lioness.

There is a muddy stream near the Shire, called the Zwei-Zwei, which cuts into the larger water in places. We passed another steamer going down-stream, and I noticed a white woman on board. Then we reached Shuanga and put some of the railway sleepers ashore.

As we were to leave the steamer soon, I packed up two bags as we were to go on in a houseboat.

We stuck on sandbanks several times daily, but soon got off. Going on in the darkness, we nearly rammed a steamer anchored in midstream without any lights showing, and there was some bad language from our skipper. As the river is only twenty-five yards broad, there is not much room in it for two steamers to pass.

On the 21st we reached Port Herald, and just before getting there I noticed two hippos lying dead at the south side of the river, and soon after a Dutchman (or Hollander), named Sinderam, came on board and told me he had shot them, and said he had caught a young one. Seeing that I took an interest in animals, he asked me to come and see it, so, as this was the end of the steamer journey, I was glad to do so. Sinderam had two *machillas* handy, so we were carried to the place where the natives were cutting up the two hippos, and where the young one was tethered to the bank with a strong rope.

At a cutting-up scene the natives yell and jostle each other to get a share, and these gatherings round a large animal are most amusing to watch and I enjoyed many such scenes later in my travels. The young hippo soon died of the wounds it had received in the neck and back. It seemed a cruel act to kill it, but natives seldom miss an opportunity of getting meat.

Sinderam was making the arrangements for *machillas* to take the party of five on to Chiromo, for though the skipper thought in Chinde that he would get that distance, he found that the depth of water in the river prevented it. The three missionaries left at 10.30 p.m., and Ford and I stayed for a time with Sinderam, as he insisted on opening several bottles of champagne and getting in a big supper for our benefit.

57

Although the clouds dropped no rain, it was a wet evening, but at last Ford and I got away about midnight, the *machilla* men going on fast through the path which leads for part of the way through the old elephant marsh. This is a great country for lions, but these *machilla* men sing at the pitch of their voices, so no lion interfered with us that night.

When Sinderam said good-bye to us he put a letter into my hand, which he told me not to open until I got to Blantyre. On reading it there, I found he had written that, if I failed to find an appointment in Nyasaland, he would be glad to put me up in his house as long as I wished to stay. As I had only seen him for a few hours, I think that was a very kind action on his part, though it was never necessary for me to accept his hospitable offer. When a country gets crowded and more artificial this spirit is absent, as the conditions make it impossible to entertain all strangers in this way. It is this open-hearted friendliness which helps to draw one to a new country, for this is the true spirit at the " edge o' beyond."

Once when Sinderam was on a trading expedition with a friend called Walker, their *ulendo* (party) was attacked by the natives, who killed a number of their carriers. I have heard men run him down, and promptly told them how he had treated me, which soon put a stop to disagreeable remarks. I always take a man as I find him, which is the best way, as nobody is without an enemy in this world.

The B.C.A. Co. arranged a small barge to take the party on to Katunga's village. In it was one cabin which the two missionary ladies occupied, and Swinnerton and I lived on an upper deck. Ford went overland, as he was in a hurry to get to Blantyre.

Next morning saw the native crew poling the unwieldy barge up-stream, and we got to Katunga's at 7 p.m. on the following day. The agent for the

B.C.A. Co. was named Hastings, and he arranged for *machillas* to take us on next morning. Noticing that he had lost some fingers from his right hand, I asked him how it happened, and he told me that he had loaded some cordite into black-powder cases and fired one from his express rifle, which was not nitro-proved. The rifle burst, with the result that he blew off some fingers. It is wonderful how careless some people are with firearms !

Next morning we left, and got to Blantyre at 6 p.m., very glad to get out of the *machillas*, which shake one up considerably. In subsequent years I hardly used the things again, doing all my trekking on foot, which suited me better.

I went to Keiller's Hotel in Blantyre, and when there heard of an appointment in The Camp, Zomba, so I went there and got the post from Captain C. H. Stigand, after I had given him a note from Major Pearce, who was then Acting Commissioner for Nyasaland, as the Commissioner, Sir Alfred Sharpe, had gone home on leave.

In Blantyre Judge Nunan had helped me by writing through to Zomba on my behalf. Several people I had met in Blantyre, like Sinderam, asked me, if I was stuck, to come and live with them for a bit, so the country seemed full of good fellows.

At The Camp I met the officers of the 1st King's African Rifles, and it was arranged that I was to have a good brick house to live in. My work was to help the Quartermaster in his office, and though I did not fancy quill-driving, I was really lucky to get the start, as billets were not too plentiful.

When I had arrived in Zomba I went to the house of the agent of the B.C.A. Co., a nice fellow named Renny. As the date was the 7th of June and I did not need to start at The Camp until the 9th, I got a bit of excitement, for on the 8th a native came to Renny and told him a lion had killed a woman about eight miles from the township. Renny would have liked to go, but was too busy, so he asked me if I would care to tackle the job alone.

To get to Zomba one day and have the chance of a shot at a lion the day after was something I had never contemplated, and I got ready at once. The native marched in front of me to show me the path, and carried my rifle. It was very hot and I was not suitably dressed for a job like this, so simply baked. The comfortable kit for tramping in Nyasaland is a khaki shirt, khaki shorts, bare legs, and boots or shoes.

At last we got to the village where the tragedy had taken place, and I was met by the headman, who took me to a grass hut, where he pointed to a body lying on the mud floor. There was a frightful smell, as the lion had eaten a good part of the woman, and the whole place reeked of blood. It seems that the husband of the woman had been in the hut when the lion got through the wall, and he immediately took a header through the opposite side, leaving his spouse for the invader. I must explain that the hut was a temporary affair, and not a strongly made hut of poles firmly sunk in the ground. It was simply made by putting in small poles some feet apart and filling up the spaces with grass to form a wall all round. Natives often make these flimsy abodes to live in until they can build a strong hut. However, lions sometimes smash their way into very strongly built huts, as I was able to see later on in my travels.

The natives soon collected, some of them having spears and a few with a bow and arrows. We beat through the heavy grass, which was still green, as it was not dry enough to burn in the annual grass fires which occur later in the season. Once we disturbed the lion, which went off, giving low grunts, but all we saw was the waving of the tops of the grass. Then we came to a large thorn-bush with a little of his mane-hair hanging to it, and also some bits of the woman's flesh which he had taken from the hut the previous night. An old man who had climbed an anthill shouted out something in an excited way, which, as I did not understand the language, I could not make out except I knew he had got a glimpse of the lion. I ran up the anthill, and only saw the grass waving about seventy yards away. I was inexperienced then and ought to have had a drive. I thought of it, but was unable to make them understand what I wanted.

As I had to get back to Zomba, and saw it was a hopeless game, I went back to the village, which was near, and the old headman brought a mat out of his hut and asked me to sit down. Then his wife brought a big pot of native beer and a dish of what I saw were roasted locusts and put them in front of me, giving a deep bow on the mat by going on her knees and bringing her head low. This was polite, but I have found that natives are usually courteous, especially the wilder type who have not been spoilt by the ways of civilization. I was glad to quench my thirst with the beer, but though I tried a locust, I could not manage it and had to eject it into my handkerchief when ostensibly trying to blow my nose.

Then the man who had guided me to the village and myself left for Zomba, which we reached a little after dark.

Next morning at The Camp I told Stigand of my previous day's experiences, and he showed me something which had to be done and left with Olivier (an officer in the K.A.R.) for the village, as they thought the lion would probably return if the remains had been left alone.

On returning next morning he told me that unfortunately, in the evening of the day I had left, they had found the presence of the corpse too much for them, so had set fire to the grass hut and burnt everything up. Stigand and Olivier, despite of that, sat up in a hut near the place and heard the lion moving about in the grass close to the village, but the fire had frightened him, and he did not attempt to come into the open and offer them a chance of a shot.

I had thought of sitting up the night I was there, but having to put in an early appearance for my first day's work in The Camp, and not knowing Stigand so well as I got to do later, I did not wish to be late. When I told him of this, he said : " Oh, you should have sent a man in with a chit, and I would have come out and sat up with you." I wished I had known that, as the lion would have been almost certain to return and give me a chance of a shot. It is possible I did shoot this lion later, as I shall shortly describe.

The officers of the 1st K.A.R. were a most pleasant lot of men and more sporting than some of the civil officials in Zomba. They were all fond of shooting, and this had been an incentive to most of them in coming to Nyasaland. There are several battalions of the King's African Rifles in different protectorates, and they were all officered by men of this manly stamp.

The native soldiers of the battalions raised in Nyasaland mostly belonged to the Yao (Ajawa) race, although there were members belonging to other tribes.

At that time there was a battalion of Sikhs in Zomba, and they were not nearly such pleasant troops to deal with as the indigenous natives, for they were always quarrelling with one another and complaining of this or that, so the whites preferred the natives of the country, and I agreed with them.

NYASALAND GNU.
This variety of the blue wildebeest is distinguished by the white chevron on face.
Photograph by George Garden.

NYALA (male).
Photograph by George Garden.

The Nyasaland troops did exceptionally well in the fighting they took part in in Ashanti and Somaliland. With good leading—and they always had the best— they would go anywhere and do anything which any native troops could be expected to do. There was a Sikh bandmaster who ran the regimental band, and it was wonderful how well the natives played and how quickly they learnt any tune. At signalling, too, they often became proficient in a short time, and before doing so had, of course, to learn the letters of the alphabet before they could take or send messages.

At the time I was in Zomba the officers, according to rank, were Captain Stokes, Captain Markham (who arrived just after me), Captain Withers, and Lieutenants Mostyn, Stigand, Olivier, McLeod, Walker, Wingfield-Digby, and Lewis. (Some of them had brevet captaincies.) Captain Stokes was ill when I arrived and died soon afterwards, and then Captain Markham took his place. Stokes had made a name in the country in some fighting, so after he was buried it was thought that the natives might dig up his body to get his heart to make " medicine." For some weeks after the funeral a guard of *askari* (soldiers) was marched down from The Camp to the grave every evening to guard it throughout the night.

Some tribes, especially the Anguru, not only dig up bodies to get certain parts to make " fetish medicine," but they eat dead human bodies whenever they can get them.

Soon after Stokes died there was a sale at The Camp of the effects left by the K.A.R. officers who had gone to Somaliland and fallen at the fight of Gumburu. I bought a ·577 double-hammer express rifle made by Jeffries, but sold it again soon afterwards as I liked my ·303 better. I never believed in large-bore rifles, and one can shoot much more accurately with a small bore, as there is no recoil to speak of. The

63

black-powder type is going out of fashion, for the smoke emitted is a great nuisance, and the recoil, though nothing to worry about, certainly influences the quality of the shooting.

Life in The Camp was very pleasant, as we often went for a week-end to the bush with tents and food. A favourite spot was the Lisanjala stream about twenty miles away. To get there one had to go to the back of the Zomba Range, where the scenery was very beautiful.

At that time buffalo and eland were preserved, but one could obtain a permit from the Government to shoot one. Permits to shoot one eland were usually given, but the one for buffalo not so readily. However, later both these species were included on the game licence, as they were becoming numerous.

Sometimes we passed through the coffee estate of Namitembo and stopped for tea with the manager, whose name was Henry.

At that time I never saw tsetse flies near Zomba, but later, when a coffee-planter named Hooker got some cattle, they began to appear and soon got so prevalent that the cattle all died.

Stigand got a week's leave and went off to shoot near Liwonde and the Shire River, and returned with a record pair of kudu horns. I measured them carefully with him, and just after being shot the measurements were: on curve $63\frac{5}{8}$ inches, on straight 45 inches, and tip to tip 45 inches. We were glad he had got such a fine trophy, for he always worked hard on his shooting trips and deserved success.

The Camp being rather a sandy place in dry weather, we often got the chigger flea in our feet. The native name for this pest is *matakania*, and the natives suffer more than the white people, as they go about with bare feet. A native " boy " (servant) is usually wonderfully proficient in taking out the egg, which after a few days shows as a dark spot about the size of a small pin-head. In the sole of the foot the pain of removal is nothing, and the only thing to be careful of is not to break the spot or bag. Otherwise it probably festers and forms an ulcer. When, however, it gets under a toe-nail it can be very painful, and in this position the bag of eggs is more easily broken, as it is more difficult to see properly. The first sign of its presence is an itching sensation.

The soldier ants are another pest, for they bite hard if a person happens to tread on a trail and disturb them. I still remember with gusto Lewis being bitten, as he got on a trail of them outside his bungalow one night. His antics were extraordinary!

Most people have read or heard of that drastic punishment ordered by chiefs of the " ant death," when the victim is smeared all over with honey (the ants love honey) and tied fast to a tree and left to be eaten alive. It must be a frightful end for the poor wretch, and I suppose he (or she) seldom merited it, as the old native chiefs often put people out of the way for very little indeed.

White ants are an intolerable nuisance, as they destroy all kinds of things, such as clothes, mats, boots, rifle-stocks, leather boxes, and in fact almost anything. All boxes should be made of green rot-proof canvas, which white ants will not touch, at least when fairly new. Perhaps steel uniform trunks are better still, especially when fitted with watertight lids. If a camp is made near a native village, rats are often a great nuisance, and are even more destructive than white ants, as they will nibble at anything. I have had all kinds of objects spoilt by them. However, they are cleaner beasts than the rats found in towns at home, as there are no sewers and that kind of thing for them to inhabit.

For a time I lived with Wingfield-Digby when the

65

roof of my bungalow was being repaired. He used to amuse me greatly when making a salad, a dish he was fond of, as he used to warble a quaint rhyme denoting the ingredients as he cut them up to put them in the bowl.

On the 30th of July a native told me that a lion had killed three men at a village, near which we used to go and shoot sometimes. Perhaps the lion which killed the woman I saw was mixed up in the affair ? Stigand and I went to a village where a lion had killed four goats in a kraal, and got another goat to tie up as a bait. We took turns to watch in the verandah of a hut which we got fenced off with reeds, but nothing happened except that two parties of eager sportsmen arrived from Zomba, the first consisting of Turnbull and Barrett, and the other Beeching, the collector of Zomba, with his assistant, Manning. The two parties, when they found that we were before them, went on to other villages. This shows the keenness of the Europeans in the country to get a shot at a lion.

When out on a shooting trip with Digby I got a waterbuck, bushbuck, and oribi. When the oribi was struck it jumped quite 5 feet straight in the air, a strange sight. The waterbuck, after I had wounded it, got into some long grass, and while following its spoor I nearly trod on it. It sprang up on its hind legs, almost hitting me in the face with its fore feet, and I fired into its chest and finished it. Of course its action was simply due to fright, and not to any attempt to do harm, although it would have been perfectly justified. I was glad it was not a sable antelope, which in the same circumstances would likely have used its horns. On a subsequent occasion, in another part of the country, a wounded sable came for me under the same conditions, but it was slightly farther off when I came on it.

66

THE PLACE STIGAND AND I SAT UP FOR A LION.
See broken goat-kraal on right.

A BUSHBUCK RAM.
Photograph by Mr. Maw.

For people who have not yet shot them, I may say that care should be taken when closely approaching sable and roan antelopes, as they are plucky animals with very powerful necks and sharp horns. I know of a case where a native was killed by a sable when going up to finish it as it was sitting under a tree. He was struck in the kidney and died shortly afterwards. There is one almost infallible rule. It is that a beast when sitting up will probably be able to rise again, but an animal stretched flat on its side is usually dead or *in extremis*; so should any large animal be sitting up, one should not approach it closely without a loaded rifle in one's hand.

In the country within a radius of thirty miles round Zomba, at that time (1903), there was any amount of game, consisting of eland, kudu, sable antelope, zebra, Lichtenstein's hartebeest, waterbuck, reedbuck, bushbuck, klipspringer, oribi, duiker, warthog, bushpig, and the Nyasaland variety of blue wildebeest, with a white face chevron. I have seen the old spoor of elephant on the plateau on the top of Zomba Mountain, and the spoor of a rhino within fifteen miles of Zomba. There was always the possibility, too, of coming on a lion or leopard, as these animals often come right up to the township.

Often we went up Zomba Mountain and stayed a night in one of the few houses there. The air was cool and refreshing after the heat of the plains, and the lovely streams of cold water reminded one of Scotland. Since then they have started trout hatcheries on the Zomba plateau, and it is an excellent idea, for trout-fishing will be a fine relaxation for the people of Zomba and neighbourhood.

I shot several bushbuck on the mountain, as I often went there, on one occasion getting a bad attack of fever brought on by bathing in one of the mountain streams. Sudden changes of tem-

67

perature often bring out fever, and for a fever patient to go to a colder place to recruit often only accentuates the complaint instead of curing it.

Coming down the mountain one day with Manning (the assistant collector of Zomba), I spiked my foot badly by treading on a large thorn while wearing rope-soled shoes. Feeling the pain, I sat down and removed my shoe quickly, which broke half the thorn off in my foot. It took some time to dig out the point, which lamed me for a week or more.

Manning was unfortunately killed in the fighting between the British and the Germans at Karonga in 1914. I heard that he was going to help one of the enemy after the fighting was over, and was shot by the wounded man, a treacherous murder. He was one of the best of the younger officials in the country, very keen on shooting, and much liked by the Europeans and natives in the country. It is strange how many of the best are the first to go!

We heard at The Camp that one of the man-eating lions had been killed by natives with spears a few miles from Zomba. They are plucky fellows, attacking a lion with such flimsy weapons.

On the 29th of August, while on one of our periodical short trips, I wounded a warthog boar which did a strange thing, as a second shot when it was running off made it turn a complete somersault just like a shot rabbit.

While up Zomba Mountain with Mostyn and Digby, we came to a wonderful precipice with a straight drop of quite 1,500 feet, at least it looked quite that. It was the sort of place that makes one dizzy to look over. There is a similar precipice in the Mlanje Mountains. Natives have gone over it in the dark, as the path passes close to the place.

An amusing incident occurred one dark night, for a hyena got into my cookhouse and removed a slab

BUNGALOW ON LAUDERDALE ESTATE.
Mlanje Range behind.
(Photograph by George Garden.)

of bacon weighing 4 lb. We found it in the compound chewed up, so it was evidently too salt for the robber, or he may have thought the salt was poison.

A swarm of bees, about this time, settled in one of the brick chimneys of my house, so I smoked them out, causing them to fall down the chimney. The torpid things crawled all over the place, and when lying in bed that night I got three stings. They took their revenge, for on being again smoked they attacked my fowls, and stung some of them so badly that the cook had to finish them afterwards. There was a hen with chicks which was set on, the poor bird getting her head and neck covered with bees as she tried to get her brood under her wings. My three " boys " ran into the bungalow for safety, and through the glass-covered door we watched the hens being attacked. Seizing a towel, which I waved vigorously, I ran out and seized the hen, which I brought in, bringing at the same time many furious bees, when they immediately went for the " boys " and myself, all of us getting stung.

Bees are very pugnacious sometimes, and I suppose the message is passed from one to another, for it is wonderful how they act together. This was a large swarm, and there must have been thousands of bees in it, for the noise of their buzzing was very loud and menacing. It was a common sight to see swarms passing overhead, and one would hear them for some time before they appeared in sight and long after they had disappeared.

I lost sixteen fowls on this occasion, but at that time fowls cost 3d. each, or a yard of calico, so it was not much of a financial loss, although I was sorry for the fowls, and particularly for the self-sacrificing old hen.

At certain times of the year swarms of bees change ground, and I think their movements are largely caused by the annual grass fires which occur from August to October, or even later if the grass does not dry up quickly. Locusts, too, come along in dense clouds, and drop all over the place, when the natives collect them to eat. Another favourite delicacy of the natives are several varieties of large caterpillars ; and white ants when they are in the flying stage. All these are roasted before eating.

About this time Captain J. Brander-Dunbar and Captain Withers arrived, the former out for a shooting trip, and the latter to take over the temporary command of the 1st K.A. Rifles. Stigand soon left for Fort Manning, in Central Angoniland, where he expected to get some elephants.

As the troops were to be given a feed for the King's birthday festivities, Major Pearce gave me permission to shoot two hartebeest (above the number on my licence), so I went off to Kumicundi's village, where I hoped to find some of these animals. I only managed to get one hartebeest, but I got a bushbuck in place of the other, which with the bullock which had been already supplied made the natives happy.

GAME ANIMAL COVERED WITH BRANCHES AS A PROTECTION AGAINST NIGHT PROWLERS.

MY THATCHED HOUSE ON KAPUNDI STREAM, NORTH-EASTERN RHODESIA.

TOWARDS the end of November the rains began to break, usually accompanied by violent thunderstorms and strong winds. During one of these storms the roof was lifted clean off the rifle store in the *boma*, and we had all to turn out to get the rifles and other stuff put in a dry and safe place. The rain poured down until the ground got so water-logged that it would hold no more, so it collected in pools and made the country like a lake, until, when the rain had stopped, it gradually filtered into the earth.

These tropical thunderstorms are sometimes preceded by heavy hail, although I have never seen it so large in Africa as in India, where we used to get it as big as walnuts, which, coming as it did when the tea-bushes were flushing, often caused the planters much loss. Hail, even when the size of peas, is capable of doing great damage, but when as big as walnuts it becomes dangerous when carried by a strong wind. I remember an old man in India being killed by a sudden hailstorm which caught him in the open. Birds are often killed in thousands, and once at Ekaruni, when the snipe were in, I found some dead, and afterwards sent out some youngsters with baskets, who collected large numbers which I distributed amongst my friends.

I have heard of large hail being driven through corrugated iron sheeting, but never saw it myself, although I have seen such material dented with hail.

71

DAYS AFTER BIG GAME

If caught in the open it is advisable to take cover quickly, as I know, for I was once nearly stunned before I got under a bridge when going between Cossipore and its out-garden of Felixstowe in Cachar. My face was very sore for a few days afterwards with the hammering it got in a space of less than three minutes when I was running for shelter.

There is something very fascinating in witnessing a really bad storm, and the relentless power of a cyclonic gale, which lifts trees out by the roots, and demolishes buildings like native huts as if they were built of cardboard. It is quite impossible to face such a wind at times, and all one can do is to rush for shelter, or lie down and wait until it blows itself out. Luckily tropical storms, at least the severe ones, are rapidly over, but they can do a wonderful lot of damage in a short space of time. In the rainy season, from December to April, the damp becomes wearisome and the long grass all over the country grows very high and thick, and the deciduous trees, which in the dry season are grey and sombre-looking, put on their green coverings.

Although it is damp, the sun often shines and makes everything moist and steamy, just like a hothouse at home, and the white ants and other insects hatch out and come in scores to the lamps at nights. All this is a great contrast to the bitter, damp cold one experiences in the long winters at home, when the days are short and everything is dismal and depressing. Britain has the most disgusting climate in the world for six months of the year, and people who have come from Canada say it is much more uncomfortable than the drier cold experienced in that country.

During the months of the dry season, roughly from May to November, the days are very hot, especially the three months of September, October, and November, although the latter month is often cooled by the

72

YOUNG BUSHBUCK RAM WITH CAT.
Photograph by Mr. Maw.

THE SHIRE RIVER, CENTRAL AFRICA.

early rainstorms. A fire is often a comfort in the early mornings and evenings, and so is a thick coat.

The climate varies slightly at different elevations in the country, and of course the higher one gets the cooler it is.

On the 27th of November I left for a shoot on the Shire River, and looked up a friend named Barnshaw at Gwaza's. From the path I shot a nice bushbuck ram with a good pair of horns, 14½ inches in length.

Barnshaw asked me to stay the night, and after dinner I noticed a very fine bushbuck skull and horns which he told me had been picked up near the Shire River. On measuring the head carefully, I found it 19¾ inches on the curve. Barnshaw later sold this head to Rowland Ward, the well-known taxidermist of London, and it then went to the Hon. Walter Rothschild's museum at Tring.

Crossing the Shire next morning, I shot an impala ram, a species I had not yet had a chance of getting. I also saw a kasania (Sharpe's steinbuck), but he was off before I could get a chance at him. These little animals are very quick, and like most of the other small antelopes, such as duiker and oribi, they do not often stop to look back after they start away.

When I got back to Zomba it took me two weeks to get my feet right, as on my trip I had raised some large blisters owing to a badly fitting pair of boots.

It is advisable to be careful in choosing comfortable footgear for work in Africa.

On getting back to The Camp the first thing I heard was that a lion had broken into a small kraal at the back of Captain Markham's house, and killed a calf and seven goats, so he asked me to come up and arrange to sit up for the lion, as he was sure to come back. There was a brick hut occupied by his native servants within twelve yards of the kraal, so we decided to knock two holes in the wall and sit there just after sundown that evening (30th of November 1903).

He asked me up for an early dinner, and just as darkness was coming on we went to the hut. Markham had had his camp-bed rigged up in one corner, on which he lay down, and I sat on a small stool opposite my hole in the wall. I had agreed to let Markham have first shot, as the incident had occurred at his house.

I had been watching about half an hour when I heard a movement, and then the lion appeared round the corner of the kraal. I whispered to Markham and he made for his hole, making the bed creak with his movements. The lion stood looking at the door of the kraal, which had been blocked up so that it would prevent him getting in too quickly, and offer more time for a shot. At first the beast was facing, and we had agreed that before firing we should wait for a good chance. At last he took a few steps forward and stood dead broadside on, offering a splendid shot.

I whispered to Markham, " Take him," and he pointed his rifle (a double, hammerless ·303 by Henry, with Metford rifling) and pulled the trigger. There was a click, and I knew that his rifle had missed fire, or he had forgotten to load it. Being a double he had his left barrel, but seemed to forget about it, so I said, " Shall I fire ? " and he replied, " Yes, fire quickly," so I let go. At my shot the lion roared loudly and reared up on his hind legs, and then fell flat on his side and began dragging himself forward slowly. Markham now remembered his other barrel and fired a shot (we found the hole of the bullet next day through one of the kraal doorposts). Then I fired again and hit the lion in the flank, as his back was now the nearest spot visible. In ten minutes the men from the other houses in The Camp arrived, and they asked who shot the lion, and Markham said I

74

did. Next day, when skinning the animal, my two bullets were found in him, showing the Enfield rifling of my weapon, and I still have them amongst a collection of bullets I cut from game I have shot. I also have the skull and skin of my first lion.

I mention this incident as it was partly through it that I decided to leave Zomba and go after elephant in Nyasaland and North-Eastern Rhodesia.

Of course there was no danger in shooting the lion, as we were in cover and it was a simple affair. The animal was very thin, and it was evident he had had a hard time lately, so he would have been a nasty customer to meet on a dark night. We heard he had killed the three natives I have mentioned, although there is no direct proof that this was the same animal.

Mostyn and I got fifteen days' leave, so we decided to go a shooting trip to Lake Chiuta, and started off for Chikala, which is near the lake.

On Christmas Day I shot my first kudu bull,[1] with a fair head. I sat for a long time smoking and looking at him before I let the natives cut off his head. What a lovely creature a male kudu is, with his bluish-grey skin with white stripes and splendid horns! When moving they are typical of the beautiful country they inhabit. Kudu are more plentiful in Nyasaland than some people imagine, as they often go to hilly ground, and are retiring animals compared with the sable, which as a rule inhabits lower country, although I have occasionally found them at a good altitude.

On this day I got my bare legs stung with the vile chitaisi bean, which is plentiful all over this country. The bean is covered with myriads of fine hairy points, which when ripe are blown all over the place, or fall if disturbed by a touch. These hairs must have some irritant poison in them, as they produce a fiery itch

[1] This was my first kudu in Nyasaland, but I had bagged one in Southern Rhodesia in 1899.—AUTHOR.

75

which soon makes a pair of bare legs or arms look as if they had been boiled. In a few hours the pain decreases, but for a time it can be most uncomfortable.

Almost a worse pest is a strong tendril about the size of ordinary string, which grows in grass and fades to the same colour, so that it is not readily seen. This tendril is covered with sharp thorns which scratch bare legs badly if one attempts to push past them. They are too strong to break readily, and it is best to step over them, unless one has puttees or leggings on, when they can be broken fairly easily.

Personally I can't tolerate anything on my legs when hunting in Africa, as puttees affect my walking and make my legs intolerably hot. In very thorny country I sometimes used very light gaiters made from thick khaki cloth, but they never lasted long with the wear and tear they got, so I preferred my uncovered shanks.

The following day Mostyn got a bushbuck, and I shot two hartebeest and two oribi for our followers, who revel in the meat.

On the 26th we got to Nafisi Hill, near where Brander-Dunbar had shot a lioness. The country round here is very wild-looking and game of the commoner kinds is plentiful. Next day, after a hot trek, we got to Lake Chiuta, seeing plenty of hartebeest, reedbuck, and oribi near the path.

I do not intend to mention every day of this trip, for, although it was interesting to the sportsman, it becomes monotonous to the reader.

We got across the lake, which is hardly a lake at this time of year, as there is only a little water at one end. Most of it is mud and swamp, and it is the haunt of myriads of mosquitoes. As I forgot to bring my net with me, I got badly bitten every night. Mundi Hill is visible and the hills round Mangoche, where there is a fort garrisoned by the K.A. Rifles.

76

Crossing the reedy swamps, we found ourselves in Portuguese territory and liable to be questioned if found shooting there. As the Portuguese officials do not go in for sport much, it was unlikely that we would be interfered with.

On the 5th of January 1904 I had one of the hardest walks of my life, for I left the tent at dawn and walked steadily until sundown, only resting once for about ten minutes the whole day. I first of all shot a harte-beest, and then found the fresh spoor of a herd of buffalo, which I and my men followed for five hours, through swampy ground most of the time. Then we found the footprints of some natives ahead of us, as they had cut the spoor from a different direction. These men were probably hunting for the Portuguese.

After that we turned for camp, and while passing along the edge of the swamp, put up a lion which was lying in a hollow where there was some grass about 4 feet high. I had passed the hollow about fifteen paces ahead of my men and kept out of the grass. They came along after me, speaking loudly, and walked through the grass and put up the lion, which ran to-wards me. My rifle was in the hands of one of the men behind, or I would have got a splendid shot at him as he crouched in some low grass. It would have been the simplest thing to have blown out his brains if I had been armed. The sickening thing about this incident was that I had only handed over my rifle five minutes before to my gunbearer, as I had carried it since I left the tent.

As the lion lay watching me I held my hand out for the rifle, and the gunbearer very pluckily ran round the lion with it. The lion, seeing the move-ment, sprang up and rushed into some thick bush to the left. By the time I got the rifle in my hand and had put off the safety catch, the lion was going strong about sixty yards off, when he stood behind a bush,

77

all that showed being his head. I was moving round to see his shoulder when away he went again, so I fired hurriedly and missed him clean, the bullet passing, I think, in front of his nose as he swerved quickly and was soon lost to sight in the thick bush.

I was greatly disappointed, and the worst of it was my troubles were not over, as one of the worst thunderstorms I have ever seen came on soon afterwards. We had got to the middle of the swamp, with water and mud up to our knees, when the brazen sky began to blaze with the most vivid lightning I had ever seen. Flash succeeded flash until gradually the storm began to creep right over us. If the ground had been dry underfoot I would have put down the rifle, which I had retained since I saw the lion, but there was nothing but sticky mud and water about, except the reeds and grass, and it got so cold with the lashing rain that it was more comfortable to keep moving.

Suddenly there was a blinding flash and the clouds seemed to open just over our heads. For a moment my men and I were quite dazed, for it had come very close. I heard several exclamations of "Oogwi!— oogwi!" which is a native expression of extreme astonishment. For the second time in my life, when very close to a descending flash of lightning, I felt the sensation of pins and needles in my body, and my hair when I stroked it was painful to the touch.

The natives of Africa are accustomed to severe thunderstorms, and as a rule take them calmly; but on this occasion the men with me were all very frightened and dazed, and there is no doubt that this might be classified as a first-rate exhibition of fireworks. Then, after hanging overhead for a time, it passed on, the period between the flashes and crashes denoting its movement, and we were all relieved, as it had been a nasty experience.

During the storm, as we moved slowly forward, I

had been interested in watching several lots of harte-beest and reedbuck standing with their backs to the driving wind and rain. One reedbuck ram, which never moved, though we passed it within fifteen yards, was shivering with the cold and standing with its head down between its forelegs. It gave one the impression that it was praying for stillness and peace to come again.

It was 6.30 p.m. when we got to camp, and I forget how many cups of hot tea I swallowed, but they were many. I fancy I tramped a good thirty-five miles that day, the going being very hard in places on account of the swamp and heavy grass. It made a fine contrast to easier days, and life without contrasts is a tame affair.

On the 27th we returned to Zomba, being disappointed that we had not been able to obtain a shot at a buffalo, which was the main object of our trip. If we had been on the ground a month sooner, we would have been certain to have had some chances, as the country we covered was thick with their tracks. They had changed ground with the break of the rains, conditions which make certain of the larger species, such as elephants and buffaloes, move elsewhere, as water becomes plentiful in places which have been as dry as tinder.

The grass fires leave lots of ash which game come to lick for the salt in it, and the new green grass supplies a lot of fresh food, and animals come a long way to feed in these places. Grass fires do enormous damage to the young trees and a great amount of animal life is destroyed, such as newly born antelopes, mice, land tortoises, insects, and young birds in their nests. Snakes also are killed, although they are wonderfully quick in escaping from the fire.

What with the reckless deforestation by the natives when they make new gardens, and these grass fires

79

which they start mainly to get the mice and other animal life destroyed, the forests of Central Africa are being rapidly denuded, and I believe the Government is now making stringent laws against both customs; and it is time, for I believe the deforestation is affecting the rainfall of the country.

Lakes such as Shirwa (sometimes spelt Chilwa), Pamalombe, and Chiuta are rapidly drying up and being filled with sudd and growth. Lake Nyasa, too, does not hold nearly so much water as it formerly did, with the consequence that steamer communication has disappeared on the Upper Shire River. Lakes in other parts of the continent also suffer in the same way, for instance Ngami in south-western Africa.

We killed a mad dog in the canteen store in the *boma* one day, but fortunately it did not manage to get its teeth into anybody. Another day a dog dashed right through my room, coming in at the half-opened glass door at the back, and instead of going out at the open part of the front door, it dashed clean through one of the large panes in the other half. I chased and shot it before it could do any damage.

While in India I had seen a number of mad dogs, and once a jackal came to a bungalow in Sylhet I was staying in and bit two dogs belonging to a planter, Curry, and one of mine, besides several ducks and fowls. We chased the jackal, but it had a good start and got away in the jungle. After talking it over, we decided that it was best to kill the dogs, so I took the three of them out, tied each to a tree, and shot them.

Again, in Fort Jameson, North-Eastern Rhodesia, a friend of mine named Langshaw came to my house and said a small dog he had was behaving in a strange way, as it was tearing up curtains and anything it could get at, so he shut it in the room. I shot it through the window of the room. This is always the

80

best thing to do when a dog behaves queerly in the tropics; although it may not invariably denote rabies, the consequences are so vital that it is foolish to take the risk, for someone else, if not oneself, is likely to be the victim.

Periodically in Assam the planters used to sally out with rifles and shotguns and kill numbers of the super-fluous pariahs in the surrounding villages, as these animals are often the means of spreading hydrophobia throughout the country.

When a jackal or dog has rabies it usually foams (though not always) at the mouth, and in running about it gets a fit every now and then and lies on the road scratching with its feet. In India we occasion-ally saw these scratches on the garden paths when going round the work, and sometimes a branch of a low bush or clumps of grass would show signs of gnawing by the teeth of the distressed animal. The inoculation, discovered by that wonderful man Pasteur, was not known at that time, but soon afterwards many victims used to go from India every year to undergo his treatment in Paris.

A well-known story about hydrophobia is the case of the young American girl who burst into the hotel drawing-room shouting, " Ain't it glorious ?—ain't it glorious ? " " What's glorious ? " said everyone. " Oh, Poppa's been bitten by a mad dog and we're off to Paris in the morning. I say, ain't it glorious ? " This is a chestnut, but chestnuts are not chestnuts to everybody, so I pass it onwards.

Having resigned my appointment, I started off for Fort Manning, not far from Fort Jameson in North-Eastern Rhodesia, on the 30th of April 1903, and put up with Maw, an assistant on a coffee estate (Likan-jala) a few miles out of Zomba, for a couple of days. Two lions had killed a bushpig not far from his bunga-low a few nights before. We hoped they would come back, but they did not do so before I left for Gwaza's.

Stopping over a day here, I went out and got a nice impala ram with a better head than the one I had shot here before. Next day, as I wanted meat for my carriers, I shot three impala males, and then went off to Matope and camped near the Matiti Hill within thirty yards of the river (Shire). There were a number of crocodiles sunning themselves on rocks, and I shot one of them, which my men recovered. The Murchison Falls were close to my tent, and the sound of the rushing water was pleasant. The noise was quite loud, and it was difficult to make the natives hear anything said to them unless they were close.

Hearing that there were hippos not far away, I went off to try to find them. At last I saw one, and waited for it to give me a satisfactory shot, which it soon did. It sank quietly under the surface, and I knew that I had killed it, as Sinderam and others had told me that if they splash at all they are only wounded.

After that I went off to the tent and had some food, leaving two of the men to watch for the hippo. At last I saw one coming towards the tent shouting " Wafa," which means dead, so I went off to see it. Not far away were the three remaining hippo (there had been four), so as the natives begged me to shoot them all, I killed another one, though I cannot say I was very anxious to do so. I hit the second one in the back of the head, the bullet fairly cracking on its hard skull as it struck. The first one had stranded about the middle of the river, but the natives went in at once, shouting hard and splashing to frighten the crocs, I suppose, although they always get extremely excited at the sight of an abundance of meat and fat.

There was some beautiful scenery here, huge bulbous baobab-trees, feathery palms, plants like euphor-

IMPALA RAM.
Shot and photographed by George Garden.

bias, and a lovely shrub with red flowers, abundantly scattered on both banks of the rushing river. The contrast presented to this idealistic scene was the horde of black-skinned Africans, each armed with a large knife, hacking and shouting as they cut large chunks of meat from the bloated body of the huge amphibian.

An hour after it had been shot the second hippo rose, which meant another performance joined by a lot of new-comers who had heard there was *nyama* (meat) about. They fairly ran to the slaughter, followed by their womenkind, who brought up the rear with a large basket for the meat, and usually a bobbing baby on their backs, uncomfortable and squalling at the lively antics of its mother. Unless something like a bull buffalo is chasing them, there is nothing which stimulates the African so much as a cheaply procured basket of meat. They will come miles to get it, and the condition is always a secondary consideration to the quantity which is to be got.

I got my men to bring the two hippo skulls and some slabs of skin up to the tent, it taking four strong men to carry each head slung on poles. That night I was awakened by something striking one of the tent-ropes, so sat up and lit my lantern. By this time the natives had been disturbed as they were shouting, so I went out with my rifle and the lamp. I noticed one of the skulls (with flesh on) was missing. Close to the place was a grooved track in the earth and sand, so the natives and I took up the spoor and found the skull about fifty yards off, so we hauled it back and turned in.

Not twenty minutes had elapsed when I heard something else being moved, so I got up again and tried to see through the slit in the front flap, but it was too dark, so out again I went with the lamp. My natives had heard something and joined me, and we found a large slab of skin had now disappeared. We tracked it for quite a hundred yards, and found it chewed at the edge by a hyena, or probably there were more than one. This slab of skin, like each skull, had required four men to carry it to the tent, and must have weighed a good 200 lb., for the back skin of a hippo is about 2 inches thick, and this slab measured roughly 6 by 4 feet. I noticed that the hyena had walked backwards in places, the sandy soil showing the spoor reversed. This shows the great power of a hyena's jaws and its strength of body.

Returning to Matope, the agent of the African Lakes Corporation, whose name was Baird, kindly lent me the large iron boat used by his company, to get myself, men, and goods across the Shire. As the men were going first, he got me a cup of tea before I left. Saying good-bye, I trekked to a place called Kaninga, this being the headman's name. Villages are usually called after the chief's name, or if some of his ancestors have been notable men, their names are retained for generations and become place-names.

When I was having my evening meal off a skinny fowl, some rice, and tea, I heard a lion grunting in the distance.

Next day I got to Mpezi, and though I went out shooting in the afternoon, I saw no game.

On the 13th I did the longest trek I had yet done, for I reached Fort Mlangeni late in the evening, passing the Government station of Ncheu. The distance was quite forty miles. When passing Ncheu the collector, Aplin, was away, but I met him at the fort, where Withers, whom I had known in Zomba, was in command. Brander-Dunbar was staying with him at the time, so we were a merry party. After staying at Fort Mlangeni for a few days, and also a couple of days with Aplin at Ncheu, I pushed on for Dedza, and Withers and Aplin came on at the same

84

time to spend a few days with Gordon, the collector there. He was ill at the time, so we all did our best for him, taking turns to sit up at night.

Dedza is called after a hill of that name quite near the *boma*, and I have been up it several times, as from it one can see Lake Nyasa in the distance. It is a favourite haunt of klipspringers, and also a likely place to get a shot at a leopard.

Leaving here, I trekked on for the Taiti River, which I reached about 2 p.m., having left early. There was an Irishman named McFadden here, who, with a partner, Moore, owned a small cattle ranch. In the afternoon I went out and bagged a reedbuck ram, and saw some fairly fresh spoor of a herd of elephants which had passed through a patch of thick grass just behind McFadden's hut. This is a good place for lions, and a man I met later, when camped here, had one of his carriers taken and killed by a lion one dark night. The scenery is wild and beautiful, as there are many high and rough kopjes in the neighbourhood, and this part of the country reminded me strongly of places I had seen in Mashonaland. The grass had not yet been burnt off, so the shooting was not nearly as good as it would be in a few months.

Marching on, I camped at Sandola's village, and next day reached Lilongwe. H. C. Macdonald, one of the best and oldest collectors in Nyasaland, was away, so I did not see him, and he was a man I wished to meet, being a very good hunter. For some years he held the record for buffalo, but this measurement, which I think was about 48 inches in spread, has since been beaten by many heads from British East Africa and Uganda. The record now is one measuring $56\frac{1}{4}$ inches outside width, shot in the Wakamba country, British East Africa. Several heads have been got in the country just north of the Zambezi River

85

measuring about 50 inches in width. A very wide head is not necessarily a prettier trophy than a narrower one, as a good deal depends on the curve of the horns, the sharpness of the tips, and depth of the frontlet.

After I left Lilongwe I did a twenty-seven-mile march to Banabanda's village. There is a collection of villages here called Gwirisi. In the rainy season lions are plentiful here, and the natives suffered so much that nearly all the villages were surrounded by stockades of poles. My tent not arriving until after dark, Banabanda allowed me to use a new hut. Unfortunately some fowls had roosted on the cross-poles above my head, and they kept me awake most of the night. In fact they were quite rude !

Next day I reached Kongoni rest-house, seeing many tracks of elephants, some fairly fresh, but most of them old. It was fascinating to me to get to a place where there were plentiful signs of such big game.

Near the rest-house were the remains of an old mud fort with loopholes in it for shooting through. I do not know its history, but fancy it was made by the Achipeta to keep off Mpseni's marauding Angoni, a race which was constantly raiding the smaller tribes. In the old days the Angoni had a great name, probably through their numbers and combination. Now they are very mixed, and not such fine fellows as many of the so-called inferior tribes in this part of Africa.

The swampy Bua River was near here, full of papyrus and matete reeds, the former very pretty when in flower. Plenty of mosquitoes were present here, and I needed to rig up my net for the night.

Next day (the 4th of June) I reached Fort Manning, a pretty place surrounded by bush and much hilly ground in different directions. Mostyn was in command of the K.A.R. troops here, and Stigand was out on a shooting trip. On the 19th Stigand returned, getting a hippo and other game.

As there is much game within six miles of the fort, we often went out for a morning or afternoon shoot and usually got something to bring back. News came in that a villager had killed a lion with a spear, which was breaking into his hut. Natives have usually a spear or two in their huts, and when they are killed by a lion that breaks through the wall, it is owing to their either being taken unawares or retreating from the spot instead of standing near and spearing him. Of course at night they have little light, as it takes some time to blow up the embers of their fire sufficiently to see well.

A medicine-man, or witch doctor, appeared at the fort and gave a performance at Stigand's house by dancing and droning incantations. He was quite pleased with a few shillings and some calico as a present for his performance, which was rather weird, as he was wonderfully dressed in skins and feathers, having a sort of kilt with bobbing cat-tails, and seeds round his ankles and arms which clicked with his movements.

I went up the hill near the fort with Stigand on the 3rd of July, and he got a nice sable bull and I shot two klipspringers. I saw eight klipspringers in small lots of two or three. When Stigand had been in Zomba, we were walking along the path one day towards his house, when we saw on the sandy ground some small tracks of a jungle cat. I said it would be interesting to make a collection of the spoor of all the game, so he agreed to collaborate in a book if I would sketch the tracks. This was the beginning of an idea which led to our writing and illustrating *Central African Game and its Spoor*, which was published by Horace Cox, of *The Field*, London, in 1906.

It was a great interest to us collecting notes and rough drawings, and we paid attention to the droppings of game, and collected the smaller varieties in empty matchboxes so as to get average specimens, for the droppings of the same species vary considerably. These I did in colour, but the publishers thought that coloured illustrations would be too costly to reproduce, so they were eventually printed in black.

An amusing incident occurred with reference to these natural deposits when Mr. Codrington, then Administrator of North-Eastern Rhodesia, came from Fort Jameson on a motor-bicycle to stay the night. He was looking for a match to light a cigar, and kept picking up box after box from a side-table, but failing to find a match, said : " What are these strange seeds you are keeping, Stigand ? " On being told the seeds were the dried droppings of duikers, oribis, reedbuck, etc., he was greatly amused at our natural-history proclivities.

It took some time to collect the spoors and other indications of all the game, as all the species do not exist in one district, so it meant covering a great extent of country to get them all. I shall later have more to say about Stigand, as he was one of the finest men I have associated with in any country.

When I was staying with Stigand we had a little excitement on the night of the 6th of July 1904. Suddenly we heard a shouting in the *boma*, which was about 150 yards from Stigand's house. He was having a bath, but he soon threw on some clothes, and we took our rifles and some cartridges and went down to the back entrance of the fort, where there was a gate. When we got to the front entrance, we found it closed, though it was usually kept open night and day. Stigand asked the guard why the gate was shut, and he said there were lions outside. The K.A.R.

SABLE ANTELOPE COW.
Shot in North-Eastern Rhodesia.

sergeant was told to open it, but nothing was visible with the light of the lanterns we had brought and the one kept in the guard-room.

Then the Indian doctor *babu* arrived, and said that he had been chased by lions, or by some animals, for he was not quite sure what they were, as he was going down to a stream about a couple of hundred yards away. He had boots on and had run hard for the guard-room, shouting loudly, so the guard had turned out. We went out to the place and found the spot where a lion had made a spring and torn up the grass a little, and then followed the spoor for some way by lamplight, which was, of course, a useless proceeding, but we were energetic then.

After this we sat up several times for the lions, but when we were at one place they came somewhere else, and we did not get a shot. All we got were numberless bites from mosquitoes and some sleepless nights.

Stigand, in his book *Hunting the Elephant in Africa*, mentions this incident, as well as many other interesting experiences he had with wild animals.

On the 10th I bagged my first eland, which had horns of about 28 inches on the straight. Although I have since then shot a number of elands, they are most inoffensive animals, and one never kills one without a feeling of regret. However, they do much damage in the natives' gardens, and, unfortunately for themselves, their meat is the best of any of the African game animals. I killed this eland with a single ·303 Mark V (hollow-point) bullet in the centre of the shoulder as he was standing broadside, at seventy yards. After being hit, the eland reared up, and then rushed off for forty yards and fell dead.

Having now got a Kodak camera from home, I was able to get some pictures, but my first attempts were very poor, as I was not careful in cutting down grass and branches in front of the lens. The consequence was that waving grass and leaves often blurred my photographs.

On the 14th Stigand and I went off to Lepenga's village, taking different ways through the bush to try to get some game. I came on a herd of Lichtenstein's hartebeest, and shot two nice bulls with horns of 20 and 19 inches, which is better than the average. Our principal object was to each get a good specimen of a roan antelope bull, a species which was fairly common there at that time.

Two days afterwards, when searching for game, especially roan, I came to the Bua River, where I heard some hippo blowing and grunting. My " boys," always on the lookout for fat, begged me to shoot some, so I fired at two—one certainly killed, the other doubtful, as it splashed before going down.

To get closer to the herd, I went into the water up to my waist, and had just fired my first shot, when something nearly swirled me off my feet and scratched my legs. This, I believe, was a small crocodile which had probably been preparing to grab my bare shanks just at the moment I fired, and the concussion of the shot near the top of the water frightened it, causing it to turn, touching my legs with the quick movement of its tail. This was a lesson I never forgot, and I was careful in future not to go into a muddy stream like the Bua, where it was impossible to see the bottom.

Next morning only one hippo had risen, so we all went to watch the cutting up. It was difficult to get this animal ashore, as she (it was a female) had stranded in some tangled vegetation and reeds. I told the natives to go for a dugout, but they said they could get it by some men swimming out with a rope to tie to the animal. An old man with grey hair at once sprang in, and when he was near the hippo, followed

CROCODILE SHOT IN THE LUANGWA RIVER, NORTH-EASTERN RHODESIA.
Length about 11 feet.

NATIVES PULLING A HIPPO FROM BUA RIVER, NYASALAND.

by five or six other natives, I saw him behaving queerly, as he seemed to be gripped by the legs. I thought at first it was a crocodile which had got him, but as I was just preparing to put a bullet into the water close to him, saw that the tangled vegetation had got round his legs. Luckily all the men were fine swimmers, so they soon got a hold of him and helped him to mount on to the hippo's back. Several others were trying to get on it too, and it was amusing to watch the huge carcass bobbing up and down, and partially turning over at times. Once the old man fell in, being rather tired, I suppose, with his previous struggle, but he was pulled back. Then two men, having fixed the rope to a back leg, swam ashore and the animal was tugged in. I promised the old man the heart and a good lump of fat, at which he grinned joyously, and he was soon hacking away with the best of them. Having told the headman to send the skull and a slab of the skin to the tent, I went back, shooting a redbuck on the way. I also saw a small lot of waterbuck, which ran before I got within shot.

When Stigand came in I heard he had got a good roan bull antelope, so all the natives got plenty of meat.

On the Bua River I saw a lot of guineafowl and ducks, but not having a shotgun at that time, I did not bother about them. When after large game a shotgun makes too much noise and frightens the animals away, so it is not advisable to use them much. A better weapon is a ·220 or ·250 rook and rabbit rifle, as it does not make so much noise and the ammunition costs less.

One night my camp-bed, which was rather groggy in the legs, came down, and the mosquito-net got over my face and body. Being suddenly awakened, I thought a lion had broken in and was worrying me, and it took a few moments to discover the cause of the catastrophe, as my arms, legs, and head were all mixed up in the net. This bed was rather a flimsy one, and when I got the X pattern type I found it a much better article.

On the 19th I killed a warthog, and soon after saw a herd of roan antelopes, which ran. When following them I saw a warthog boar with very nice tusks, so stalked it behind an anthill and killed it. I kept the skull and have it at home, as well as the skull of a sow with nicely curved teeth which I shot later in North-Eastern Rhodesia. Notwithstanding persecution by the natives, who often hunt pig with dogs and spears, and the attacks of lions and leopards, warthogs were wonderfully numerous in all the country I shot in, so they must be prolific animals.

After sending the remains of the pig to camp, I went on and found a herd of roan, and fired a long shot at a bull, which fell dead. Unfortunately, his horns were rather poor, but he was my first roan, so I was glad to get him.

All the meat was eaten by my carriers, personal servants, and the numerous villagers who are always begging for meat, and it is remarkable the amount of flesh a healthy native can swallow and digest. I have seen a man eat at least 10 lb. of meat in an evening when squatting over a fire. He cuts it into strips or small lumps, and puts them into the hot embers of the fire ; then, when cooked slightly, he puts an end into his mouth, gripping it with his teeth, and with his blunt knife (a native's knife is usually blunt) he saws away and pulls until a large mouthful is separated.

A favourite type of native knife is a piece of the soft-steel banding often used for binding boxes or bundles of goods. This he flattens with a stone, and breaks off a piece from 12 to 16 inches long. Round one end he wraps native string, or in some cases

NATIVES WITH A WARTHOG, NYASALAND.
The blood on flank is exit-hole of a raking shot from left shoulder.

NATIVES CARRYING A BUSHBUCK TO CAMP.
The head has been removed.

reim (hide thong), and he has a weapon which, although no use for stabbing, makes an excellent meat-knife if it is kept moderately sharp by rubbing on a stone.

The hunting-knives sold by cutlers and stores are useless weapons except, perhaps, for stabbing, as the steel is too hard and the blades too thick to be easily sharpened. Then the high temper of the edges makes them chip easily. A common type of sheath-knife, often used by sailors, and all men in the wilder parts of the world, called by names such as " Bushman's Friend," " Green River Knife," and so on, are much better tools, as the blades are soft-tempered. For skinning and cutting meat these soft-steel blades take a rough, saw-like edge (if examined through a magnifying-glass), and this is the kind of thing to get for hunting purposes.

Selous always carried a single-bladed pocket-knife with a blade about 2½ inches long, fairly soft steel, and made by Rodgers. I always preferred a two-bladed knife, keeping the small blade very sharp for fine work, but usually carried a sheath-knife on my belt for rough work, and for finishing off game at times—although, if I had plenty of cartridges with me at the moment, I did not mind using one to save an animal pain. If I did not intend to keep the headskin, I fired a finishing shot at the back of the head, in the neck; or when the headskin was to be retained, I put a bullet through the animal's heart. Shooting is cruel enough at all times, so the first consideration of all humane-hearted people should be the saving of prolonged pain to dumb animals. Some, not all, gamekeepers at home are very callous regarding the sufferings of game, and I have often seen a man pick up a hare or a game-bird, and carry it for some way before thinking of dispatching it. If I employed a gamekeeper who did this more than once, I would dismiss him on the spot.

There can be no excuse for premeditated cruelty, even when it is caused by thoughtlessness.

On the 23rd of July I shot a very old roan bull. I saw him walking towards me through sparse bush, so managed to run under cover and cut him off. He was mooning along in the great heat with his head low, and was apparently so old that he was in his dotage, as he never once looked up until my bullet hit him through the shoulder. He made a rush and fell dead. His horns, which I still possess, are very gnarled and chipped at the bases with many a fight, and his tail was missing, having been bitten off some time before by a lion, as he had some deep scratches on his rump, long since healed.

There has always been a controversy amongst big-game hunters how the larger carnivora kill their prey. While in Cachar and Assam I have seen thirty or more carcasses of domesticated buffalo, oxen, cows, and goats killed by tigers. A tiger, according to my observation, almost invariably seizes his prey on the shoulder with one paw, gripping the top of the neck near the body with his teeth, and with the other paw seizes the face of the animal, pulling it towards him, thus causing it to fall forward and often (but not always) dislocating the vertebræ of the neck. It is possible that on rare occasions, when an animal is very close, he may grip the throat, but this is certainly exceptional.

On the other hand, panthers (or leopards) almost invariably seize a large animal by the throat, although with a small beast like a goat or dog they may seize the nape of the neck on certain occasions.

The leopard tries to perforate the windpipe, and I have seen several goats, which had been rescued from a leopard, breathing loudly through the holes of the leopard's teeth in the throat.

A lion kills in almost a similar way to a tiger, and

the following account may be considered a fairly exact description of the method in which a lion seizes his prey on a dark night. When he goes on the prowl he probably moves up or across the wind so as to scent game. Then he gets a taint of (let me say) a herd of buffaloes, a favourite prey of lions. He approaches near enough to the buffaloes not to be heard, and then squats and waits behind a bush or in the grass. When an animal gets near enough, he makes a sudden rush, which may start off his victim. Owing to his great muscular development, the lion accelerates quickly, and is soon up to the buffalo, when he rears up on his hindlegs, and seizes his prey by the nape of the neck fairly far back, using (if on the left side) his left paw to drag the buffalo's face towards him. If the buffalo is still moving, the lion still keeps his hindpaws on the ground, advancing with the buffalo by hops, so to speak. The weight of the lion and the tearing of the face backwards make the buffalo stumble, with the result that he often, although not always, breaks his neck. If not, the lion, having him down, breaks it with his teeth. If he seized his prey under the throat, he would often be rushed off his feet; and the above account is fairly correct, judging by many of the kills, and places where they happened, which I have seen.

With lighter game such as a zebra or kudu, both species often preyed on by the lion, it is likely that the energy of the attack and the weight of the lion bring the game to ground almost at once.

I have seen places where a lion, when he had got his grip with paws and jaws, had hopped for some way alongside his victim before he was able to bring it to earth. A well-made lion in good condition weighs somewhere about 400 lb. (sometimes more has been recorded), and when one considers his phenomenal muscular development and the deadly energy he exerts

at the moment of attack, anything less than a buffalo
would seem to stand little chance of escape. Yet I
have seen a good number of animals I have shot
(such as zebra, roan and sable antelopes, eland and
kudu) which have managed to get away. Considering this fact, there must always be a fair percentage
of game which has undergone the ordeal and lived to
recover.

In Africa leopards kill a great number of the smaller
antelopes such as bushbuck, reedbuck, impala, duiker,
oribi, and klipspringer. All the carnivora—lion,
leopard, hyena, wild dog, and jackal—must kill many
fawns just after they are born.

As to the correct way to measure lion, tiger, and
leopard, there is only one method which can be called
really practicable, and that is to put a peg in at the
nose and another at the end of the tail just after
the animal is dead. All measurements taken from
skins, which may have been soaked in water for some
time, are fictitious and should never be accepted, as
a lion skin (or any skin), when soaked for a night in
a tub, can be pulled out quite a foot longer than the
skin measured when stripped off the carcass. Curve
measurements of animals are also unsatisfactory, as
the tape cannot be kept tight, and some men keep
it as slack as they can when they are looking for a
record. For standing height a peg should be put
in at the top of the shoulder, and another under
the pad or hoof when the leg is held in a natural
position.

Most people who know the proportions of the skin
of any animal can soon see when a skin has been
stretched, as naturally the more it is pulled out, the
more is the width reduced. Only steel tapes should
be used, as they do not stretch or shrink so much as
cloth ones.

There is a story of an old Indian Colonel who was

96

boasting in a smoking-room of shooting a 12-foot tiger. An angler sitting near immediately told a story of catching a skate a quarter of an acre in extent. The Colonel promptly challenged him to a duel, so the angler said, " If you'll take two feet off that tiger, I'll see what can be done with the skate."

Chapter IV

MUCH has been written on elephant-hunting by Selous, Neumann, Stigand, and others, although nothing which can be written about it can quite express its intense fascination, as it is not only the most exhilarating sport in the world, but it is about the hardest a man can undertake.

Nowadays elephants, especially the large tuskers, are not so plentiful as they used to be, and the animals, being more hunted, trek much longer distances than they formerly did, and in some places will not visit a drinking-pool two nights in succession. Man is more than ever their dire enemy. They also make for thicker country, which means that it is more difficult, when one has got up to them, to get a good shot.

All these changed habits compensate for the vast improvement of modern rifles and their increased range and killing power. There is a great difference between a modern high-velocity double ejector ·470 cordite rifle and the old muzzle-loading 4- and 8-bore black-powder weapons, which took some time to load, and when loaded kicked like infuriated mules. Then there was the dense cloud of smoke from the black powder, which hung like a blanket in front of the hunter, giving a splendid signal to the wounded beast if he felt inclined to be crusty. The old hunters were plucky fellows to tackle game with these cumbrous weapons.

98

ZEBRA WITH MY GUN-BEARER MUMBA, NORTH-EASTERN RHODESIA.

Most practical modern hunters prefer a single or
magazine rifle to a double, as they are lighter to
carry, and most of the large-bore magazine weapons
can hold three cartridges in the magazine as well as
the one in the breech.   This gives one four shots instead of two in the double, which is undoubtedly a
great advantage.   Certainly for two quick shots the
double scores, but a third and fourth prevent that
fumbling which usually takes place in loading a double
quickly.

The best large-bore magazine rifle I know of is a
·416 Rigby-Mauser, although Jeffery's ·404, Westley
Richard's ·425, and Gibbs's ·505 are all excellent
weapons of their kind.   I have owned many types
and bores of sporting weapons, from a single 4-bore
black-powder rifle to ·256 Mannlichers.   For several
years I used ·303 rifles, and later a ·318 "Axite," ·350
old-pattern Rigby-Mauser, and ·350 "Magnum" by
the same maker, which was a fine weapon with its
flat trajectory and shock-giving qualities.

The difficulty of getting cartridges for many of
these rifles induced me to get a 7·9 mm. Mauser from
Rigby, as cartridges of this size could then be bought
from several stores in the country.   So as to get it
quickly by post from home, I had it made with a
24-inch detachable barrel.   This rifle weighed 7¼ lb.,
a very nice weight to carry on long tramps through
rough bush.   I was very successful with this little
rifle, and killed nearly every species of game in Central
Africa with it, from bull elephants to duikers.

I have written a good deal on rifles, but do not
intend to say so much in this volume except to give
my personal experience with different bores as I go
along in my story.   One thing, however, I would like
to say, and that is that when the young hunter gets
to know his weapon, it does not follow that he will
do better with another rifle which may have the

99

advantage of a flatter trajectory, as he will likely find that the type of weapon and action he has become accustomed to will suit him best. It is a mistaken idea that new things are always better than old, for gunmakers often form their theories from the behaviour of a weapon at a target, which is a different proposition to its use against tough African game.

A good many books have been written on rifles by men who have a good theoretical knowledge of their points, but little practical experience of their use in the field, so in the case of a youngster he is better advised to copy the experienced hunter than the experienced theorist.

Very light bullets are a mistake, though they naturally tend to give higher velocities and flatter trajectories, but they break up more readily and do not penetrate efficiently in heavy game. This is where rifles such as " Magnum " ·256s, ·275s, and ·280s fail. There is a happy medium in bullet weights if one is to get an all-round proficiency in practice. With an ordinary high-velocity rifle, say a ·256 Mannlicher with a bullet velocity of 2,300 foot-seconds, there is always a tendency to shoot too high, so with a " Magnum," say a ·280 Ross, the fault may be accentuated as it has a bullet velocity of 3,000 foot-seconds.

One of the best rifles I ever tried was a ·318 " Axite," but I got a bad batch of cartridges with it, so disposed of it, telling the buyer I had had several missfires, which he said he would risk, but he told me later that he got them replaced by the gunmaker for a lot with better caps, as it had been found that the caps were defective.

Single-falling block rifles are very nicely balanced tools, like well-made double rifles, and this is their chief advantage over magazine weapons, which seldom balance well. I had a lovely little ·303 falling-block single by Fraser of Edinburgh with which I bagged a lot of game, and it handled almost like a rook rifle. It was no weight to carry on a thirty-mile tramp through rough bush, but it had a bad defect, as the side lever sometimes failed to eject the empty case, and on occasions I have had to put the butt on the ground and press the sole of my boot on the lever to force it open. This fault got worse when the chamber got slightly corroded with the powder gases, and is one of the old drawbacks against the ·303, as I never found this happen in any rifles I owned regulated for Axite or Troisdorf powder. Magazine rifles, such as Lee-Enfield, Mauser, Mannlicher, and Mannlicher-Schönauer actions nearly always eject efficiently. The Mauser is supposed to have the strongest action, and the Mannlicher-Schönauer works smoothest and is the most silent.

I have not had much experience of the Ross straight-pull action, as I have only handled one or two belonging to friends, though by comparison I thought the Mauser a better action.

The old-type ·256 Mannlicher is loaded either singly or with a clip (not a charger) holding five cartridges. I have had one or two jams with it, and found, when used with a ·375 barrel and cartridge, that the magazine spring was too weak to force up such heavy cartridges, and it jammed frequently.

Personally, unless I was expecting to make a living by elephant-shooting (it can hardly be done now with the limit on licences), I would not bother to buy an expensive rifle such as a ·470 or ·416, but would shoot my couple a year, or whatever was allowed on the licence, with the small rifle I used for lesser game, using, of course, solid bullets, and the rifle I would pick would be a ·318 regulated for the 250-grain bullet, and with a 24-inch barrel.

Now I will get back to Fort Manning, where I was busy with Stigand arranging matter for the projected work on spoor, which entailed trips of various durations to find suitable tracks. I intended later to go to North-Eastern Rhodesia to get an appointment to see me through the rains, and there resume operations in the bush for spoor-sketching and note-taking.

On the 31st of July, a glorious day with a hot sun overhead and a cool breeze blowing, Mostyn and I took a walk down the old Kongoni road, and he then returned to the fort to work. With my hunter " boy," whose name was the staggering one of Kacha-kapaenda [1] (I used to call him " Katcho "), I struck into the bush on the left side of the road, he carrying my ·303 Jeffery rifle, and I a new short ·303 sporting rifle I had just got out from Gibbs of Bristol. I had never used it except to try three shots at a target to test the sighting, so I was very keen to blood it on game, the bigger the better.

We kept walking up-wind and looking all round for game, as there were plenty of tracks all over the ground showing that we might see something at any moment. Suddenly the " boy " picked up a chewed leaf and said in his language, " Elephant are near, master," so I looked into my cartridge-bag to see how many solid bullets I had with me, as I always made a point of having a few in the bag. I only found five, and wished I had had more, but I loaded the short Gibbs rifle with them, and we took the spoor.

I suppose we had gone slowly for about half a mile when we heard branches breaking just ahead, and we soon got a glimpse of three elephants. The distance

---

[1] This man's adult name was Wagwa. Natives often change their baby name on reaching adolescence to another, and for some reason object to the first one being used. Sometimes, on being asked their names, they forget the last one and give the former, and it was so in this case when I first asked his name.—AUTHOR.

separating us was not more than twenty-five yards, and the country consisted of large bushes with a few scattered trees here and there, but nothing, I noticed, which might have been good cover if anything happened in the way of a charge. Then I saw a fourth elephant beyond the others which was almost hidden by the bush.

I was preparing to shoot at one with fair tusks which was standing broadside on, when " Katcho " told me one in the act of twisting a large branch off a tree was larger, so I shifted the sights on to him. His head was up, exposing the base of his throat where it meets the chest, and knowing that this was a deadly shot for all the big antelopes, I aimed carefully and pressed the trigger. This is always an exhilarating moment when firing at big stuff, as the subsequent proceedings to a shot may be very lively. It was so in this case, for the elephant gave a shrill scream, piercing in its intensity, sent the branch which he had just broken off flying through the air, and subsided backwards in a sitting position. I have shot a good many elephants since, but never saw one of them fall exactly like this. One on the left began to make a deep rumbling sound, and all of them were uttering loud screams of what sounded like anger mixed with fright and consternation.

Then one stopped screaming and began to advance, flapping his big ears on his sides ; but fortunately the other two had started off, which induced the pluckier one to follow, and he turned sideways, receiving a bullet in the shoulder. He then put up his tail and bolted hard after the others, which by this time were going hard.

The one on the ground was not dead, so I used my remaining three solid bullets in putting him out of pain. Then I did what was a foolish thing—but I was raw then—for I filled the magazine with Mark V hollow-point bullets and followed the wounded elephant for some way, luckily not finding him as he had gone clean away. Had he waited for me, I doubt whether I could have stopped him with these expanding bullets, though I had decided in my mind to shoot for his body, and not his head, if we did meet.

I came back to the dead elephant, and we cut off his tail and started for Fort Manning, on the way putting up a splendid roan bull, which bolted and came to a stand about a hundred yards off. He dropped to my shot, and I ran in and finished him off before he could get up again. We cut off his head (the horns were quite good) with a small knife, which took some time as the heads of all the larger antelopes are hard to remove with a diminutive blade, and carried on for the fort, which we reached about lunch-time.

Next day I brought my Kodak and got some pictures, which turned out poorly as the grass had been waving in the breeze across the lens of the camera. I had also brought plenty of solid bullet cartridges, so, telling the men whom I had brought along to start getting out the tusks, I went off on the spoor of the wounded bull of yesterday, and tracked him for a long way, but found the three animals were all going strong, the wounded one running and walking with the others, showing he was not severely wounded. I found subsequently that once a wounded elephant goes for a few miles without stopping, it is almost a hopeless quest to go after him.

Coming back to the carcass, I found the tusks almost out and the natives had been careful not to chip the ivory. They have a strange superstition about removing the large nerves which run up the tusks, and an old grey-headed man took them off behind some bushes and lighted some grass, which he passed over the base and into the holes after he had pulled out the nerve-matter. They believe that should a youth or maiden see this done, they will never be able to have children—a queer idea ; but the natives have some extraordinary beliefs, probably founded on some occurrence which happened in the misty past. The immemorial appeals to them.

The usual mob of villagers arrived in scores, the women with their squalling babes being jostled about as they ran to seize big chunks of meat flung out to them by their menfolk. Some most amusing scrimmages took place, and one would see two old hags fighting like wild-cats for a juicy lump of flesh or a greasy mass of fat. However, they seldom come to blows, but they make up for this in screams and lamentations when unsuccessful.

Elephant meat is greatly appreciated, more than any other game, as the natives think eating it gives them strength and bravery in danger.

On getting the tusks to the fort, I found they weighed 34 and 32 lb. respectively. Their length was 5 feet on the curve, and they were a nice, un-blemished pair, not being cracked or broken in any way.

Wishing to get my second elephant allowed by licence, I had men out often to try to get news of them, so at last a man came from Kamwendo's village to say a good bull was coming to the maize-gardens near that place. I went out, and we at last found his spoor leading into some very high, tangled grass. Fortunately, there were a few large anthills sprinkled here and there, so from one of these we at last got a glimpse of the back of the elephant standing sleeping. I noticed there was an anthill close to him, so decided to get to it if possible. When in the grass nothing was visible and it was hard to keep a true direction.

I may say this elephant had been dusting himself with reddish earth from anthills, so when I got near

I thought I saw the anthill, and was preparing to go to it when Kamwendo touched my arm and said, " Njovu, bwana." I now saw that the object close to me was part of the elephant, so we promptly retreated in the grass, which was horribly thick, and made a detour, at last seeing the anthill. I crawled up its rather steep sides, and " Katcho " crawled behind me with the second rifle. Getting a beautiful sight at the elephant's earhole, I was just pressing the trigger when " Katcho " put his hand on a dry reed and made it crack. Like a flash the elephant wheeled right round, and the bullet, which I could not stay, hit him in the ribs and not the brain. He bolted through the grass, the up-and-down movement of his body with each stride making him rise and fall, so it was difficult to shoot straight. I tried to break his back, but failed to do so, and I am sorry to say I never got him, though I tried my best to overtake him.

When he was standing asleep, I noticed that he swayed slightly backwards and forwards. I was very annoyed with " Katcho " for spoiling my shot and losing me the elephant, as he had a very nice pair of long tusks. The sun was frightfully hot, and we were a tired and disappointed party when we got back to camp.

In the interval of waiting for news of elephants I used to go out into the bush and shoot a buck occasionally such as a sable, hartebeest, or reedbuck. One day I got a warthog sow, which was a plucky animal, as it tried to come for me, but I killed it easily with a second bullet before it got close enough to use its tusks.

In a few weeks I was successful in getting a second bull elephant with large tusks, and the tallest elephant I have ever seen. Kamwendo, who has been at the death of over fifty bull elephants, told me he had never seen a taller animal, and afterwards, when he had been out with Europeans and seen many more good ones killed, he still asserted that this one was by far the tallest he had ever seen. Unfortunately, it fell against a small tree in dying, and though I got the tree cut down, we could not get him in a natural position for a measurement.

The tallest elephant I ever measured was 10 feet 7 inches from the top of the shoulder to the flat of the forefoot nearest the ground, and he was much less than the one I have referred to. Kamwendo was also present at the death of this one, so I asked him to make a mark where the tall one would have come to if lying in the same place, and the mark he made was quite a foot more. Of course, this was not good enough for any authenticated measurement, but natives are very observant, and this tall elephant was known in the district as a monster for height. He was called the " Great One " in the district. I spoored him some way from the grain-fields of a village called Mponda's, and he had visited the village the previous night with a herd which had broken into some of the natives' grain-bins (*n'cokwe*), and I had had to turn out in the dark and help them drive the animals away with flares made of dry grass. We got up to this bull, which had separated from the herd, in two hours, and found him in an open glade dusting himself with sand which he was sending over his back and sides, all the time making strange abdominal rumblings. These internal rumblings ("colly-wobbles" they might be called) are sometimes the first thing heard when following an elephant in thick bush. I suppose they denote that his digestion is giving trouble, or working at high pressure.

As this elephant put down his head to suck in some sand, I fired at his forehead, a silly shot to take at an African bull elephant. When the bullet struck him he gave a scream and started in our direction, not quite hitting "Katcho" and myself off correctly as he went past, getting two bullets in his side when passing. He then ran through some men I had left behind, including old Kamwendo and Mponda, and I was startled by a piercing yell, and the sound of the elephant thumping something with his great feet, which, I may say, afterwards measured 58½ inches in circumference. Loading up my rifle, I ran with "Katcho" towards the sound, but could not see exactly what the elephant was doing owing to the thick bush. I saw his head, however, though he kept moving it about violently, and put several bullets into it as fast as I could pump them out, as I thought he had a man underfoot. Then he collapsed against a tree and died, as the last shot had brained him.

I could not find out exactly the bullet which had caused him to stop in his violent rush, though I think it was my second shot, which possibly injured the neck-bone, as I found a tiny hole near the middle of the neck. The man who screamed was Mponda, who had been knocked aside by his rush, hitting a tree and taking a patch of skin off one leg.

The right tusk was chipped at the point, and the two measured 6½ and 6 feet, and weighed 53½ and 47 lb. Like all the elephants in this part of Africa, the ivory was of very good quality, being called " soft " in contrast to the " hard " ivory often got in West Africa and Uganda.

I returned to Fort Manning to rest for a bit after the hard work of hunting elephant. It is without doubt the most arduous sport that any man can go in for, as the elephants usually take the roughest country in their wanderings.

In the dry season water is scarce, and any taken out in gourds or water-bottles gets hot with the terrific sun which blazes out of a molten-looking sky, fairly frizzling up the moisture in the human body, until

CUTTING OUT IVORY, NORTH-EASTERN RHODESIA.

THE MEAT-LOVERS AT WORK ON AN ELEPHANT.

one's tongue becomes so dry and swollen that it is sometimes difficult to speak fluently.

After struggling on the spoor of elephant, often for six hours or more, one is tired with the hard going and burnt with the torrid heat, the dust and sweat have got into one's eyes and mouth and the strain of searching out the spoor and the intense glare have blurred the sight, often just at the moment when the game is sighted, and when one needs all one's best energies to settle the business. Under these circumstances it is best, after sighting the elephants, to take a breather, though there is not always time for this as the beasts may be suspicious and on the verge of departure.

If the selected bull is in the middle of a large herd, there is the added difficulty of circumventing the others so as to obtain a satisfactory shot at him; not always an easy matter, as the small bulls and cows are often more wary than the patriarch of the herd. A cow with a calf may make herself unpleasant, or just as one is preparing to shoot at the bull some of the others may move into the way. Then, to cap everything, the bullet fired into the bull may not kill him, and he runs off, having to be followed quickly, though the hunter is so tired already that he can hardly drag one leg after the other.

The wind is the primary point to be considered, as a whiff of a human being will send elephant off immediately, or it may make them more inquisitive if they are disinclined to bolt. However, the rule is that they go as fast as they can, as the usual instinct of wild animals is to escape.

At the end of the dry season—September, October, and November—the wind is often very shifty due to the heat and those strange phenomena, dust-whirls (also called dust-devils), which are caused by vacuums formed by the heated atmosphere.

Once when lying resting on my camp-bed under a shelter of branches and grass, I had my handkerchief lying on my chest when a dust-whirl came along, picking up leaves, strands of grass, and even small branches, and lifted the handkerchief into the air, where I watched it get higher, until it passed on with a circular movement into space. It was interesting watching the corkscrew kind of spiral of the handkerchief as it disappeared.

I suppose these whirls are on land what a waterspout is at sea, though I never saw any water go up in them as they passed over the Luangwa River, where I used to see them frequently. I have seen several waterspouts in the Indian Ocean.

A good way to test the wind is to carry a tiny bag of fine flour and shake it occasionally, or wet a finger and hold it in a wind, when the side nearest the wind gets slightly cooled. Another plan is to take a handful of fine sand, or put a few downy feathers plucked from a fowl or game-bird into one's pocket.

Stigand and I went off on the 31st of August for a shoot into Portuguese territory, but the pleasure of the trip was completely spoilt for me by spiking my knee with a thorn a few days before. The thorn broke off under my left knee-cap, and the heavy walking made it fester, and I shall not easily forget the pain these long marches caused me, for I became such a cripple that I had to hobble along with the help of a stick. When it had festered for some time I managed to get the thorn out, and then it soon healed, though too late to do much hunting on that expedition.

Stigand got a buffalo and had several unproductive chases after elephant, the approach being spoilt by the changing eddies of wind which I have just mentioned, and which are such a nuisance to the elephant hunter.

Soon after this I went to Fort Jameson, where I stayed for a few months. When I got a few days' leave I used to go out to some village within forty miles for a shoot, and got various game such as roan, sable, hartebeest, kudu; but these trips were very tame after shooting elephants.

In November we heard that a white hunter named Johnston had been killed by an elephant he had wounded. Later I saw the tusks, as the elephant had died soon afterwards. The elephant had broken one of them into several pieces with the force of the blows, probably striking a rock or the hard ground underneath. The fragments were covered with blood from the unfortunate hunter.

On the 8th of January 1905 a violent wind and thunderstorm came along and blew the galvanized iron roof off the Victoria Memorial Institute, some of the pieces being carried quite a hundred yards by the force of the gale. I remember seeing a strip sticking straight out of the trunk of a tree which it had struck with a great velocity. This gives a fair idea of the power of a tropical storm.

In January 1905 I left Fort Jameson for Mzazas, on the Luangwa River, very glad to see the last of that seat of light and learning for a space. I never liked life in an African township, or work at a desk, so it was pleasant to get out into the bush again and breathe more freely.

The rains had broken, and I had a rough trip to the Luangwa, as it poured hard almost every day. Before leaving I had bought a large 10-bore double Purdey rifle, but sold it later to an officer in the K.A.R. who was going a shooting trip in North-Eastern Rhodesia. Personally I would rather trust to a small ·303 than one of these big black-powder weapons, which are bulky and difficult to shoot with. The volume of smoke, too, is an intolerable nuisance, especially in damp weather. In a wind it soon blows clear.

Even in this bad weather the men were fairly cheery until we came to a range of hills over which I took a short-cut. The path here was little used, so the high grass enveloped it and made it difficult. Central African natives loathe cold, as it almost paralyses them. It seems to affect their brains too, as they get quite dazed and stupid. At such times they will sit down and say they are going to die, but a little forcible persuasion on these occasions is quite good for them, as it seems to warm them up. Before such a thing as beating is contemplated, it is far better to make a few jokes, as they are very susceptible to humour and sarcasm. One can get a few extra miles out of them (especially if they belong to a dominant tribe such as the Awemba) by telling them they are behaving like women or children. They hate that more than corporal punishment.

Most of the successes of a hunter will be due to the long-suffering efforts of his carriers, and also the help of the villagers, who often supply men who are really fine trackers. A really good white man will probably beat the ordinary villager after he has spent years in the bush, but he will never equal the best of them.

Kamwendo (who was an Achipeta, I think) was a marvel on elephant-spoor in his own locality. He often instinctively knew where to pick up fresh spoor, and how an elephant would go ; and I have only seen one other man who could equal him when after elephant. He was a good man to get at that time, for he was always going from village to village after native beer, and he thus picked up news of elephant. In 1904 he was a middle-aged man, so by this time he will be old for a native, as he is now probably over sixty years of age.

MY HUNTING CAMP, BUA RIVER, NYASALAND.

SHELTER FOR TROPHIES AND STANDS FOR COOKING MEAT.

The atrociously wet weather made camp life very uncomfortable, and it was a bother keeping my rifles clean, as they soon get rusty in a damp climate.

On my trek to the Luangwa I did not see much game, although I often went out shooting in the afternoon. The grass was getting long and the country was flooded, so all the game had scattered far and wide.

On the 20th I had a hard march, as I had to get through a great marsh with two streams flowing through it. My men were very plucky, as they were often nearly swept off their feet in the rush of water. The thick reeds, however, gave them something to hold by, and eventually we all emerged on to comparatively dry land (it was pouring hard) with all the loads and men intact.

Close to the path I noticed a large tree with a notice-board fixed to it on which was written, " Reader, prepare for death," and a date and name—Jeanie Gilchrist, a missionary who had been buried here. As we had just passed through a veritable " slough of despond," I was rather amused at the epitaph on the board, notwithstanding the sympathy I felt for the victim in meeting her end in such a dismal place. I suppose she had been ill with fever when she reached this vile spot, and the hardships she had endured had ended her sufferings. It was no place for a delicate white woman, as I can testify.

At the camp I had formed that evening the rain simply poured down until my tin boxes on the floor of the tent were standing in several inches of water. I was interested in seeing a label with the name Siliguri on one of them. Siliguri is a station under the Himalayas, in India, so they must use a tenacious kind of gum there for a label to stand much of this kind of thing. I had had this box in India with me.

At last the rain kept off for a time, and I was able

to get out, with a shotgun I had procured before leaving Fort Jameson, and shoot four guinea-fowl. I browned them, getting two for each barrel, as I was out for the pot, not for sport, and guinea-fowl are most excellent eating after tough buck or stringy village fowls. I saw three small wild-cats and some monkeys, and a good deal of game spoor, during my evening walk.

As I sat in the verandah of a good rest-house I had come to, there was a gorgeous sunset with some lovely reds in the sky, paling off to the most delicate tints. This rest-house was one used by the native Commissioner on his visits to this district, and was called N'gucha.

Next day I got a headman of a small village to guide us to Mzazas, promising him a few yards of calico for his trouble, so we got on better, as we did not make a mistake by taking the wrong path when there were several crossing each other. Native paths are almost like a spider's web in places.

On the 23rd I shot a warthog, which gave us a little fresh meat, and the carriers were so happy that they sang for several hours in the evening when sitting over their camp-fires.

Next day I reached the Luangwa River, which was in flood with the heavy rains. While passing through the mopani forests near the river, my Irish terrier, named Tim, ran after a small herd of impala, spoiling a chance I might have had to shoot one.

The Luangwa at the spot I struck it was a good 150 yards in breadth, and we had all to wait an hour before the natives on the other bank heard our shouts and brought over a leaky dugout. I must say I did not much fancy this vessel, as when loaded with ten men and the kit there were only a few inches between the sides and the water, and an upset in the raging torrent would certainly have meant disaster. Tell-

THE LUANGWA RIVER, NEAR NAWALIA, NORTH-EASTERN RHODESIA.

RHINO BLOWN AFTER THREE HOURS IN A HOT SUN.
Note dried mud on body.

ing the men to keep still, we all got over in three trips, and then I had some tea before walking a few miles down the west bank to Mzazas, shooting an impala ram on the way. I came on this impala in a lovely forest of mopani trees.

African rivers rise very quickly, especially a river such as the Luangwa, which is fed by numberless streams flowing from the great Muchinga range of mountains, which run parallel to the river for a great distance.

Although there were plenty of tsetse-fly not far away, there was a small herd of cattle at Mzazas belonging to an Italian named Paolucci, who had asked me to look after them when I was living in a hut here which belonged to him. It was my intention to study the game in the vicinity, and make notes and sketches of the tracks.

On the opposite side of the river from Mzazas was the Luangwa Game Reserve, so I had asked Mr. Codrington, Administrator of North-Eastern Rhodesia, for permission to shoot in the Reserve, promising not to interfere with a herd of giraffe which lived here, the only giraffe to be found in North-Eastern Rhodesia, and the main reason why the Reserve had been made. I kept my promise, and only examined them at times and got some drawings of their tracks. They were beautiful animals, and the shooting of such splendid creatures can afford little satisfaction to anyone, as they are absolutely harmless and there is little interest in any trophy they can supply when dead.

My most exciting remembrance of Mzazas was an occasion when lions visited the place on a dark night and pulled down a line of reim I had cut from hide and stretched on some trees.

Tim, the Irish terrier, never minded leopards, as he used to run out at them, and in the end got killed by one when I had given him to a friend to keep when

I was shooting in tsetse-fly country. The great roaring of the lions, however, made him shake all over with fright, and no wonder, for they were within twenty yards of the hut when they started their ear-splitting chorus. The rain was sweeping down with a strong gale which was blowing at the time, and the night was as dark as a pool of ink. The crickets, which usually enlivened the night with their monotonous chant, were all silent as death as the resounding vibration of the mighty music rang through the night.

I had a few small windows in my hut, and I went to one and tried to see the marauders, but it was hopeless, as I could not see a yard, and my lamp which I had brought with me was immediately blown out by the wind. My " boys " lived in huts behind mine, and they too kept as quiet as mice, for they knew terror was abroad. Then the great cats went off and pulled down the reim, and next day I found their spoor on a path leading to the river, where they had gone for a drink.

I have often heard lions roaring, but never so close as this, and I may say that there is a vast difference between their roars at two miles and twenty yards. After each roar one could hear the in-drawing of their breath and the deep sigh of what seemed satisfaction at making such a glorious noise.

Selous, in his first splendid work, *A Hunter's Wanderings in Africa*, mentions how he once lay in the bush on a rainy night and heard lions roar close to him, and he describes in most fluent language the tremendous power of their voices when heard at close quarters. It is quite impossible in writing to give the reader a true impression of the intensity of these sounds, as the only way to appreciate them is to have the experience of hearing them under such wild conditions of place and weather.

After the lions had gone and the storm had abated

116

I called my hunter " boy " and took my rifle and a lamp and went down to the cattle kraal to see if the cattle were all right, as an old bull had been roaring too, but in a weak minor key compared with the great cats. Cattle often " speak " when lions are about, and an old bull is invariably one of the first to object strongly to their presence.

The lions had found the thorn palisade round the poles too strong, for I found next day they had had a sniff at the kraal. Finding the cattle were safe, I returned to my hut and bed, quite cheered by the lovely concert I had had during the evening.

There is something fascinating, in fact exhilarating, in listening to the voices of wild creatures on the prowl, for such sounds are the most primitive on the earth, and I suppose the day is coming when such incidents will be a thing of the past, the only records being those left by the men who have experienced them.

This night, and the one when I sat with Shave in his bungalow in Cachar listening to the fight between the tiger and the buffalo, are two of the most interesting I have had the luck to experience, and both are a lively remembrance to me.

I had been very ill with fever for some time, and this terminated in a bad attack of blackwater fever which came on coming back from Serenje, a station sixty miles off on the Muchinga Plateau. Taken ill when I left there, I struggled back to my hut and lay pretty bad for about a month. Fortunately I had plenty of milk, of which I used to drink great quantities when warmed up. I never saw a doctor, as the nearest was at Fort Jameson, about 150 miles away, so I had to do the best I could without one, and managed to pull through, mainly by the help of the milk, as of course I could eat no solids for some time.

It is thought now by the medical profession that the use of quinine is an incentive to getting an attack of blackwater. Whether this is fact I do not know, but I do know that after such an attack one is not so susceptible to malarial fever, as the more serious complaint seems to clear the system of the germs of malaria.

When out after a rhino one day I found a pretty land tortoise, the shell of which was just like the tortoiseshell of commerce, and not the dark-greenish colour of the usual variety commonly seen, so I kept it and have it at home.

The most numerous species of game near Mzazas were waterbuck and impala, though bushbuck were also fairly common. The waterbuck (*Cobus elipsyprymnus*) is perhaps the toughest antelope in the country, as they are extremely tenacious of life when not mortally hit at the first attempt.

I have noticed that an animal after a shot may get a kind of paralysis of the nervous system, which enables it to withstand wounds which, if given in the first instance, would have proved fatal. Other hunters have noticed this fact and mentioned it in their writings, without expressing any opinion as to the cause of this insensibility to pain. I noticed it on many occasions with various wounds, so could not decide in my mind the injury which was mainly responsible for causing it, except that I am sure it has something to do with the nerve centres of the anatomy.

When out shooting in the Reserve I came on a pack of wild dogs and shot two of them. I have read accounts of shooting in which the wild, or hunting, dog is accused of being a nasty customer to interfere with, though I never found them really dangerous. When come on they have a way of stopping to look back at the intruder, and are often slow when retreating. If the grass is higher than they can see over

118

WATERBUCK BULL.

Shot and photographed by George Garden.

they stand up on their hind legs to have a look, giving short barks and a sound like "yak-yak-yak." I shot some near Fort Manning, and on several occasions came on them, but if I was after any special game I left them alone as not being worth a shot, for they are usually mangy, as they seem to suffer from a skin disease which makes the hair fall out.

Once I saw a pack chasing a waterbuck, going steadily on in a relentless way, the front dogs keeping their noses on the spoor like a pack of foxhounds, and running mute except for a cackling sound at times. Any animal they chase is probably doomed unless he can cross water, as the dogs are persevering and have wonderful endurance and fair speed.

The waterbuck was going all out and was about half a mile ahead of the dogs when I saw him, running parallel with the Luangwa, and I wished I could have told the hunted animal what to do by crossing it, and so escaping the pack behind. The dogs were coming on steadily, and at the time they did not seem to be going as fast as the waterbuck, though I had not the least doubt that they would wear him down in the end.

These animals are a scourge in a game country, as they hunt the place clean, or rather frighten the animals they do not kill so much that they leave the locality for a week or two. Possibly, if a pack met an unarmed native, they might go for him if ravenous with hunger, but a white man with a modern rifle is a different proposition altogether.

Baboons, which I never found inclined to act on the offensive, are given a bad character in parts of Africa, and I suppose no definite rule can be made about the behaviour of any animal.

Most dangerous animals attack when they think it is the only course left, or when a bad wound prevents them moving away fast enough to escape. The only exception is a female with young. Then the sense of protection which Nature has given to the mothers of all life comes into action, and the lioness will come on to save her cubs, and the cow elephant to guard her calf. This, however, is not an absolutely infallible rule, as I have known of cases when many animal mothers left their offspring, possibly thinking they were left hidden from observation, but probably because the sense of fear was stronger than maternal affection.

Natives have told me that a pack of wild dogs will sometimes attack and kill a single lion. I fancy, in such instances, that the lion is an old animal almost finished with life, as I could never imagine an adult lion of normal activity falling a prey to such animals.

Lions in Africa, as well as tigers in India, often lame themselves when killing a porcupine by getting a quill in their foot, which festers quickly in such a carnivorous animal. Such an accident prevents the animal hunting, and is sometimes the cause (as other accidents may be) of lions and tigers taking to man-eating. The difference between a man-eating lion and tiger is that a lion may pass from game to man as opportunity offers, whereas a tiger usually sticks to humans once he has found how easy they are to kill. Another distinction is that man-eating lions have no hesitation in breaking into native huts; whereas the tiger nearly always lies in wait for his victims near much-used roads or paths.

I have heard of leopards which killed a score or two of people before their career was ended, and they are really worse than lions and tigers in being more cunning, and being smaller are more difficult to find. Leopards prefer a woman or child to an adult man, as the former are, of course, easier victims, and they sometimes come right into villages on dark nights and grab a native child while passing from one hut to

120

another, and then drag their prey into the bush to eat it, unless driven off by the men. I have known several African natives who, with an axe or spear, have killed a leopard which came for them, and seen a few who were badly marked by the claws and teeth of a leopard which had sprung at them when in the bush. Probably in these cases the man nearly trod on the beast in thick grass, and thinking itself cornered it acted offensively, and this is by no means a rare occurrence in Central Africa.

The natives round Mzazas belonged to the Asenga tribe, not a very fine lot in many ways, but I suppose they had been so badly treated in the old days by the raiding tribes, such as the Angoni, that the spirit had been knocked out of them and they had never got it back. The women wear the *pelele*, or lip ornament, which makes them infinitely more hideous than they naturally are. This adornment, I believe, was originally invented by some chief who wished to make his women so ugly that marauding tribes would be so disgusted that they would omit to carry them off. When one comes to think of it, this was quite an ingenious thought for a native to conceive, as they seldom suffer from too much imagination in preparing for the future, leaving a lot to chance, and then putting it down to witchcraft.

Every malign happening is connected with some superstition. If a man, woman, or child dies, an enemy has bewitched them. If a person is killed by a lion, an enemy's spirit has passed into that animal and revenged itself. If a man's wife forgets to put a pinch of salt into his food, she has committed adultery; and so on *ad infinitum*. From the time they emerge from babyhood to the day when they sit in their grey-headed dotage, on a mat, blinking in the sun, they seem the victims of a malignant fate which holds their minds in thrall. If education is to be effectual, it must be given to the young, for the old people are hopeless, because their minds are atrophied. An old native's brain is crammed with superstition and myths, but as far as that goes civilized people are not a whit better.

I remember going to India in a Clan liner which carried a cow which went sick. A lady on board, of the Roman Catholic faith, hung a medallion round the cow's neck and assured us it would get better. It did, but none of us could understand the cow's opinion of the proceedings! As long as people can believe in symbols and their effect on human or animal fate, something is wrong with the reasoning powers of such believers and they are little removed from the veriest savage.

To me it is questionable whether civilization, with its so-called education, tends to make the natives happier. I am certain that they would prefer our room to our company, for they would be quite happy living their natural lives and settling their quarrels in the good old way with spears or knobkerries. I think the fact of our presence is reflected in the attitudes of a lot of the older people, who sit and ponder over the past when they were free to do as they liked. The lawful peace which now reigns is enough to atrophy their minds and make them think that life is no longer worth living, and I don't blame them. By far the best missions are the medical and industrial, which really do much good amongst the natives.

I seldom, in this volume, use the word " nigger," as many people at home imagine it to be a derogatory term. Most people in Africa call a native a nigger without meaning it as a term of reproach, or insinuating that he is any worse or better than a native of Africa.

I heard an amusing yarn about an old headman who came to a missionary and asked to become a member of his church. The evangelist asked him how many wives he had got, the first question a parson would naturally ask. The native, being a truthful man, said, " Three," and was told that his request was quite impossible as a Christain is only allowed one squaw. He was told that when he had only one wife there might be a chance for him, so he departed, musing deeply on the quaint ways of white men.

In three months he returned with a benign smile on his countenance, and again made his request, so the parson said, " And how many wives have you got now ? " " One," said the beaming nigger. " And where are your other two wives ? " said the missionary. " Oh, I've eaten them," said the headman as he gently patted his tummy.

THE elephant is a dangerous beast to tackle under any circumstances, and the more he is hunted the more is he likely to take reprisals, although I cannot see that he should be blamed for this. An animal which has been plugged by several hunters in non-vital spots of his anatomy cannot be expected to look on it as a pleasant game which only one can play, so he often tries his best to make a very flat pancake of anyone he can get a hold of.

When at Fort Manning with Mostyn and Stigand, we took a pride in flooring an elephant with a small bore such as a ·256, ·303, or 7·9 mm. (·311 bore) ; and there is no doubt that it gives one a pleasant feeling of satisfaction to do the work with as small a bullet as possible. This might be called the supreme art of elephant-shooting. The small bore, however, although perfect for the brain shot, may be rather small for the heart or lung shot, as the animal does not die so quickly, so for body shots I certainly think a ·416 or ·470 H.V. rifle is more humane.

Even with a large bore, when hit in the heart, an elephant may run some distance before falling, and it depends a good deal whether the top of the heart, where the large arteries lie, or the bottom has been punctured. This makes a considerable difference in the time the animal will live after being hit, and whether the elephant, if charging, has sufficient time to do damage. In several books I have used the expression that a small bullet in the right place is better

124

ONE OF MY BEST BULL ELEPHANTS.

Shot near the Nyamazi stream, North-Eastern Rhodesia.

than a large one in the wrong place, and I still think it is, although I would qualify that statement now by saying that for the inexperienced hunter the rifle producing the greatest striking energy (that is, a large bore) is by far the safest to use against all the heavy game. To stop a charging elephant, rhino, buffalo, or lion, a heavy bullet driven at a great velocity is a good type of life insurance. The man who puts in a carefully aimed first shot will not be charged very often, though it is quite impossible to prevent it occasionally happening if the country is covered with heavy grass or bush, where a very close approach is necessary.

By far the worst country to tackle dangerous game in is heavy grass, often so tangled that it is almost impenetrable at any pace, so it is impossible, at times, to do anything else than stay where you are and await events. Another bad kind of cover is thick patches of thorn, which is almost worse than heavy grass because the thorns catch in the clothes, and also in the skin, quite preventing one swinging the weapon. Thick grass also stops one moving the rifle, and no one can shoot accurately at a running object with such obstructions in the way.

People at home, or in more temperate countries, have no idea of the thickness and strength of tropical grasses and reeds. In India, in swampy country, reeds as thick as the human wrist are common, and in Africa, although I have not seen the stuff quite so huge, it is hopeless vegetation to be enveloped in when matters become serious.

Should a herd of elephant or buffalo charge in the open where one is visible when standing, the only thing to do is to lie down, preferably in a hollow, if one can be found, and either shoot when the animals are close or stand up and wave your hat or arms. In such a case the herd almost invariably splits up and passes on both sides, for the game gets such a fright that it seldom thinks of charging straight at the hunter.

It is a marvellous sight to see a herd of elephant bolt in tree country where there are many saplings about, as they crash against and through the timber, often uprooting small trees with the shock of impact. The dust fairly flies with the avalanche of flesh. I remember seeing a bull (tuskless) run between two small trees, pretty high, but not more than a foot in diameter. The two trees seemed to spring out of the ground as they were uprooted and came down with a crash.

Where elephants are numerous they clear large patches of small timber to get the masuko plums and a kind of fruit called a Kaffir orange. I have seen places where they have dug for succulent roots, though some experienced hunters doubt this. It is certainly not a very common habit, but there is no doubt that they occasionally do it, because I saw an elephant chewing a root he had just pulled out of the ground.

There is a vast difference between being an expert hunter and a capable observer, for a man may have shot a hundred or more elephants and know less about their habits than a man who has only shot a quarter of that number, because the former may be after the ivory for the cash he gets for it, and the other may be more interested in the natural-history side of the subject. Some men are better at deductive reasoning than others, and that is why the native is often so inferior to a white man, as immediately something occurs which is new to him he is quite at sea. He is not a Sherlock Holmes in any sense!

If a good tracker is taken from, let us say, Nyasaland to British East Africa and sees a spoor which he could not possibly have seen before, he will find a name for it from the names of those he has already seen. I think when a native spoors well he partly does it by instinct; at least the best tracker of elephants I have seen (Kamwendo) did his best work through knowledge of the habits of the elephants in his district. It was attained by knowledge, not deduction.

In my *Wild Life in Central Africa*, published by *The Field* office, I gave a chapter on the risks of big-game shooting, so I do not wish to repeat the details of men killed and wounded by wild animals which have come under my notice. While in Central Africa I heard of the deaths of eight white men who were killed by elephants. Some of these men I knew, and most of them were experienced, although a few were killed by their first elephant.

Anyone who has watched a bull elephant breaking down a good-sized tree, or twisting off a branch the thickness of a man's leg, is bound to think a bit when he goes close up to a large tusker with the intention of waging a life-and-death struggle with a weapon shooting a bullet the diameter of a slate pencil. He begins to wonder if he should have made his will before starting out on the trip; though probably all he has to leave will be a rifle or two, perhaps a few cattle, some very ragged garments and boots, a copy of Rowland Ward's *Records*, and a few notebooks of his wanderings, and game-bag.

When he sees that tree-limb being ripped off, as we peel a banana, a strange crepitating feeling runs down his spine and he may give a slight shiver, because he is mightily tired and perhaps shaky from fever. Leaving some of the men behind and taking a quencher of tepid water from a gourd covered with some green leaves, he hitches his belt up a hole, sees that his rifle is loaded, and puts a spare clip or two in his pockets. Then his gunbearer, with the spare rifle (if he has one), and he test the wind carefully and find its natural drift, although it will likely be shifty if it is late in the dry season, caused by the heat waves which occasionally strike his roasted face and sun-glared eyes until he feels like a hot cinder.

The tusker is just visible, but there are two smaller bulls near him, and several cows ; so the problem is how to get past them and escape their sensitive trunks, which will catch the slightest trace of tainted air. There is a fair amount of scrubby bush about, enough to enable him to get within forty or fifty yards if he is careful, for although the elephant depends mostly on his smell and hearing for safety, a moving object at fairly close quarters may catch his red, bleary eyes and make him go or come. He has shot elephants before, so he has a certain amount of past experience to guide him, although it is impossible to get the conditions the same on every occasion, which lends a contrast to this entrancing game that he is playing, with his nerves twanging and his head buzzing with the tense excitement of the stalk.

To get round some of the elephants who are in the way, he has to make a detour, passing a female within ten paces as he and his plucky native creep past, now on their knees, which are being scratched by the hard ground and thorns. Then he has reached a thick bush which gives him satisfactory cover, but he has to be careful, as the cow he passed has evidently heard something, for she is suspicious and on the *qui vive*. However, she moves slowly away, giving her ears a few flaps, and making a low rumbling which sounds like water gurgling in a cistern.

Up to now the hunter has not had a very good view of the bull owing to the dense vegetation, but the movements of the wary cow have attracted his attention and he takes a few steps towards her, exposing both his tusks. " A good sixty pounds each," says the hunter to himself as he prepares to shoot by

128

pressing over the safety-catch of his Gibbs's ·256—
"the little marvel," as he once heard a friend describe
this rifle.

Now the hunter's past experience is coming into
action, for he knows if he takes him now it will be
most difficult to reach the brain in the frontal position he is in, so there is another lapse which makes
everything feel very tense and ominous. Except for
the sounds from the elephants and the rustling tread
of the advancing bull, all is still in this land of space.
The hunter feels a bit lonely, so he turns to look at
his gunbearer, Kalenje, and sees a face turning a
yellowish-green colour and a pair of staring eyes fixed
on the advancing tusker.

· It is difficult, even afterwards, to analyse the
thoughts that pass so quickly through the brain.
Some are afraid that they are to be pulverized, others
are exhilarated by the pressing danger, and some
there may be who decide that never again will they
put themselves into such a risky position.

Fortunately, the bull swerves to get round a large
anthill, and in doing so exposes the left side of his
head. Now is the moment for quick action, and the
hunter puts his bead a few inches forward of the earhole and presses the trigger. Just after the shot rings
out, a series of crashes like an avalanche rushing down
a hill-side are heard as the frightened elephants run
here and there before they bolt away. The bull is
out of sight, but several gurgles are heard coming from
behind the bush, so the hunter goes round a little
way and comes up behind the elephant and sees it
on its knees. He notices the great bulk of the
animal, which, as he watches it, gives a shiver and
dies. The elephant has been brained and quickly
killed, but the hunter wonders if a hunt with such
monsters will always end in such a satisfactory way.

The men left behind now come up smiling, one of

them bringing a native-made basket containing a small kettle, and some tea, sugar, and biscuits. Choosing a bush with shade, the hunter sits down and lights his pipe, probably having made a few measurements and taken some photographs before he rests. The " boys " are all grinning as they look at the huge carcass and discuss between themselves whether he will have much inside fat. It is impossible from the external dimensions of a beast to tell this, and one must get inside to find out. One of them, who has evidently come recently from the Salisbury mines, as he wears a pair of khaki slacks, is so over-joyed that he comes up and shakes hands, so one asks him if he ever saw so much meat in Salisbury, and which is the best country ? In his native language he makes one understand that " there's no place like home."

It is mighty hot in this bare, dried-up forest, as only some of the evergreen bushes give shade, but it is pleasant sitting there and looking at the grand beast and the fine trophies in his head. One thinks of the friends who were in similar scenes, and the last day when something went wrong, which meant the end for them.

I have heard of men who drugged themselves before attacking elephants, but whether this is a fact I cannot say, as one does not like to question men on their habits, and none of them ever told me he did this. It is a foolish thing to do, just as it would be to swallow half a bottle of Scotch whisky in the same circumstances. Narcotics may dull the nerves and produce a feeling of daredevilness, but they also act as a clog to quick observation and movement ; so a man who requires stimulation of this kind should leave dangerous game alone.

It is difficult, when one has shot a number of elephants, to pick out the most exciting incidents of

TREE BROKEN BY A BULL ELEPHANT IN NYASALAND.

Under break the circumference was 52½ inches.

130]

the various hunts, as many of them are similar up to the moment one gets in sight of the bull, or the herd he is with. There are certain streams which are very pleasant memories, for there one camped close to the water or the pool selected, and started out on many an exciting day's sport; sometimes being lucky in getting a good tusker, or dragging one's legs along with fever on one, and grievous disappointment at wounding and losing a fine bull.

What a difference success makes on one's mentality, and even strength, and how depressing and weakening is failure, particularly in the early days before grim experience has made a man philosophical and patient!

Two streams, the Rukusi and the Nyamazi, were favourites with the elephant-hunters of North-Eastern Rhodesia in these days. In the rains they were rushing rivers, but only dry sand, with here and there a pool, in the dry season. There were a few rhinos, as well as many elephants, and the country round was inhabited by many species of antelopes.

While camped on one occasion at Katema's village, I had picked up the spoor of a large bull elephant at the pool about half a mile from the tent, where he had drunk with others. On leaving he had gone off by himself, as the larger bulls often do when not associating with the females at a certain season. I had a ·303 Lee-Enfield rifle and a single ·400 falling-block cordite at that time, the latter bought from a hunter named Crood. He, or someone else, had tampered with the lock, and it was a tricky weapon, for suddenly, although set at " safe," it would go off. It had once played this game with me, so I took it to pieces and thought I had cured it, as it seemed to work efficiently.

As there is no saying how soon one will see an elephant when followed in dense bush, I loaded it and the ·303, which I carried myself, for I have always believed in carrying a weapon to save losing a chance of a shot.

Although carrying a fairly heavy rifle during a long day's march through rough African bush is at times a nuisance, it is a wise proceeding to do so, as I have proved on many occasions.

My spoorer was leading, I came next, and a " boy " named Machila had the ·400. We were walking along a native path for a short distance, when suddenly there was a bang just behind me, and I turned to see Machila on his back and the rifle lying on the ground. He had both his hands over his ears and was saying that he was dying. Luckily, just at the moment the rifle cartridge exploded there was a bend in the path where five other men were coming along in the rear, one with a basket containing a kettle, etc., the others with spears or axes. I found they were all on their legs, so knew the bend had enabled the bullet to clear them. As this rifle was a ·450/·400 cordite loaded at the time with a solid bullet cartridge, had these five men been in line (which they had been a second or two before), the bullet would have likely raked the lot.

On picking up the treacherous weapon, I found it was still on safety, so Machila had not moved the catch. The violent kick, as it was held loosely near his ear, had dazed him badly, so I told him to go back to camp and take it easy, and ask my cook for a chunk of *nyama* (meat), so off he went. I decided I would not load the ·400 until it was time to use it, as it was a dangerous tool to have about.

The crash of such a charge early in the day, when the tusker was perhaps only a mile or so ahead of us, was an unpropitious start : which it proved, as we found, on going some way on the spoor, that he had started running for a bit, and then settled down again

132

to his ordinary fast walk along the elephant path he was following, evidently making for some spot ahead to spend the hot hours of daytime.

On and on we went, getting hotter and hotter as the blazing sun got higher in a sky molten and copper-coloured with the heat. Yes, it is hard work spooring elephants, and I often longed to have the steady, long-winded gallop of the hunting-dog when after a trekking pachyderm.

The paths in this district were most interesting, as the elephants had used them for ages, and with the constant rubbing of their feet had worn them below the level of the earth in places. It was wonderful, too, how they always chose the easiest gradient over hilly ground, selecting their path as ably as a civil engineer could have done with the aid of his instruments.

There is no doubt that the elephant is a highly intelligent animal, although the stories told of the Indian species and their wonderful performances are usually founded on an incorrect basis. Nearly all the marvellous things the Indian elephant does are taught them by their *mahouts*, and from the natural intelligence of the animals, which enables the untrained ones to imitate the actions of their trained companions.

The bull's spoor at first passed though fairly open tree and grass country. At one place I found a small snake (a young puff-adder) which the elephant had trodden on when passing. Once before I had found a small field-mouse crushed by the foot of an elephant, and it is not a common thing to find anything they have killed in their colossal movements.

Three hours passed in a steady footslog, and then we came to a lovely valley evidently fed by a small stream, as the trees were beautifully green and shady in places. My " boys " immediately said, " He will be there," as they looked and pointed towards the oasis ahead. Thinking they were all probably correct, I told them to sit down and have a rest for a bit, and lit a pipe, after getting a few tepid mouthfuls of water from a gourd. The tobacco-smoke gave me a good index as to the direction and steadiness of the wind, the most important question as a preliminary to getting closer.

Having rested twenty minutes, we carried on, and soon got into the valley, which looked very beautiful after the sun-scorched bush we had been traversing all morning. The droppings, which had been fresh when we started, were getting fresher, as we could see them steaming when we broke them with our feet. This is a useful thing to do when coming upon an elephant, as the dung dries very rapidly in the blazing sun.

I decided, as the big rifle was untrustworthy, not to load it except in an emergency, or when I got so close that I could load up quickly again if it played me false.

Suddenly we saw the bull, a very fine beast with good tusks, but unfortunately he had left the denser bush, and gone into an open glade with only a few fair-sized trees here and there. I could not get nearer than eighty yards, as he was very suspicious owing to the shifty wind. Although he had not smelt us, I think he heard a branch break which one of my men had foolishly trodden on. As I saw he would soon bolt, I decided to use the ·400 instead of the ·303 and try to get him in the heart. This was a mistake, for the untrustworthiness of the rifle made me shoot too quickly, for I thought that the beastly thing might go off prematurely.

There was a sapling about 8 inches thick right in the line of the heart shot, and I thought I could clear it, so fired. At the shot I saw a piece of bark fly from the sapling, though I hit the elephant all right, as he gave a loud grunt and nearly fell.

Now was the time I should have seized my ·303 and put several bullets into him, as he was still much in the same position, though moving slowly across us. Slipping another cartridge into the ·400, I was just lifting it to my shoulder when the thrice-accursed thing got one of its nasty turns and went off, twisting the rifle out of my hands and taking some skin off my right hand. I let it lie and got hold of the ·303, but the bull had got into a hollow in thicker bush, and was now going for all he was worth with his tail up. Naturally I was disgusted, as he had a lovely pair of tusks, long and nicely curved.

We followed that elephant till dark, and found he had lain down twice and got up again and gone on. Fortunately, we came to another valley where we found a little water, so we built two grass shelters and spent a fairly comfortable night, except that I was a bit bothered by mosquitoes, and a lion which came to drink at the stream. The men were snoring loudly under their shelter and their fire had gone out. The lion grunted as he came along and woke me up, so I blew up my fire and got hold of my ·303 and awakened the men. It was pitch dark, so nothing could be seen much beyond the glare of the fire except the twinkling stars in the heavens.

After we left the elephant spoor I had shot a zebra for the men, so they sat up until past midnight gorging the meat and then slept like logs. As I do not like zebra flesh, I made a little soup in the kettle, and with two biscuits had not done so badly. The tea made in the same kettle tasted strongly of zebra, as it had not been washed out very clean.

We heard the lion drinking, and he lay some time near the stream, and then went off in the opposite direction to the remains of the zebra, and he did not seem to get the wind of the meat and bones lying around our little bivouac. If he had got the smell, I think he might have tried to get a hold of something to eat ; but, then, if he had smelt the meat at the bivouac, he would also have got the taint of the dead zebra and gone for it, as it was within seventy yards.

I shot several good bulls in this district at one time or another, but somehow the unsuccessful days have a greater hold on my memory than many of the successful ones, because the disappointments were so bitter. Most authors deal almost exclusively with their lucky days and forget, or dislike, to mention their lost animals, and such accounts are by no means a fair description of hunting big game. The blank days are those to furnish lessons for the future and to test the grit of the hunter.

About fifty miles from this valley I had followed a fine bull elephant who left the drinking-pool with two smaller males, and had taken us the usual hours of tracking to come up to. It all depends where the elephants intend to stand to pass the heat of the day. If there is much shade to be found, they will probably slow up sooner, as when hot they cannot resist good shade. But a few hours extra for an elephant is nothing compared to the difference it makes to the hunter, with his comparatively short legs and the broiling heat.

Elephants dislike heat as much as humans, although I think the African species is less susceptible to it than the Indian elephant. Their dark skin, too, is not the best colour as a non-conductor of the sun's rays, and I have often wondered why elephants do not become bleached like many plains-loving antelopes. This may be accounted for by the fact that they do the most of their feeding at night, and try their best to keep in the shade between about 10 a.m. and late afternoon. If, however, they are subject to much molestation, they will trek much farther and pass many suitable standing-places because they are afraid to risk being overtaken.

The spoor of the bull and two small ones led us to a low, bushy ridge, and we got quite close to them before we knew exactly where they were. Then we heard elephants moving on both sides, in fact the bull had taken us into a crescent of elephants and we were surrounded by them on three sides. It might have been safer to retreat by the back door, and in fact my men suggested doing a bolt ; but I was very keen to shoot that bull, as I believed him to have good ivories, so I got behind a bush and waited.

When inside a crescent of elephants, it is absolutely certain that it won't be long until they get the wind. Some soon did, and they began to make rumbling sounds in a deep tone, and I could also hear squeaks from some of the cows. This put the bull on the alert and he came walking back, and when he got to where we were, he put his sinuous trunk over the bush and swung it about almost over our heads. At the same time he rattled his enormous ears against his sides, making a noise like a lid of a heavy box falling shut. All I could see through the interstices of the bush was a huge grey mass of flesh and bone towering above me, and that snaky trunk feeling about close to our heads.

Suddenly I got a glimpse of one of his small, wicked-looking reddish eyes, so, as I had to do something pretty quickly, I tried to get my solid ·303 bullet up the eye orifice, and fired. Instead of coming on, which I thought was probable, he almost sat down on his stern with the shock in his head, but he was not killed, as I had hoped when he crashed backwards, for he got up and bolted.

I was shooting with a single ·303 which jammed

after almost every shot, and I had to use a rod to push out the fired case. I was just preparing to do this when the crowd of elephants on our right, frightened by the shot, dashed over the ridge, making the usual crashing and shrill screams, which, heard at such close quarters, are rather menacing. We "froze" like frightened hares, and were relieved to see their large sterns disappear after the bull, who had run off with the elephants which had been close to him on the front and left.

A long chase after the bull ended in disappointment, as it invariably does with an elephant which escapes with a head wound, or even a body wound unless in the heart, lungs, or kidneys. The advantage of the head shot is that an elephant very seldom dies from the result, as he probably does with a bad body wound.

When shooting near the Nyamazi stream in 1905, then one of the finest countries for elephant in Northern Rhodesia, I had excellent sport, getting some fine bulls. Every night they came to drink in the stream in great numbers. Some parts of the stream were full of reeds. Here grew pretty papyrus and a horrid reed called by the natives *matete*. All the spiky leaves of this obnoxious growth had a point as sharp as a needle, which was rather dangerous to the eyes, and pricked bare legs and arms painfully. This grass, or reed, is common on the Luangwa, and on many other rivers, and of course elephants think no more of it than they would of an ordinary hayfield at home, and neither do rhino and buffalo. The larger animals are so powerful that they will face any cover likely to be seen in this country. After they pass through *matete*, the stalks spring back and trip up human beings, and are so strong that one has to step over them, as pushing forward will not break them.

138

One day I followed three bulls through this stuff, as they wandered in it for over two hours before they went off to the dry timber country, covered underfoot with matted grass. I came on the elephants asleep, all standing in the open. It was amusing watching their bulky bodies swaying backwards and forwards, and an occasional movement of a hairy, pointed tail. There is something extremely ludicrous in viewing an elephant from behind, as he looks as if his trousers were coming down, and the oscillating movement accentuates this impression.

The Indian elephant, while in captivity, has been known to live well over a hundred years, so I should think a wild African elephant probably sometimes reaches the age of one hundred and fifty years. If a young man of twenty-five years shoots a very old elephant, it is strange to think that the animal may have lived in the time of his great-great-grandfather.

On one occasion, when stopping at Dedza, in Central Angoniland, the magistrate (Gordon) showed me about thirty stones his natives had found in the stomach of an elephant he had shot. On several occasions after this I found stones inside them, once getting as many as would have filled a good-sized bucket. They probably swallow these stones when drinking at a stream, and also when eating anthill mud. It is unlikely they are swallowed by mistake, as an elephant is too sensitive an animal to do this.

When I was staying once with Selous I told him of this, and he said he had never thought of looking for stones inside them, as he did not know they were inclined to swallow any. This, like the grit fowls and birds eat, may prove a help to their digestive organs, the only reason which seems to account for the habit.

Many African elephants' feet show a fifth toe-nail, usually immature, however, and it is a mistake to say they have only four, and not five, toe-nails like Indian elephants. Two large African elephant feet I have among my trophies clearly show a fifth nail, although, as I have just said, it is not so large as the four others.

Elephants are most interesting animals to watch in a wild state, and, having seen large numbers (at least two thousand), I have spent some enjoyable hours when near them. Elephants will help others off when wounded, as I have seen them do so on two occasions. On one of these instances I hit a bull in the head, and he fell dead as I thought, but was only dazed, and lay motionless with his tusks fixed deeply in the ground, as he fell directly downwards and not on his side. He lay quiet for about a minute, and two of the other elephants came and began prodding him and stroking him with their trunks. Then he awoke and tried to get up, but failed at the first attempt, and I could not get another shot in as the two others were in the line of fire. At last he got on his feet, but was dazed and silly, as he rocked about like a drunken man. I had become so interested that, instead of trying to fire, I stood watching them closely. As the elephant showed signs of collapsing again, the other two got one on each side, and every time he lurched over, the elephant he came against would give him a bump to steady him.

This all took place as they retreated at a slow walk, and I was so fascinated that, instead of running in and trying for another shot, I forgot all about killing him. Once the wounded beast stopped, still dizzy with the hard rap on his skull, and the two hustled him on until they were in the timber, gradually getting up a faster pace, though as long as they were in sight they never broke from a walk. As I was certain this elephant would recover, I did not go far after him, but I went far enough to know that the three of them had run at last.

On the other occasion I saw elephants help each other, I had not hit one, but someone else had, as there was a small wounded bull in the herd. They were going through some open bush, and this small bull (his tusks were not more than 20 pounds each) lagged behind. He seemed slightly lame in a back leg, but it was not broken, as an elephant cannot move with a fractured bone in his hind leg. It is not certain I could have killed him had I wished to, as I shall shortly relate. When he lagged behind, an old cow came back to him twice and hustled him by pressing against his stern.

Some natives who were out for honey crossed the wind, and the elephants got the taint and they ran. As far as I could see, the injured bull did as good time as any of them as long as I could see them. We shortly met these natives, and I bought some honey from them and sat down and made some tea and ate some of it.

This herd had not a decent bull in it, so I did not attempt to follow them.

Now when anyone tells me it is all nonsense that elephants ever think of helping each other, I simply smile if they doubt what I tell them.

At that time there were many bulls going about with tusks of 40 pounds' weight and over. If one was extremely lucky, one might even get an 80-pounder, and two men I knew were fortunate in getting a bull with tusks of over 100 pounds each.

A friend named Allport shot one with tusks just over 100 pounds each. This elephant had been nearly killed by a farmer named Purchase, who knocked it down, and fired the remainder of his cartridges into its head, and failed even then to slay it, for it struggled to its feet as he helplessly stood aside and watched over 200 pounds of splendid ivory walking off, and not a round left to stop it. If he had only put his shots into its shoulder instead of the head, he would certainly have killed it.

The easiest brain shot is into the orifice of the ear when standing slightly behind the elephant. If dead broadside on, about 4 inches forward of the earhole is correct. It is all a matter of angle according to the position of the game and the hunter. Nothing can beat a small bore such as a ·256 for the brain shot, but for body shots I believe a larger bore to be more efficient, as the bigger the bore the greater the striking energy (as a rule).

The heart is below an imaginary line drawn horizontally through the centre of the body, not above it, as a bullet placed at the edge of the ear (as some recommend) is too high. If such a shot kills, it is because it gets the lungs, not the heart.

A good shot at any game is through the middle of the neck, as the vertebræ may be broken. A similar result will be got by breaking the spine, but this wounds, and does not kill quickly, like the neck shot.

Wounds in any of the joints or legs are crippling, but not so sportsmanlike as the brain or heart shot. I have heard hunters advise a shot in the foot, but personally would leave this out, not only because it is rather cruel, but because it is unsatisfactory, as the cover usually prevents one seeing the feet properly.

The result of a brain shot is instant death, so if a beast struggles much, one may be sure the animal is only dazed and will soon get up, although he may fall and keep down for a minute or two. Should an elephant fall and struggle, if the shot has been taken at thirty or forty yards, there is often time (if other elephants are not too near) to run in quickly and slightly behind and shoot into the ear orifice, or at the back of the skull where it joins the short neck.

If, however, the animal looks as if it will be up before one can reach the place for this shot, then keep behind and shoot at the middle of the spinal ridge which rises in the centre of the back, taking it fairly low, about 2 or 3 feet forward of the base of the tail. This shot, especially with a large bore, will almost invariably anchor the elephant; and to save it unnecessary pain, one can then move round and administer the brain shot with another cartridge.

When hit in the heart, I have seen an elephant fall immediately, though the usual action is a rush forward for any distance up to a mile according to the section of the heart struck. Should the bullet have cut the heart near the top, where the arteries are placed, death occurs more quickly, and an elephant so struck generally comes to earth within a hundred yards.

With a shot in one lung he may get clean away and be lost, but when he has got the bullet through both lungs he will usually stop and die within half a mile or so. Such a wound sometimes produces a strange result, as the wounded animal will rush off and then suddenly stop and put his trunk straight up in the air, sending streams of blood flying, and then sink down and die fairly quickly. I have seen this happen on several occasions, and although it is not a pleasant sight to witness, it gives one the satisfaction of knowing that one has got the elephant, as I never saw an elephant doing this without dying where he stood.

When shooting near the Luangwa River, in November 1908, I found the spoor of a large herd of elephants, which my men and I followed for five miles before we got up to them. This was not a great distance to follow and come upon the animals, as anything under ten miles may be called an easy trek. Most of the herd was in thick bush, but a few in more open country where one could see them fairly well. About midway between us and the

143

elephants was a small stream, which was dry at that time, as it was extremely hot weather.

None of the three bulls I saw was very large, the best being one with tusks about 30 pounds each. This elephant was broadside and offered a satisfactory position for the brain shot, so I aimed a little forward of his earhole and fired. He collapsed as if brained, and I thought he was down for good, but he wasn't, as he soon began to make the most strenuous efforts to get up, screaming loudly as he struggled violently to rise. The herd ran at the sound of my shot, and some of them came round towards us, so we had to run for the timber, as we were out in the open. Before going I gave the wounded bull a shot in the shoulder, but it did not seem to hurt him much.

Getting amongst the trees, I picked one of the best of them, but only about a foot thick, and stood behind it, with my Awemba gunbearer, Kalenje, just behind with my cartridge-bag. The other men disappeared into the bush and ran some way. When I looked at the wounded bull, I saw he was coming straight for Kalenje and myself, and coming very fast, too.

I had a Gibbs ·303 fitted with a large magazine holding ten rounds when full, but I never put more than eight into it, as it did not work quite so well when full up with the ten rounds. Having fired two shots, I had six left, and I needed them all.

The elephant, as I say, was coming at his best pace, and he was swishing through the short grass, making a loud rustling at every step. His trunk was curled and held low in front, and he never made a sound except with his feet as he came rushing at us.

By the time I was settled comfortably against my small tree, there was a distance of not more than sixty yards between us, and it was being reduced very quickly, so I began to shoot steadily at the spot where the trunk joins the forehead. There is a hollow in the skull here. Two bullets clapped on his hard skull, and all he did was to shake his head and come faster still.

I was quite cool, but cannot say I was not a bit anxious. When the second shot failed to stop him, it struck me that I was going high, as that is the usual fault with the frontal shot. I then aimed lower and got him, for, while coming at his maximum pace, he went clean over on his left side, hitting the earth with a splendid bump, and with the momentum slid to within a few paces of the tree. I thought his left tusk would have been broken, but it was un-injured.

Kalenje, who was a very plucky fellow, was looking green, as he usually did when close to elephants, but the sport had a fascination for him notwithstanding his natural fear of the animals. This was the best kind of bravery, as it is nothing to be brave when one is not afraid. I may have been green, too, but I did not have a mirror handy to look at my face.

The men were quite delighted with the show, and ran up and patted me on the back in the most sym-pathetic way, and I must admit that I was mightily pleased, for after I had failed to stop him with my second shot, I began to wonder whether he would pick Kalenje or myself first.

This is the finest sight I witnessed during the time I was hunting in Central Africa, and although I killed another elephant which was coming for me, he was not coming at anything like the pace of this one, nor had he the relentless look of silent fury which that animal displayed.

Of course, I have had elephants rush past me and almost over me many times, but only twice have I seen one come straight for me knowing that I was " his meat," so to speak. Some people who see game rushing towards them call it a charge, which is absolute nonsense, as the animals are simply trying to escape, or get up against the wind, for all animals try to get the wind in their faces so as to have the power of scenting danger from their front. They may run down-wind for a bit when they are scared, but soon begin to swerve up to the wind. By knowing this fact, one can sometimes cut across and get a shot, and this was a favourite move in the old days in South Africa when a hunter was chasing game on horseback. Selous in his books often mentions doing this, and so do others.

The day I shot this charging elephant happened to be my mother's birthday, and when I left camp that morning I wondered if my luck would change, for I had been having a lot of terribly hard work in the sun every day with poor results, as I had not got up to an elephant for two weeks. Then after the elephant was dead, I thought of it again, and again wondered if there is any occult influence which can favour or protect man. I am not superstitious, and really cannot credit such a force, especially after the horrible carnage in the Great War, when thousands of mothers, and thousands of sons, prayed in vain for an immunity which was not granted to them.

When the business was over, I also marvelled at the luck I had had, for a frontal shot at a charging African elephant will not come off once out of ten times, especially with a small bore like a ·303. With a heavy cordite rifle, such as a ·416 Rigby, the shock of the bullet is so great on impact that, if not brained, an elephant would likely be so stunned that he would fall, and then, of course, one could run to the side and finish the matter easily.

On one occasion, when I was going along a native path, I saw a small herd of eight elephants feeding on masuko plums in the sparse cover near a *dambo*, so I went up to them with a "boy" who had a spare rifle. As they were moving in a certain direction, I got ahead of them and sat down behind the stump of a large tree. I noticed two cows each with a calf a few months old, and it was interesting to watch one of them trying to suck when the mother was engaged feeding. Several times she gave it a hard smack with her trunk, which made it give annoyed squeals.

This cow soon got rather too close, as she came within twenty yards of my stump, and the "boy" (one of my house "boys" who had never been so close to an elephant before) looked faint, and his face got the usual colour of a native's who is really frightened. The calf ran up to the opposite side of the stump and began to rub itself against the rough bark, just like a cow does on a post.

On again looking at the "boy," I thought he would bolt, for his eyes were starting out of his head with funk. For a joke I leaned out and gave the calf a lusty pat on its posterior, and it gave a squeak and ran towards its mother, who began to look nasty. As I had no wish to shoot the cow, I stood up and waved my hat, and she went off, taking the others with her, and there was not a shootable bull in the lot.

I did a really foolish thing with a cow elephant once near the Rukusi stream, which there is no reason why I should omit in my yarns about the habits of elephants, as it shows how fearless they can be under certain circumstances, although some people, who have never seen a wild elephant, may say it is boasting!

My men and I had been looking for a good bull, and had got to some pools, one of which was most interesting, as many elephants had used it as a bath. It was a hole in the mud about 16 feet long and half that width, and the sides, which had been lately used when I came on it, were wet and rubbed as smooth as an enamelled bath.

On that day in October the heat had been terrific, in fact one of the hottest I can remember. When we got to the pool, we had tramped a good fifteen miles, and we were all rather fagged with the intense heat. Not far from the pool was a rocky rise with a few trees on it, so I went there to rest for a bit. We were perhaps 50 feet above the surrounding bush, and the place was excellent as a look-out over the country.

I had lain down in the shade, with my hat over my eyes to keep the glare away, when one of my men said, " Elephants, master," so I got up to have a look, and soon saw them coming to the pools, for there were several in the dried-up stream which wound down the valley. These elephants were doing something that is not often seen at midday—drinking —and what had caused it was the extreme heat, of course, as it was exceptional at the time.

Two elephants made for the bath-shaped pool and had an argument which was to use it, and a large cow with nice tusks got first dip. When she was in it, she drew water up with her trunk and blew it over her back and sides, and rubbed herself vigorously along the edges of the hole. Then she got out and did more rubbing against a tree, which I had noticed before with mud all over it.

We saw three herds come to the water, but except for small bulls with tusks not more than 20 pounds or so, there was no big tusker amongst them. After staying less than half an hour, they wandered off into the bush, so we came down and took much the same direction, as it was the way to camp. While going along in some fairly thick timber, we came on the first herd, and spotted the muddy cow standing under a tree, apparently asleep. She was separated from the others, so I decided to try to get as close as possible to her, and three of the men came just behind me.

We got to within thirty yards (I stepped it afterwards), when she woke up, so some of the men and myself, for a bit of fun, began to throw stones at her, hitting her often. When a bit of rock hit her she stamped her feet heavily and flapped her ears, but she did not scream, which elephants usually do when much annoyed. This went on for some minutes, and she began to be seriously annoyed, so I stopped the men, as I had no wish to shoot her.

While this was going on, I may say we had not given her our wind, as I had purposely walked upwind. I now decided to test her in the wind, and walked round her, keeping about fifty yards away. As soon as this elephant, which had been hit quite twenty times with stones, got the wind, she went off at once and took the rest of the herd, about a hundred yards away, with her.

Afterwards I wondered if she was blind, though her eyes looked all right, and they were the usual reddish, bleary optics of an elephant, so I have no reason to think her sight was defective in any way. Whether she was too lazy with the terrific heat at the time, or whether her sight was bad, I cannot say, but I know that the affair happened exactly as I have written it.

I again say it was an extremely foolish thing to do, and I would not do the same thing again unless there was a condition that I could shoot when I wanted to. Of course, if she had come on I would have given her a shot, but at that time the tusks would have been confiscated if I had reported the matter, and possibly the further allowance on my licence cancelled at the discretion of the magistrate who decided the case.

The incidents of slapping a calf and stoning this cow elephant got round Fort Jameson and district through my " boys," and I was asked by different people if they were true. On my assuring the questioners that they were both according to fact, I never heard any rumour that my word had been doubted. I mention them here as interesting notes as to the habits of the game and how one can take liberties with them at times, although it is risky to do so.

I remember hearing of an officer in British East Africa who used to often slap the sterns of rhinos as a joke, when these beasts were more numerous and much tamer than they are to-day.

Regarding the size of elephants' feet, it does not follow that the largest tuskers have the biggest feet. The heaviest, though not the tallest, elephant I ever shot had moderately-sized feet, and he was an enormous animal in bulk. However, it may be taken as the usual rule that a big spoor is worth following when one is out to pick up tracks.

When I was in the Terai Dooars (India), a half-grown elephant which had been noosed was brought in by some men, and while they were resting they tied him up to a tree close to a native hut. I was passing on a pony at the time, so stopped to look at him. Whether it was the sight of me or my old pony I do not know, but he suddenly got furious and attacked the thatched roof of the hut with his trunk, making the grass fly all round. Then he broke loose and went for another hut, and did it considerable damage before the noosers with their tame elephants got a hold of him again.

I never believed that the natives killed many wild elephants by surrounding them with a grass or bush fire, as I once saw a herd go clean through a grass fire. They went so fast that they escaped damage, though they may have been slightly singed by the flames.

I have shot several elephants with festering sores on their bodies, which I think were caused by their rubbing on a tree which had been on fire and possibly gone out, leaving hot embers on the trunk. A dead tree, when it catches fire, may smoulder for a long time, as personally I have seen one doing so two months after I first noticed it.

What elephants dread most is swamp, as they soon get bogged and helpless, for the harder they struggle the deeper they go, until they are doomed. Certainly the natives killed numbers long ago by driving them into swamps and then spearing them when too weak to move.

Pitfalls, too, were common, and these were not so large or broad as is supposed, as all that was needed was a tapered hole which jammed the feet and legs of the elephant so hard that they could not move. If the pit was large enough for them to move round in, they would soon break it down with their feet and tusks and get out.

On several occasions I have seen a disturbed herd of elephants run over a steep river-bank, and what they do is to stretch their forelegs far out, and then sit down and do a splendid slide on their buttocks until they reach firm ground, carrying away masses of earth or sand with them.

In newspapers and magazines, etc., one reads accounts of elephants' dying-places, where they are supposed to go when they feel their days numbered on earth. In these places there are supposed to be great quantities of ivory waiting for the lucky man who finds it. This is pure nonsense, for the damp and heat of one rainy season in tropical Africa will completely disintegrate ivory, making it soft and valueless.

I knew an elephant poacher (it is not necessary to give his name) who got some good elephants in Portuguese territory, the ivory of which he could not dispose of at once, so he buried it near a stream, and left it there for the rainy season, intending to get it away next dry weather after the necessary arrangements for its disposal had been made.

When staying with him for a few days, he told me about it, so I remarked that it was probably rotten by this time, as it had been underground for some months. He wished to bet me £1 that it was all right, so late one evening, when the natives were otherwise engaged, we took our rifles as if we were going to look for a buck, and also a hoe out of which we slipped the handle, my friend putting the head inside his shirt, so as not to excite the natural curiosity of the " boys," who might have stalked us to see what we were up to.

He had marked the spot with a few stones in a slight hollow near the stream, so we started to dig, and had to go quite 3 feet before we came to the ivory. There were eight tusks (some quite good ones), and not a single one of them was sound, some, I noticed, being quite soft to the touch if pressed with the thumb-nail. He was very sick, as ivory of this good quality fetched about 15s. a pound at that time. As the tusks would have averaged about 25 pounds each, this was a serious loss for him after his hardships and adventures in poaching the elephants.

Possibly, when lying on the top of the ground, ivory might remain sound for one rainy season, but I am sure two or three would soon rot it.

It is wonderful how few elephant remains are found, except the numerous skulls and bones of animals which have been the victims of white hunters. Round Fort Manning many skulls could be found, as the officers stationed there nearly all got their two every year, and other hunters added to the number, as the district was for long the haunt of good tuskers.

When in Fort Jameson in 1904 I met a very good fellow named James B. Yule, who had a ranch up-country, though he used to spend a lot of his spare time hunting elephants. During his career he had shot many elephants and other game, and was very experienced.

In 1914 I heard he had been killed by a bull elephant he had wounded in May of that year. The animal charged at once with a scream, knocked down Yule, and first seized his rifle and threw it into the bush (according to the testimony of his native " boys "), and then put one of its tusks through the lower part of his body, throwing him about for a time, and then left him. The natives returned when the scrimmage was over and carried him to his tent, where he died next day. After that they carried the body to his farm, where he was buried.

This account (which is abbreviated slightly from one in the *Nyasaland Times* of the 25th of June 1914) is given as a warning to beginners to be very careful with their first shot at dangerous game, as so much depends on where that bullet goes. All the subsequent proceedings hinge on this ; so to place well, it is safer to get close than to risk long shots and then have the danger of following up a wounded animal, which is sure to be infuriated with the pain of its injury.

N O man is capable of writing the complete life-history of any animal, as the habits of a particular species vary in the different localities where it is found, and it would entail an extensive experience to get such opportunities.

For instance, the behaviour of rhinos and buffaloes differs considerably in different parts of Africa. In British East Africa (now Kenya Province) both these species are said to charge on very little provocation, whereas in the territory farther south they are not often inclined to take the offensive unless after being wounded.

All generalities, however, are a mistake, for I have heard of exceptions to this rule. It is quite impossible to say how any animal will behave under given circumstances, as one may run off and another do the opposite. Therefore it is advisable to keep a rifle handy when in the bush.

When I first went to Nyasaland the buffalo and eland were strictly preserved, but later a certain number were allowed on the licence, six of each per annum. Rhinos were not very numerous in Nyasaland, and I only occasionally came on their tracks ; but in North-Eastern Rhodesia they were quite plentiful, so I saw a number at different times. I did not bother much about them, as I was usually looking for elephant when I found their tracks in the bush. A rhino treks a fairly long distance from his nightly drinking-place.

After I had got a few horns as trophies, I had no

wish to shoot more for the little one could get for the horns and skins, as I never believed in making money out of anything except ivory. The tuskers were bound to be shot by somebody, and I thought that, if others went for them, I might also, and the more I hunted elephant the greater became the fascination of the game.

In my previous chapter I have given an account of some of my experiences with elephants, and could give many others if I did not wish to say something about the other game of the country. My first rhino took several shots to kill her. One of the shots fired from a heavy, kicking 10-bore double Purdey rifle upset me, as I was sitting on the side of a large ant-hill. The rhino bolted and (after my men and I had finished laughing) was almost out of sight in the bush, so I ran after her with a single ·303 and killed her.

On another occasion I found a bull rhino asleep, and hit him as he was snoring, with a single ·400 H.V. rifle. He woke up and was on his feet in three seconds, and came puffing past us into some long, sun-dried grass which threw a strong glare into my eyes as I chased him. I was so dazzled with the reflection off the bright yellow grass that I almost collided with the rhino, which had stopped to look back. Being dressed lightly in shorts with bare legs, I was fairly agile, so did an excellent swerve, passing the angry beast within a few paces, until it seemed safe to pull up and look back.

The rhino wheeled round to keep his eyes on me, and offered an excellent raking shot on the point of his shoulder, so I gave him a solid ·303, as I had grabbed that rifle after firing the single ·400. He collapsed at once and soon died, for I found afterwards the bullet had cut the large arteries above the heart. The first bullet raked his left lung, and he might have got away if I had not run after him quickly.

It is a mistake to fire at game sitting, as it is difficult to locate the vital spots when an animal is in that position, so the best thing to do is to whistle or clap one's hands sufficiently loud to excite the beast's suspicions, but not so loud as to make him bolt quickly.

Rhino are much easier to kill than bull elephants, and I put them on a par in this respect with cow elephants, which die quicker than the bulls.

The black rhinoceros feeds mainly on thorn twigs and seldom eats grass, like the white rhinoceros, which feeds solely on grass. There are no white rhinos in Nyasaland and Northern Rhodesia, and they are a South African species which through a short-sighted persecution are rapidly becoming extinct, owing mainly to the love of slaughter displayed by some of the South African colonists who are not nature-lovers or thinkers.

There is a variety of white rhino in the southern Sudan and adjoining territory, but I have never been there, so all I know about it is what I have read on the subject.

I think the black rhino occasionally eats grass, as I have seen grass in their droppings on several occasions. Thorn-tree twigs seem a most indigestible kind of food for any animal, as they are hard and stringy, but so does some of the stuff that elephants eat, and there is no accounting for taste.

Why the names black and white were given to the two species of rhino I do not know, for when examining one of each in the Cape Town Museum it was difficult to say which was the whiter of the two. Both names are wrong, as their colour is a darkish grey, just about the colour of an elephant's hide.

One of the rhinos I shot had a third rudimentary

RHINOCEROS BULL.

Shot and photographed by George Garden,

horn about the size of a prune, and my friend George Garden, of Mlanje, Nyasaland, shot one exactly similar in Portuguese East Africa. There is a record of one which had five horns—three rudimentary, and the ordinary two which are usual.

A rhino is a very strong animal and capable of doing much damage, so when spooring one in thick cover, it is best to have a rifle ready for action, for although all the large game seem bulky and slow, they can come at a great pace when they want to. The pace of an animal running away, even when frightened, is no criterion of his speed when coming for one in an infuriated condition.

Many people scoff at shooting now, so they take telephotos of game, sometimes pretending that a beast is charging when it is not, as an expert can see at once. They get up quite a reputation for courage amongst people who do not know the ropes, and who admire their fine pictures (some of them are certainly good). As a matter of fact, there is seldom much danger in approaching game with a camera, because the first instinct of any beast is to bolt.

On the other hand, it is much more dangerous to follow a wounded animal into thick cover with a rifle, for one is much more likely to be charged when doing so, than by taking a photograph of the same beast when unwounded.

In mentioning this, I have no wish to decry the pluck of the telephotographers, as they are brave men, but I do wish to dispel an erroneous idea which is prevalent amongst people who know nothing about hunting. Some of these " charging " photographs give themselves away at the first glance, as the beast is seen at an angle, whereas a real charge is straight on, if photographed from the front. Of course a charge at someone else could be taken from the side, but one does not often see that kind in books or magazines. Few animals charge unless wounded, except, possibly, a female with young. When game has been much molested, instead of wanting to charge at sight, they want to run away as quickly as possible.

In British East Africa, for many years after the buffaloes and other game were decimated by the rinderpest (about 1895), the buffaloes were preserved. Therefore they got accustomed to the sight of human beings and would hardly move away; in fact at times they would advance to make out an object which interested them. Then, when shooting at them was allowed, they retained this trait of curiosity.

On the other hand, animals which have been wounded slightly are inclined to resent their injury on the first human creature they meet, unfortunately not always the person who deserved the attention; but it is often the way in life that the innocents suffer and the culprits escape—for example, the politicians in the war.

Nobody can give sound advice as to the best thing to do when knocked down, for the victim is probably stunned or dazed; and an elephant, buffalo, lion, or leopard does not waste much time in these circumstances, but gets busy very quick.

When buffalo-shooting was allowed in Nyasaland, I went to the Chiromo Marsh and spent some time shooting round Machinjiri and other villages under the Cholo range. It was hot work, as the grass was long and unburnt, and when it had been burnt, some of it, being green, had not gone, so it was all tangled, and the place was black with ashes, which made one filthy in a short time. The ash dust got in one's throat, as it rose in the air when disturbed.

One of my most exciting days with a buffalo was when I found a fine bull with two others one morning at dawn. He had just left a maize-field, where he had been feeding with the others in the night, and gone into heavy grass near.

We spotted the animals from an anthill, and the bull's head and neck were the only part of him visible as he stood half hidden behind a bush. I had a ·404 Jeffery-Mauser with one of those drag pulls on the trigger—that is, the trigger came back slightly before it released the striker, and I never liked this kind of pull on a rifle. Aiming at the bull's neck, the drag pull made me shoot low, but I hit him hard and he rushed off with the others, leaving a lot of blood on his spoor.

We followed for many miles through horrid thick grass, and I got another chance, knocking him down for a moment. After this he left the others and went off by himself. He was a tough old beast, and it was wonderful how he managed to keep on in the intense heat, wounded as he was. Fortunately he left the grass and got into timber country, which was much better going, and less dangerous for us.

At last he got winded and stopped, when I got up to him and gave him a bullet. He now came towards us at a trot, and my men went up trees. Molilo, my gunbearer, stood fast, so we got behind a bush and waited for a good chance. At last he stopped under a tree, so I finished him with a raking chest shot from my Rigby 7·9 mm. rifle, and he fell and made that long-drawn bellow which buffaloes usually give before they die. I admired the pluck of the fine old animal.

I was very pleased with the result of the day, as we had tracked him for a good six hours under a scorching hot sun, and through the vilest of country.

Another day I shot four buffalo near Machinjiri's village, principally on account of the natives, who were hungry as their new crops were not yet bearing, and they had finished most of their last harvest.

159

Two of these animals ran into a dense mass of reeds growing in a swamp, with mud up to my knees, and I did not much fancy going into such cover after buffalo. The wise thing would have been to wait for an hour or so to give them a chance of dying or stiffening up before tackling them, but I was hot and tired and wanted to get back to camp as soon as possible. Besides, I wished to put them out of pain.

Tracking the one which looked most badly hit, I was fortunate to find it just dead, for it was lying on its side in the mud. I did not see it, however, until I had got within five yards, so decided I would take great care when going after the other, as I had only my small 7·9-mm. Rigby-Mauser with me. Getting on the spoor of the other one, we went very slowly indeed, stopping every few steps to listen carefully.

At close quarters one can often hear a large animal breathing if there is no noise, but we did not manage to hear this buffalo make a sound, as everything was quiet, except the squelching of the mud as we moved carefully forward.

Suddenly we found ourselves within two paces of the buffalo, which was sitting in the mud. He saw us, of course, when we came into view, and tried to get up by raising his hind quarters (as all the ox tribe do when rising) ; but failed to recover his feet owing to the slippery mud. I might have put a bullet into his body, but not into his head, as it was moving about in his efforts to rise.

On his second attempt he bent his neck, exposing the line of his vertebræ, so I put a bullet there, and he fell, and immediately began to bellow loudly. I was greatly relieved to see him collapse, for had he got up one of us would likely have suffered, as it was most difficult to move quickly in the swamp and reeds.

Buffaloes are very shy beasts, and keep as far from

160

BUFFALO BULL, PORTUGUESE EAST AFRICA
Shot and photographed by George Garden

human beings as they can when much hunted, although in wild districts they, like other game, often come to the native fields to eat the dried stalks of maize and millet. Like elands, which are also heavy beasts, they will break down rough fences to get to these places.

The shape of African buffalo horns varies considerably, even in one locality, due mainly to the age of the animals, so it is absurd (as a German professor of natural history attempted to do) to classify them as different species, because their horns vary according to their age.

Of course, the small red-haired buffalo of the Congo, and the varieties found in Senegambia and other places, show a great variation in size of bodies, skulls, and horns, compared with the common or Cape buffalo, so they can justifiably be separated through this distinction.

This tendency to differentiate by home naturalists is partly due to ignorance, as they think that the immature horns will develop on the same lines throughout the life of the individual.

Take an animal like a Lichtenstein's hartebeest. There is a vast difference between the early spikes and the fully developed horns. A bushbuck, impala, or any animal which develops curves from early spikes, in the course of a few years is a good example of the impossibility of classification without full knowledge of the differences caused by age. The same mistake is sometimes made with skins, which also vary according to age.

When a herd of buffalo is startled, the beasts often rush towards the hunter in their attempt to get upwind, and this rush can never be called a bona-fide charge. A real charge is one made with intent, and herds of animals never (or very seldom) act in combination against human beings. It is fortunate for the

161

hunter they do not, for if they did there would not be many hunters left.

The calves are a brownish colour, and gradually change to a blackish-grey, the aged animals, like old eland, getting almost hairless in the course of time.

At certain seasons the old bulls consort, and run separate from the cows and younger animals.

Lions often follow herds in their wanderings, but generally attack cows or young animals in preference to the large, well-horned bulls, which can put up a gallant fight unless they are taken unawares.

A bull buffalo is tremendously powerful, particularly in the neck. I remember suddenly surprising a herd of buffalo lying in a dense thorn-brake, and it was marvellous how quickly they disappeared through the matted undergrowth, which looked thick enough to stop anything on four legs.

Buffaloes are one of the first species to retire before the advance of civilization, as they like quiet ; at least this has been my experience in South Central Africa. They are fond of swamps, where they can refresh themselves in hot weather by rolling in the mud and water, although they are likely to retire into thick, shady bush to sleep. I once came on what I at first thought was an albino buffalo, as it was white all over. I soon found he had been rolling in some chalky mud, which accounted for his colour.

In South Africa, where they were so plentiful in the early days, they were supposed to be responsible for the spread of the tsetse-fly (*Glossina morsitans*), for when they were driven from certain localities the fly went too. I do not think this applies to the country north of the Zambezi, because the fly there do not specialize on buffalo blood alone, and suck the blood of any species of game they come across.

Like all game, buffaloes cannot keep their tails quiet for long, as they are always swishing their backs

162

and flanks with their caudal appendage to keep away the numerous flies which are perpetually bothering them in the daytime.

In old shooting books illustrations were sometimes shown of a buffalo charging with his head lowered, although he was some distance from his intended victim. This is all wrong, as a buffalo only dips its head when within striking distance, and the action is a continuous sweep from the moment he lowers his horns to the instant he lifts them. For this reason it is almost impossible to instantly kill a charging buffalo, as he has his nose straight out, and to brain him the bullet would need to go up one of his nostrils in a straight line for his brain.

Any moving animal rises and falls as he takes his quickly repeated strides, which makes it practically impossible to hit such a small mark as the brain, so the best thing to do is to rake him by putting the bullet low in the centre of his chest.

A buffalo's heart lies lower in the cavity of the chest than the heart of most game, which I have often proved by cutting one up for an investigation.

Until the beginner knows the internal anatomy of the game thoroughly, he should make a practice of watching them being dismembered. A good plan is to leave the heart, lungs, and kidneys inside, and with an axe split the upper ribs off along the spinal ridge, allowing the vital organs to remain in their natural position, and then make a rough sketch of their relative positions. Of course these organs in an animal flat on its side will not assume exactly the position they would do when the beast is standing up.

The kidney shot, although not often intentionally used, is a very deadly one, as it not only sickens an animal, but causes severe internal hæmorrhage.

Vital shots are purely a question of angle, and this matter of angle is the best reason why long shots should not be taken, for at a distance of more than 150 yards it is impossible with the human eye to discern the angle in which an animal is standing. A small antelope at that distance will be blotted out if the front sight is large; so for really good work the foresight should not be larger in diameter than the head of a small pin, which will be found to be $\frac{1}{10}$ inch.

I can hear a reader say, " Why all this detail ? " I would reply that unless one pays a close attention to detail, results will suffer, and so will the game.

Although there are probably more interesting things to say about the buffalo, I must get on to another animal and will make some remarks about the hippo and my experiences with them in various rivers such as the Zambezi, Shire, Bua, and Luangwa, where they were very plentiful when I was in Central Africa.

I have always been rather sorry for the hippo, as he is at the mercy of anyone with a rifle who happens to see him, although when shot at often he gets extremely wary.

Previously I have mentioned how some people, who seldom know much about shooting, blaze off from the deck of a moving steamer at any hippo they see within 200 yards without the slightest hope of killing him, or of getting the body if they should make a lucky shot.

In cold weather a dead hippo may take quite six hours to rise to the surface, as the cold water prevents the gases generating inside from natural decomposition. When the water and air are warm, they often rise in less than an hour, especially when they hold a lot of inside fat.

If shot in a rapid river, they are often carried some distance from the place where they were killed, and it is usual, after one has been shot, to send one or two natives to watch for the body rising. They rise very

164

gradually, as the gases slowly accumulate, and all one sees at first is a bit of shiny skin bobbing about in the water. It is best to leave them until about half of the body rises above the surface, as they are easier to get ashore when quite buoyant, for naturally they do not get fast in the mud or on the sandbank where they are to be cut up.

My first hippos were shot above the Murchison Rapids in the Shire River, just opposite Matiti Hill. The late Lieutenant Henry Faulkner, in his book *Elephant Haunts* published in 1868, gives a vignette on the title-page showing the Murchison Cataract and Matiti Hill. I remember reading this book when a boy, and wondering if I would ever see any of the elephants and other game the author mentions hunting. As I was sitting amongst the beautiful scenery there waiting for a hippo to rise, I recollected my early ambitions and the vignette in the book, and it gave a touch of romance to the scene, which was just as wild as when Faulkner was there in the sixties of last century.

The hippos in the Zambezi River were very numerous during the years I was in the country, but they had rather a hard time, as the Portuguese soldiers who occupied the forts along the river constantly fired at them with old Snider rifles. As most people know, the bore of the Snider is ·577; and the bullet, though large, is soft lead and has not enough penetration for head shots at hippo. The consequence was that there were a good many wounded animals about which occasionally attacked the native dugouts and sent them to the bottom, sometimes drowning the occupants if they were far from the bank.

I did several trips on the Zambezi in houseboats, which were ordinary large boats of the European type with a shelter fixed at the stern made of wood, or sticks and grass. Twice a bull hippo came at the boat I was in, but I always had a loaded rifle handy and was able to stop the animal before he got close enough to do any damage.

Coming down the Zambezi from Tete to Chinde on the sea in December 1905, I saw between the places mentioned quite 150 hippos, mostly in small lots of from three to a dozen animals. I had several men who were paddling hard every day, and they were always keen to get meat, and so were the natives of the villages we passed occasionally on the banks of the river.

On this trip I shot four hippos and a crocodile, which was also eaten by my men, as some of the Zambezi tribes will eat anything that can be eaten.

The following year I was again on the Zambezi, and had stopped to have a talk to a Portuguese officer at one of the forts. He told me there was a herd of hippo near which had been doing much damage by upsetting the native dugouts. Several people had been drowned, and one man so badly bitten in the leg that he died soon after he was got out.

I promised to kill a few if I came on the animals, which I did about two miles above the fort. We saw them some distance away near a nice sandbank, so I stopped the boat and walked up the bank towards them. I had not the slightest difficulty in getting to the edge of the water on the sandbank, taking care, however, to only move forward when their heads were down, or when they were facing the other way.

I had with me a new ·303 single Fraser falling-block rifle, a most accurate little weapon with a very fine enamel-faced foresight, and the only shots I had yet fired with it were some at a mark to test the sighting.

The hippos were from twenty-five to thirty yards off, and I fired at four, all sinking without a splash, so I knew they had all been brained. The first two were hit close to, or through, the eye orifice, as they were slightly at an angle, and the others between the ears at the back of the head, the best shot I have found for hippo.

There were exactly twelve hippo in the herd, and I could have shot several of the survivors before they began to get away, but I did not wish to butcher more, although there was no doubt that this was the herd the Portuguese referred to as being so dangerous. All the hippos had old wounds, and I picked a flattened Snider bullet from the head of one, which had just got under the skin and stopped against the hard skull.

I took the half-cleaned skulls of these hippos on to Tete, and there was a bit of a smell in the boat before I got to that place, as the Zambezi valley is one of the hottest places in Africa.

On another occasion, when travelling on the Zambezi, I shot a hippo on a Christmas Day when I had camped on a sandbank in the Lupata Gorge. The gorge widens out slightly in one place, and close to us were four hippos; so, wanting some meat for my men and myself, I killed one, which rose in an hour. As I sat eating my Christmas dinner of tough hippo steak, some boiled rice, and tea, I thought of my friends at home who were enjoying roast turkey and other delicacies of the season. However, I did not envy them much, as I was quite happy in the wilds of Africa. The wildness of the scene was accentuated when I heard a lion grunting some way off as he came to the river to drink, and later on in the night I was awakened by him, or another one, roaring loudly in the bush.

I had a strange experience with a bull hippo one night when tied up to a sandbank. It was the night following the shooting of the four with four consecutive shots, and I forgot to mention it in its proper place, so will give a short account of it now.

As it got dark on that evening, the herd, which had gone up the river, came back to near where I had shot the four; and the bull which I had not killed was very angry. Evidently they got the smell of the blood from the skulls, skin, and remnants of the cutting-up scene, so the bull was grunting his displeasure as they worked up closer in the fast-gathering darkness.

When they got to within thirty yards or so, there was enough light to see their dark bodies, but not enough to shoot with any accuracy, so I let them alone, and had my evening meal as I listened to them grunting. At times the bull gave a regular roar of rage, which I have seldom heard a hippo do. The men got rather frightened at these sounds, as they said he wanted to break the boat, so I sent them to some reeds on the sandbank and told them to collect a lot of the dried stalks to make a fire.

As the darkness got deeper the bull got angrier, and he made several violent rushes through the water towards the boat, so I had to do something.

Besides the single Fraser ·303, I had brought from home a double ·400 cordite H.V. rifle for elephants, so I got it out of its case and slipped two cartridges into the breech, and left the fire where I had been sitting and got behind the boat to wait for the bull. He may have seen me go there, as for a time he kept a little farther off; but as I intended to turn in soon in the shelter at the stern of the boat, I thought I would have to scare him off. So when I saw the dark mass again, I let go both barrels of the ·400 at his body. The first barrel seemed to get him, but the second missed, as I heard the bullet slap into the river; anyhow he had had enough, for just after that we heard them all go puffing and blowing down the river, and we were all pleased to hear them depart, as we were sleepy. Nevertheless, I slept with the ·400 alongside me under the small mosquito-net so as to be prepared for

168

another visit, but nothing happened except the violent snoring of the boatmen on the sandbank. One of them was the most sonorous warbler I ever heard, and I am sure a lion could have heard him a mile off.

Arriving in Chinde after a Zambezi trip, when I had shot several hippos, I had brought some large slabs of hide to try to dispose of in the place. The hippos had been shot about a week before I got there, and the skin had been lying in the bilge-water in the bottom of the boat. In a few days the smell became atrocious, and everything that had touched the decomposing hide was impregnated with the aroma.

When unloading some elephant tusks wrapped in canvas at the African Lakes Corporation store in Chinde, which the natives had taken to the office, one of the white assistants, spotlessly arrayed in white cotton drill, came up to me and asked me, with his handkerchief held over his nose, what in the world was wrong with the tusks! I told him that the smell was only slight, and if he wanted the real thing, to come down to my boat, which was tied to the bank near. He did not come, but got some of the natives to take the tusks off to a godown (storeroom).

After that I went off to the boarding-house where I was to stay until the ocean steamer arrived, and shaved off my beard and had a tub. When I looked at my face in the glass, I looked a regular wild man of the woods, as I had not shaved for some months while on trek; and my old khaki shirt and frayed and bloody shorts were hardly fit for a civilization where the young men wear stiff collars, ties, and spotless drill.

As I was going to have lunch, I got a note saying that the Portuguese commandant of Chinde presented his compliments, and requested me to remove the hippo hide as soon as convenient, as it was poisoning the inhabitants; so I called my head " boy " and sent him up-river (which was also down-wind) with orders to put the stuff on a sandbank and cover it up.

The man who had asked me to bring him the hide no longer wanted it, so I suppose some of the hyenas on shore, or the crocodiles in the water, were the only creatures who benefited in any way.

The smell was so pungent and penetrating that when I unwrapped the canvas off the tusks at home, nearly two months afterwards, the delicate scent immediately wafted me back to the lovely Zambezi and its denizens.

Smell has a wonderful way of refreshing and stirring up the memory, for a heap of rubbish burning in a garden can take one back like a flash to a camp scene in the bush, the aroma of a cup of tea to a day when we cooked a kettle near an elephant just shot, and the taint of a butcher's shop to many a cutting-up scene in the wilds of Africa.

When I shot hippos I usually did so for the natives, as they like the meat. After all they pay well for it, as the animals often raid their gardens when made near a large river and do immense damage. I may say that elephants and hippos often do so much harm to the crops that in small communities they almost cause starvation. Therefore I had seldom any hesitation in shooting a hippo or two for the natives.

The natives dried the meat over fires and kept it some time, probably eating the last of it when it was seething with maggots and green with heat and damp.

I have seen them eating the flesh of an elephant I had shot which had almost decomposed to pulp, and as one watched it slowly cooking in front of a hot wood fire, the maggots were dropping out of it in hundreds. One would imagine they would suffer from eating food of this kind, but it takes a lot to kill a healthy nigger.

Hippo sometimes trek across country from one river to another, and I once saw the spoor of one quite eight miles from the nearest water.

170

In the old days the natives, when they found a small herd in an isolated pool, would surround the place with men and camp-fires, until they starved them sufficiently to kill with spears. Then they would have a glorious debauch on meat, and eat until they could hold no more.

Wanting some milk goats when on an elephant-hunting trip, I had been asked by the natives to kill some hippos in a pool in the Luangwa close to my camp. The natives may be very hungry and not kill their goats, as they are averse to reducing their stock unless in the last extremity.

I promised to shoot some, but told them that each headman who got a hippo would have to supply me with a nanny in milk, as I was hungry for milk. Several agreed, so I shot the requisite hippos, but when it came to getting the goats it was a different matter, as they nearly all wanted to palm off young billies or barren nannies on me. However, by this time I knew the native, so I told them that not a knife would enter the skin of one of my hippos until the goats arrived at my tent. Then they began to arrive to the number of three, and my tent began to resemble a goat kraal.

There were six hippos belly up at the side of the river, but three headmen said they had no goats, so I said bring fowls to the number of one dozen. Two of them said that a dozen fowls were too much for one hippo, so I tried to explain that twelve African fowls weighed at the most 30 lb. and a hippo weighed close on 7,000 lb. avoirdupois; but it was difficult with a native to explain in thousands, as he can only count up to ten on his fingers or toes; and " avoirdupois " quite beat me in the native language, as they did not seem to have a word for it !

I got twenty-four fowls and one hippo was still left, and the headman who had been promised it for a goat or fowls had not arrived. Soon, however, I saw him running along the path which led from his small village with something in his hand. On arrival I found the object was a pair of khaki slacks which he told me his son had brought from Salisbury, in Southern Rhodesia. I told him I never wore khaki slacks, as they were too floppy for hunting, so he suggested I should cut the ends off to make " shorts," and he would keep the bits to make garments for his young family. I said " No," as I thought he must have some goats or fowls, and the old fellow nearly wept as he looked towards the river and saw the crowds round the other hippos, and making stands on the bank to cook the meat when cut in strips.

My head " boy " came up from the river just at that moment, and I noticed his cloth was rather worn, so the thought struck me that he might be the recipient of the slacks, as he was a hard-working fellow, so I told the headman to hand him the trousers, which I did not care to handle, and get along to his meat, and I never saw a more sudden change in a native's face, as disappointment was replaced by joy.

Hippos often contain a lot of fat, as do elephants, and it is excellent for using as lard for cooking. The natives render it down and refine it by boiling it in large pots, taking the dirt and scum off like a cook does when boiling jam. It should not be washed, however, before cooking, as this prevents it lasting long and it goes rancid. If cooked well (and not washed), it keeps for months in a sweet condition, and I seldom used anything else for cooking.

I shall now say a little about the lion, which, although fairly plentiful in most of the country I hunted in, was seldom seen. At night, however, one often heard lions grunting, and on occasions roaring, and I used to marvel at my bad luck in not seeing more, considering the amount of ground I covered through rough bush. In British East Africa it was the same, as men who had been a long time in that famed country for lions never saw or shot one, and others who never even troubled to look for them were constantly seeing them.

Several times when after elephants I put up a lion, but the cover was so thick that he got away without offering a chance, giving short grunts as he rushed off.

My most exciting experience with a lion was when staying with my friend George Garden at Mlanje, in Nyasaland. One day a native came and told Garden that a lion had killed a bush pig in some long grass near his village, which was about five miles off. Garden was busy with his work and could not go, so I decided to go myself, although two rifles would have been better for such work. The path led up hill and down dale, as the village was on one of the foothills of the Mlanje range.

When we got to the village, a number of men were waiting armed with spears, so we all went off to the place where the bush pig had been killed the previous night. It was a particularly nasty place, as the grass had not been burnt and was about 10 feet high, and also very thick. I liked it so little that I almost got cold feet!

I was told the pig's carcass was not far in, so I prepared to have a look at it, telling the men to keep close behind me. After advancing about fifteen paces, I caught a glimpse of the defunct pig, and just as I did so there was a rush in the grass, and some menacing deep grunts from the lion as he came towards us. I stood my ground with my rifle pointed towards him, but he did not advance near enough for me to see him, being a most cunning animal.

The men behind me bolted for the open, and I was left alone with an annoyed lion very close, and I confess I did not like it a bit. In fact, I liked it so little that

I retreated slowly backwards, also towards the open, because the heavy stalks of the grass made it absolutely impossible to swing my rifle sideways, and this is not the kind of cover to tackle a lion in alone. In fact it was a mad proceeding. Had Garden been there, we certainly would have polished off the beast, but it was not the job for a single rifle owing to the difficulty of quick shooting.

When I got outside to the cleared bit of maizeland on one side of the cover, I stood back about twenty yards with the men behind me, and told them to collect stones and lumps of earth and bombard the lion in the hope that he would come out and offer a shot. He would not show up, however, although whenever a stone or clod landed near him he rushed to the place, thinking possibly there was a man there.

An old headman was sitting on a rise about a hundred yards away, and he shouted he could see the lion, so I ran up to him and saw the animal's back through the stems of the grass, so lay down and had a shot. He disappeared and I thought I had got him, but was mistaken, for we saw the grass swaying as he passed through it towards the thick bush.

Then he departed faster as we got on his tracks and found that he had run. There was no blood about, and I am sure I missed him, although from the sudden way he disappeared after my shot I thought he was hit at first. He did not grunt or make a noise after I fired, so I believe I shot over him; but it was a difficult shot, as he was very indistinct in the matted cover.

A few days after this a small troop of lions came round, and Garden and I followed their tracks for some way, putting them up once. Through a bush I caught sight of what looked like a lion, and as I was trying to make sure, I saw it slip away. The cover round Mlanje Mountain is very thick, and lions often

174

came round the villages and took domesticated pigs out of their flimsy houses.

On one occasion Garden got a leopard, and after having had it skinned, the carcass was left near his bungalow, and a lioness came and took it one night and ate most of it. Garden followed her and, getting a good chance, killed her.

Another time a lion took a large pig from Mr. Harry Brown's house on Thornwood Tea Estate, and Garden and I tried to spoor up the troop he was with; but although we followed for some distance, we failed to find them in the thick bush. It was so difficult to move quietly in such country that the lions always heard the trackers and cleared out.

An old official once told me a story which he asserted was the truth, though it sounded rather improbable.

An old native woman was hoeing her garden, which was close to the bush, when a lion came at her. She struck at its head with her hoe, and killed it on the spot by smashing in its skull.

At first I rather doubted the story, but when one thinks it out, it does not appear altogether impossible, for these old women are very strong in the arms with their hard work in the mealie-fields, and a hoe is often as sharp as an axe. Such a weapon driven hard on a lion's skull might easily fracture it and kill the animal.

I may say a shotgun, even with heavy shot such as S.S.G., is not much use against a lion, unless at a range of less than a dozen yards or so.

I once saw the skin and skull of a large lion shot by a youth, Monty Foord, the son of Mr. J. A. Foord, who had a farm near Fort Jameson at that time. He had disabled the lion with a ·303, fortunately hitting its spine, which paralysed its hindquarters. He then blazed at it with a 12-bore shotgun and S.S.G. shot at thirty yards, and, running out of cartridges, approached and tried to lay it out with an axe, which was plucky,

175

but rash. Later he got hold of more rifle cartridges and finished it off.

The skin of the head was full of holes, and there were several flattened S.S.G. pellets still sticking in the skin. They had failed to even crack the skull, and none had penetrated, as I examined it carefully.

After coming in from a shooting trip, I met Monty, who had just arrived from home, where he had been at school. Being fond of shooting, his father had promised him a trip before starting work, and meeting me, he asked how I had got on where I had been shooting. He went to some of the places where I had just been, and, like me, was bitten by tsetse-flies, which were numerous there. Apparently he had been inoculated with the germ of sleeping-sickness, for he was sent home, and died, the day the steamer reached Southampton, of that deadly disease. He was a fine stamp of young fellow, plucky and very fond of shooting, as I think all the best type are.

When I was staying once for a night with my friend Martin Ryan at Government Farm, near Fort Jameson, he had another visitor named Grimes, who had gone in to see the doctor in Fort Jameson to hear the result of an examination of his blood, as it was thought he had sleeping-sickness. As it got dark we saw Grimes walking up the avenue to the house, and when he came in, he told us that he had got it and had to go home for treatment. Amongst the specialists who tried their best to cure him was my cousin, Dr. G. C. Low; but he was a hopeless case, like several others whom I have known in North-Eastern Rhodesia who contracted this vile disease.

I think it was poor Grimes who was put in a kind of refrigerator to see if intense cold would kill the germ in his blood, but it was no good.

In 1911 I went with two other men for a shoot in British East Africa, and had to leave them to get back

DEEPDALE DRIFT, BRITISH EAST AFRICA (KENYA).
Where Postma shot the lions.

ELAND BULL IN NYASALAND.
Note typical thorn-tree country.

to North-Eastern Rhodesia, so I did not get much shooting in that fine country.

The evening of the day we got to Deepdale Drift I had gone out by myself to hunt through the rocky hills near there, but saw no lions. Next evening, on the way back to Kijabe, I was camped at a small water-hole in the plains, when I heard a wagon coming along the road close to where my tent was pitched. On seeing my tent, the two young Boers came over to see me, as they wanted to give their oxen a breather. One of them was named Postma, who spoke broken English. After having a cup of tea which I got prepared for them, they started off for Deepdale Drift, which they expected to reach early next morning.

Some months afterwards I heard that Postma, just after he had inspanned to go on from there next day, saw a large troop of lions coming for his oxen. My friend J. G. Millais asked Postma about it in Nairobi, where he saw him in 1913, and Postma told him that the lions rushed up in two lots at the oxen. His rifle was on the wagon, and he shot nine of them at close range, and wounded two others, which managed to get away. The oxen do not seem to have been hurt much, as the yokeskeys protected their necks.

Postma must be a cool shot to have laid out so many in such a short time, as the whole affair was probably over in five minutes or so. But what a chance to get at lions!

The night Postma and his friend stopped at my tent they had a large dog with them, something like a Great Dane, and I have wondered since what the dog did in the scrimmage.

There was a farmer a few miles out of Fort Jameson named H. K. Brown, who kept a fine pack of these big dogs, often in Rhodesia referred to as " lion " dogs. Some of them were all gashed with the tusks of wart-hogs they had tackled, and they were a great protection

177

in keeping lions and leopards away from the cattle kraals at night.

A farmer near the Kapundi stream, where I had a small cattle ranch for a time, lost some pigs killed by a lion which broke into a large shed they were in. He was disturbed, and jumped through the poles at a height of quite 15 feet from the ground to get out, and in doing so he went through some thick thorn-branches which had been strongly fixed against the poles on the outside.

A lion, when he breaks into a kraal, almost invariably forces his way through near the ground, and will not risk jumping over, or through, the more open places high up. But if disturbed he has no hesitation in jumping up and through the top spaces to get out. This shows that he remembers what the place is like outside when he will jump out of, and not into, an enclosure.

If a lion cannot get through the walls or doorway of a native hut, he has been known to jump on the thatched roof and make a hole through the grass and top poles to get in.

A white man, whose name has slipped my memory, did a very plucky thing on the Serenje Plateau, where he had a cattle ranch. One night a lion broke into the cattle " boys' " hut and killed two of them. Some natives in another hut came to tell the farmer, and he took his lamp and rifle and went to the hut to try to save his " boys," although he found afterwards that the lion had killed them immediately he got in. At last, by the feeble rays of the lamp, he saw the lion, and with a fine shot laid it out on the top of the dead natives.

A few months after this one of his " boys " came to tell him that there was a dog in a trap for small antelopes the natives had laid, but it was so fierce that they could not get close enough to free it, so the white man went off on his errand of mercy. When engaged freeing the dog, it bit him in the hand, and a few weeks afterwards he developed hydrophobia and died.

This was a particularly sad case, as his mother (a widow) had come to live with him on his farm, so his horrible end was a veritable tragedy for her, and I believe she left the country soon afterwards.

The natives firmly believe it is useless hunting certain lions, as they are not lions at all, but forms in which the spirits of malignant people have taken up their abode; so it is difficult sometimes to get information about a man-eater, as the informant thinks that, if he gives it away, it will avenge the act. Much the same thing happens in India when the Sahib tries to hear of a man-eating tiger.

A native, in telling me about a man's death by a lion, said the lion had severed the head and taken it to the grave of a chief, where he was supposed to have left it as a peace-offering.

The inhabitants of Central Africa are very careless about sleeping in the open where lions are known to be dangerous. They will make a camp-fire and let it go out, and as they sleep very soundly, a prowling man-eater has little difficulty in getting some meat.

A friend, L. S. Norman, who was running some cattle from North-Eastern Rhodesia to Salisbury, told me that one night a lion came to his camp and seized a bag of coarse salt and went off with it, but dropped it when he found out his mistake. I expect he smelt the aroma of the carrier on the sacking, and thought he had got hold of something succulent.

The mail runners bringing the home letters to Fort Jameson were attacked on the road, and lions grabbed some of the bags, and a letter in one of them, from my mother to me, had a hole caused by a lion's tooth through it. The post-office authorities had a small notice printed describing the disaster, which was brought to me with the damaged letter, and I still have them.

Martin Ryan once told me of a peculiar experience with a lion one dark night when he was staying in a rest-house. He was awakened by the natives shouting " Mkango " (lion) and got up, picked up his rifle, and went out to the verandah. In the compound he saw a large animal standing, and fired a shot at it, making it run off.

Next morning he examined the spot where it had been standing, and picked up a flattened Snider bullet smeared with matter, which he is sure came out of the lion, his bullet having hit an old wound, which had opened and released the ball which was in it. He showed me the bullet, and I smelt it, and found it was still septic.

When travelling by steamer up the East Coast of Africa, I met a German named Huebner, who was one of the three white men in the railway carriage when Ryall, a police officer in British East Africa, was killed and taken out of the compartment by a man-eating lion. The three men, Ryall, Huebner, and Parenti (an Italian), were sitting up for the lion in a railway carriage which had been shunted into a kind of siding, off the main track, where the soil was rather soft and sandy. Some of their native servants, who had prepared some food for them before beginning their watch, were in an end compartment leading out of the side corridor.

I may say that Selous and Patterson have both given an account of it in their respective books ; but, having met one of the participators, and Selous having given Parenti's account as he met him in British East Africa, I think it interesting to give Huebner's story.

Ryall had agreed to keep first watch, so he sat down in the seat close to the open window and Huebner got into a top bunk, Parenti deciding to sleep on the floor.

180

The light in the roof was left burning, but the spring blind was pulled over it, which made the compartment almost dark, but not enough to prevent a person seeing dimly,

Huebner and Parenti both fell asleep, and the former told me that he was awakened by hearing a choking sound, and immediately became aware of a strong smell of lion. The choking sound was Ryall being killed by the lion, as it had got a hold of his neck, which it was believed had been broken by the teeth of the man-eater. Parenti woke up to feel something heavy pressing on his body, and he too smelt the putrid stink of lion, as the beast's body was touching him.

Huebner admitted that he lost his head, though his rifle was lying in the bunk alongside him, but he forgot all about it and jumped down, touching the flank of the lion as he did so. Parenti managed to free himself and took a header out of the window farthest from the lion and ran to a tree, which he climbed, and stayed in until dawn. Huebner ran along the corridor and tried to get into the end compartment, where the servants were ; but they thought it was the lion trying to break in, and held the door, but Huebner, being a heavy, muscular man, threw his weight on it, and burst in, afterwards locking it with the catch.

The lion, when he jumped into the doorway at the end of the carriage, shook the whole thing with the jar of his jump and weight, and the door, being a sliding one, automatically closed itself, so the lion had shut himself in and could not retreat by the way he had come. What he did was to jump through the centre window, which had been open, and the marvellous thing is that he took Ryall's body with him, as the partly eaten remains were found some distance off in the bush next day.

It is likely that Ryall, when watching, had gone to sleep, and the lion had come close to the open window and got the scent; for when it came along the corridor and through the door—which was open, unfortunately—instead of taking Parenti, who was nearest, it stepped over him and seized Ryall, whose scent it had got from outside.

This, in my opinion, is an interesting point which, I think, neither Selous nor Patterson in his account mentions. It shows that the scent of Ryall formed a set purpose in the lion, as otherwise why should he have left Parenti alone when all he had to do was to take the first person he came on, which was Parenti ?

Of course, everyone knows that when a dog distinguishes his master from a number of other people, it is through his distinctive odour. At a distance he may work by hearing when called, but smell is the predominant sense in all four-legged creatures.

It was never known whether the man-eater was afterwards killed, although it was suspected that a lion caught in a cage was the culprit.

This story, which is exactly as it was told me by one of the actors in the tragedy, is absolutely authenticated, strange though it may seem.

There are two vital points which, if carried out, would have saved Ryall. The first is that by going to sleep he failed to see or hear the lion when it came, and the second, that none of the three men thought of shutting the door leading into the corridor through which the lion came. Had Huebner picked up his rifle when he awoke, he would not have done much good, as Ryall was probably dead then, and he might have wounded the lion instead of killing it on the spot, which would have meant that he and Parenti would have been mauled and possibly killed.

There is a difference, as I have written before, in the method with which lions and tigers seek their prey, but hardly any in the way they kill.

Those fond of thrilling stories of tigers should

read Major-General N. Woodyatt's interesting book *My Sporting Memories* (published by Herbert Jenkins, Ltd.).

When lately reading that work, I noticed that his experiences of how tigers kill an animal corroborate my statements about the kills I saw in Eastern India.

Chapter VII   A FEW EXPERIENCES WITH ANTELOPES

IN several of my former works I gave detailed lists of all the antelopes in Nyasaland, North-Eastern Rhodesia, and in adjacent territory; so I will not enumerate them in this way, only giving a few of my experiences as they occur to me.

Everyone who is interested in horn trophies should get a copy of Rowland Ward's *Records of Big Game*, as he not only gives the best horn measurements, but supplies much detailed information about the habitat of the different species.

Having mentioned in past volumes details such as native names, weights, and measurements, I do not wish to repeat such information here, as it would be monotonous, and hardly in keeping with the title of the book.

I was always interested in trophies, and two of my most pleasant recollections are visits I made to the private museums of the late F. C. Selous, and to J. G. Millais's grand collection of trophies.

It is likely the beginner in South Central Africa will fire his first shot at a duiker, oribi, reedbuck, or bush-buck, as they are among the commonest game to be found in that country. At least my first victim was a duiker, and I remember how I rushed after him when wounded, and my disappointment when I thought I would not get him. However, my natives managed to catch him after running some way. When his head was skinned, I spent hours polishing the skull, until it shines like polished ivory to-day.

184

ELAND BULL.
Shot and photographed by George Garden.

184]

There is a wonderful exhilaration about these happy first days and the glamour with which one starts out for a shoot, and the amount of energy one will expend in tramping miles to get some small animal which is new to one.

Duikers supply good meat, and they are sporting little animals, which often commit suicide by stopping to look back before they depart for good. Nearly all game does this, except animals which have learnt by sad experience that the man in a felt hat and ash-covered shorts is not a safe person to know.

It is most interesting to hunt a recognised animal and get the better of his cunning, after one has missed him several times with difficult shots, or failed often to stalk him closely.

Everyone knows the story of the man who used to chase a jack-snipe which frequented a pool near his bungalow, and which he missed so often that he almost wept when at last it flew into his charge of No. 8 shot and died. He felt he had murdered a friend !

The hartebeest (Lichtenstein's) is usually supposed to be an arrant fool, which looks for trouble and gets shot for his pains ; and there is no doubt that he is very tame, until he finds most of his friends depart for good. After this he can become as cunning and wary as a bull sable or kudu, and it needs the best hunting to get the better of him.

I remember such an animal when I had a cattle ranch on the Kapundi stream, in North-Eastern Rhodesia. When I wanted meat, I went out to the bush surrounding my hut, and I often came on a herd of hartebeest, which at first consisted of eleven animals.

At various times I got one, but never the best-horned bull of the herd, which occasionally went about by himself, sometimes joining a herd of zebra which was often about. I was constantly seeing him, or his spoor, which I always recognized, because he had a chip out of his right hoof which showed clearly in his tracks—that is to say, when the tracks were distinct on damp or on sandy soil.

That bull gave me a lot of fun in my spare time, as I used up all my cunning to get the better of his. I barked my knees, often doing a crawl of several hundred yards on the hard ground, ran thorns into myself, and scratched my legs and hands profusely trying to get within range, but he never would wait. Naturally I took care to study the wind, but that did not help me, as the beast's eyes were what he was depending on.

At last I did what I think was a mean thing, because a hartebeest could not do it. I climbed a large tree near where he used to come and sat amongst the green branches, and waited one evening, taking up my post a good two hours before his usual time to come to the glade where he fed. He came as it was getting dark, and I could see his anxious glances all around to detect his chief enemy in life, and he got so near that I saw his moist nostrils twitching with excitement. I am sure he thought it was quite a good game he was playing with that ugly biped who could only boast of two legs and could never catch him fairly. He died, and I helped to eat him ; but if the thing were to happen again, I would kill him fairly or let him go, as I do not consider I quite played the game.

I killed several good sable antelope bulls near the place which this hartebeest haunted, one with a good head over 43 inches on the curve ; but one day I lost a splendid animal. When using a new rifle I was sitting watching a *dambo* late one evening, as I liked to watch the game coming out of the bush to feed here. If not needing meat, or tempted by a good head, I sometimes simply watched animals moving about through my field-glasses.

On this evening I had been watching a herd of roan antelopes through my glasses for some time, but none

186

of their heads were exceptional, so I did not move after them. I had a small native boy with me who carried my Kodak and the case for the glasses. This youngster was only about ten years old, but he was a marvellous tracker for his age, as his eyes were sharp as needles when on the spoor. He was as keen to go shooting as a young spaniel, and used to behave in much the same way when he saw me with a rifle going off into the bush, for he would run after me and ask to carry the camera, or anything I was taking along, such as a cartridge-bag.

As the sun went down, I was just thinking of coming away when the nipper whispered, " Mpala-pala, bwana " (" Sable antelope, master "); and on looking where he was pointing, I saw a grand sable bull with the best head I had ever seen coming out of the bush into the *dambo* to feed. We edged round the small bush we were sitting behind to get better cover, and watched him as he began to work closer to us. When within a hundred yards or so, I aimed at his shoulder and he fell, but began to kick, and I should then have given him a second shot, as it is a bad sign when an animal falls quickly with a body shot. With a heart or lung shot a beast nearly always rushes off hard for some yards before he falls for good.

Walking within fifteen paces of him, I turned to the boy to take my camera from its case, and when I was in the act of drawing it out, I heard the sable moving, and the boy said, " He is running away, master." I seized my rifle from the boy's hand, but by the time I was quite ready the sable was into the timber and going hard ; and the quick shot I fired, with a rifle I did not know well, missed.

We followed his blood spoor until it got too dark to see it ; and for two days I came back and followed his tracks for many miles, but did not find him.

On the following day he stopped leaving blood and

187

was going strong, and I knew he would get better. I believe I creased him—that is, touched the spinal column with my bullet, which paralysed him for a few moments, causing him to fall when struck.

I had the tantalizing experience of seeing this animal twice afterwards, as he continued to come to the *dambo* occasionally, but seldom arrived until almost dark.

One evening, when the light was almost gone, I was crawling up close enough to get a good shot, when a number of guinea-fowl got up in front of me, making such a noise that the sable went off immediately.

A month before my experience with him, I had shot the sable mentioned with horns over 43 inches, which is quite a good head in that locality. The horns of the lost animal seemed to be a good 8 inches larger, as his head looked enormous.

It is seldom the hunter has the luck to get the best specimens amongst the game he sees; in fact, he is very fortunate if he gets half of them. I lost the best elephant, sable, roan, eland, and impala I saw, and I only fired at the sable roan and impala, the others getting away without being fired at.

The elephant I need not describe, except to say its tusks were whoppers, and he got the wind of some natives who were following me against orders when I was going up for my shot. I think it was mainly the fault of the wind changing on that occasion, although the natives should have waited where I left them.

In the case of the roan antelope, I was tramping from the Luangwa River to Fort Jameson, and was near the Sasare Gold-mine (the only gold-mine in North-Eastern Rhodesia at that time). It was raining hard, so I put my rifle in its cover, and was walking ahead of my carriers when I saw a bull roan feeding in a *dambo* near the path. He had the longest horns of any roan I had seen, and I had seen hundreds.

SABLE ANTELOPE BULL, NORTH-EASTERN RHODESIA.

It did not take very long for me to grab the rifle and begin to take it from its cover, but I had to load it from the magazine, as I never leave a cartridge in the chamber when a rifle is in its cover.

Unfortunately, the roan saw us on the path, and just as I was ready he bolted. I do not believe in taking running shots at unwounded game as a rule, but these horns were too much for me, and I tried a shot. I was cold and soaking wet, and whether my muscles were cramped, or whether I pulled too far ahead, I don't know; but I missed him. He got into some rocky country where the tracks were almost invisible, although I had an excellent elephant tracker with me, and could spoor fairly well myself, as it was my chief hobby; but it took so long to get along for a few yards on the bad surface that I left the spoor and took a round, hoping to pick them up in better ground.

The rain begun to lash down, and we were all tired, as we had done a good twenty miles before we saw the roan, so we gave it up and went on to Sasare.

My friend Martin Ryan, who lived near Sasare Mine for a time, told me that several people had seen, and been after, this roan bull, as his head made him a prize worth having, but I never heard he was bagged.

The eland was a female which I saw in a small herd on the upper waters of the Lutembwe stream, in North-Eastern Rhodesia, and she had the longest horns I have seen on an eland.

I may say eland cows have much longer and more slender horns than the bulls, but it is seldom that one gets a head over 30 inches on a cow.

Although I spoored the herd for some time, darkness came on and prevented my getting up to them, and next day I had to go on, as I was making for the elephant country.

The impala I saw near Gwaza's, on the Upper Shire River, and I made a bad miss at him as he stood looking at me through some thick timber. I had to shoot between two small trees, and, as often happens in such a case, I hit one of the saplings, which deflected my bullet.

When living for about a year at a nice hunting camp I made on the upper reaches of the Bua River, I had excellent sport with eland, sable, and roan antelopes.

The assistant magistrate at Fort Manning (after the K.A.R. troops stopped being stationed there) gave me permission to shoot several eland above the number allowed on my licence, as the animals did much damage to the native crops in the vicinity, so I was able to get some very large bulls.

A bull eland is a splendid-looking animal as he strolls along with his cows feeding in some forest glade. Age makes him lose most of his light-brown colouring, as the hair is rubbed off, leaving him a bluish-grey colour. He usually retains thick hair on his neck, and develops a large tuft of long, matted hair on his forehead. A full-grown bull is quite 6 feet at the shoulder and is very heavy in the body and neck, and is faster than he looks when followed on foot.

The oldest and heaviest bull I got was a magnificent animal with lovely chocolate-coloured hair on his neck and down the nasal bone, and his hairless body was that bluish-grey which is a sure sign of age in both eland and buffalo. I gave his measurements in my *Wild Life in Central Africa*, but will again mention them here, as he was by far the heaviest eland I have seen out of probably three thousand or more.

	Feet.	Inches.
From nose to end of flesh on tail	13	4
From nose to root of tail	11	5
Circumference of body at middle. . . .	9	6
Circumference of neck at middle	7	0
Height from top of shoulder to flat of forefoot .	6	0
Horns on straight	2	2

NATIVE BOY WITH ELAND SKULL.
Horns 29½ inches on straight.

ELAND BULL SHOT IN NYASALAND.
Note chocolate-coloured pad of hair on frontlet.

In the book mentioned I gave a fairly good photograph of this splendid animal, and I have found amongst my collection of photographs another print taken from a second film I took at the same time. The foreground of the photograph is out of focus slightly, but the eland comes out well enough to notice the thick patch of chocolate-coloured hair down the nasal bone. I never saw a bull eland where this patch, and also the same-coloured covering of his neck, was so thick and abundant.

The weight of this animal I should put as quite 2,000 lb. It took twenty-five strong men to carry all the meat to my camp, and of course when cutting up the beast there was a lot of blood and offal removed. None of the men was carrying less than 70 lb., and some carried much more, as each haunch, when tied to a pole, took two men all their time to stagger under to my camp.

At the same time as I shot this splendid animal I killed another bull half an inch higher at the shoulder (the big one I believe was more than 6 feet, but he fell crumpled up and I could not straighten his forelegs, so the 6 feet is under-measured) and with horns 29½ inches long; but though he was a fine beast, he was nothing like the one whose measurements I have given.

These elands were both in a herd of about thirty animals which had been feeding in the maize-fields of Zulus' village, and I had not to follow far before getting a shot. I first wounded the large bull, and he ran, and then I saw the other, which I killed. Just after knocking it down, Kadango called out that he could see the large bull, which looked lame, and I killed him with a second shot from my 7·9 mm. Rigby-Mauser.

I was so surprised at the colossal bulk and the amount of chocolate hair on the forehead and neck, that I sat long admiring him before I would allow the natives to cut him up.

I may say we tried to straighten his legs out to get a fair measurement of his height, but I had wasted some time gazing at him before I began my measurements, and then found that the men and myself were unable to get his legs straight, as his shoulder muscles as well as his legs had stiffened and contracted until it became impossible. The photograph clearly shows the position he fell in.

It is advisable, when a hunter wants measurements, that he should take them quickly before rigor mortis sets in.

I think I mentioned before that the only true measurements are those taken between pegs for height and length dimensions.

Once, near Mauzi Hill, in South-Eastern Nyasaland, I shot a good bull for the Transvaal Museum in Pretoria. He was a fine beast, but his measurements were much smaller than the big bull I have written so much about.

Soon after I got the one near Mauzi, it came on to rain and I had great difficulty in saving his skin, and had to make a shelter with poles and grass, and a platform under which I kept fires burning. As his thick neck skin, quite an inch thick, began to go bad, I pared it down, and to do this used a good pair of ivory-handled razors, which the work did not improve. I had to grow a beard afterwards until I got them sharpened properly.

This eland skin, with others of buffalo, kudu, sable, hartebeest, etc., I sent to Lourenço Marques (Delagoa Bay) to be forwarded to the Museum in Pretoria, and a wretched Portuguese harbour official put the large package in a wet store, with the result that when it reached Pretoria the Museum people found that most of the skins had gone bad and were useless for setting up. I lost about £60 over the business, and could not recover the money at such a distance—such are the woes of a hunter's and collector's life, for it is no joke skinning and preparing heavy skins for natural-history purposes ; as besides the work of shooting and skinning them, they have to be watched most carefully until packed. The Bacon beetle (*Dermestes ladratus*) soon gets at skins and skulls, and one of my difficulties when collecting was to get the natives to keep seething skulls from the skins, as they had no hesitation in putting them close together at every stopping-place.

When I was on this collecting trip, I shot a fine bull kudu one evening about dark, when I was about ten miles from my tent. He was with a herd which, when disturbed, ran round the base of a small stony kopje, and I made a lucky running shot and dropped him. If it had not been so late, I would have preferred to follow him rather than risk a chance running shot, as they do not always come off ; and I am against doing so unless at a wounded beast which may otherwise escape.

Knowing that if I left the kudu out all night the hyenas would rip him up, or a leopard come and eat part of him, I decided to skin him at once, so got my " boys " to collect dry wood and make a big fire close to the dead animal. We soon had a fine blaze, as there are always heaps of dead branches in the bush, and it took over an hour to get his skin off his body up to his neck.

I left the head on the skin and wrapped it up, and returned to my tent by starlight, scratching my legs badly on thorns and getting many a hard bump on stumps as we threaded the rough bush which lay between us and camp. A ten-mile walk on a dark night is no joke, as one flounders into holes and strikes impediments with one's bare legs. The eyes, too, are apt to be spiked with thorns or the points of half-burnt reeds, which are sharp.

On the day previous one of my men who was just

behind me gave a grunt, so I asked him what was wrong, as he stooped to look at his leg. I found that a stalk of grass he had hit had penetrated completely through his right calf, and I pulled it out. This was an extraordinary incident which I would never have believed unless I had seen it, but it is a fact nevertheless. As I have said, burnt grass gets hardened with the heat, and I suppose the point hit his leg in a direct line from its base, so was not deflected in any way.

The natives always went about in bare feet, though some of my men used to ask me for skin to make sandals when there were many thorns about.

To get back to the kudu. I got to the tent about 11 p.m., and put the skin with head in it up a tree, so that any prowler such as a hyena or leopard would not get it. Next morning, just before having my breakfast, I gave it to my head " boy," whom I had taught how to skin specimens to be set up—and started him on the head, telling him to leave the part round the eyes for me, as that is the most likely spot to suffer damage from a false cut with the knife.

After breakfast I strolled over to see how he was getting on, and found that just after he had begun operations he had cut a hole several inches long in the skin, completely spoiling it for a museum specimen.

I was naturally annoyed with such gross carelessness, as he had done the work properly a good many times before, so I kicked his posterior with the light elk-sole boots I wear for shooting in Africa, and called up my men and left to look for another kudu; which I may say I did not find for over two weeks.

I shot a warthog boar and came back to camp, and found that my head " boy " had run away and taken my *sukampika* (dish-washer) with him, and I was really not very sorry, as they were both rather useless specimens.

The cook was rather funny about it, as the dish-washer is the youth who washes dishes and pots, and I thought he would be sulky at having to do the work himself. He came to me and said, " Master, you should kick Chapuka and Bonali," meaning two of the carriers who were rather lazy about bringing him the necessary firewood for his culinary operations.

Cooks in Africa, like everywhere else, are rather bossy individuals, and tact with them goes a long way, so the next time I heard Chapuka and Bonali arguing with the cook, the elk-hide soles came into use again and peace reigned.

While I am on the subject of personal native servants, I might mention an amusing incident which occurred at my big camp on the Bua stream. To make bread one often uses English hops, which come out in sealed tins. The cook mixes a couple of spoonfuls of hops, some sugar, and a little salt, and puts the lot with water into an empty whisky-bottle and corks it. The cork should be tied on to prevent the fermentation blowing it out.

The term for " Mr." in the native language is *Che* used as a prefix. Well, one day, as I was sitting having tea on my verandah, I heard a bang just like a gunshot, so I asked the " boy " standing near to go and see who was shooting. He came back with a broad grin on his black face, and said " *Chehopassi, bwana,*" meaning " Master, it was Mr. Hopbottle." As the cork had not been tied down, it had blown out.

At the time I was hunting the country near Mauzi Hill there were great numbers of sable antelopes about, perhaps the finest species of antelope in Africa, though some people admire the kudu more and give it first place.

Possibly the kudu is really the more handsome, but he is seldom found in the open, being fond of cover and hilly country with plenty of thick bush about.

The sable goes to the hills, too, mainly to get rid of

flies and for coolness in very hot weather; but he is fond of the open and does not mind showing himself.

Many is the time I have lain and watched sable feeding or coming to drink at a pool or stream in the evening. The Boers in South Africa called him " Swartwitpens," which, I believe, means " black with white belly," and this describes his colour, but does not give a full impression of his beauty.

They begin to turn black about the third year, and the younger animals are a rich rufous brown. The females as well as the males bear horns, although they never reach the thickness or length of the bull's fine headpiece.

There is something quite fascinating in seeing a troop of sable coming along in an open *dambo*, particularly if they have been startled into a gallop, with the sun glancing off their rich black hides and horns, as they make for temporary cover. During the heat of day they lie up in the bush, and come towards the open about 4 o'clock in the afternoon, like most of the other antelopes.

My first good bull sable was shot near Fort Manning when I was out shooting one morning. I saw him standing amongst some half-burnt grass, and stalked to within 150 yards and got him. His horns were a little over 40 inches on the curve,[1] and his skull is now above me as I write. It is close on twenty years since I shot him, but when I look at his head (by no means a very large one, but my first) I seem to see him standing looking towards me, with his jet-black coat and white belly shining, his nose stretched out, with the long horns thrown back on his haunches just as

[1] There is a variety of sable antelope in Angola which grows immense horns, probably due to the phosphates in the feed. H. F. Varian, who knows that country so well, gave me a lovely pair of horns measuring 58½ inches on the curve. The record of 64 inches belongs to J. G. Millais.

SABLE ANTELOPE COW.
Shot and photographed by George Garden.

the fatal bullet took him in the shoulder and laid him low.

One sometimes thinks, especially at the time, that it is cruel to slay such lovely animals; but how much better a well-placed bullet than a lion's tearing jaws and claws—for sooner or later death will come for creatures which live near the great cat, whose life means death.

In all the country I have tramped over roan antelopes were very common, in fact they were among the most numerous species. Like the sable, a roan is a plucky animal, fond of the open at times, when feeding in those numberless grassy glades termed *dambos* in Central Africa. All over the country, especially where the land is undulating, these openings in the bush occur. During the rainy season water collects in most of them and they become swampy. The edges near the timber-line are often sparsely covered with bush, which gradually thickens into timber country.

Many of the *dambos* have large anthills scattered here and there, which form splendid stalking cover for the hunter; particularly the larger ones, which are often covered with thick grass, or in some cases bushes. If it were not for these anthills, many an animal which died would be alive, or at least would have lived many more years than it did. Another advantage of the anthill is that it enables the hunter to get above the level, so they are good spots as lookouts.

Near my ranch on the Kapundi stream there was a high kopje named Manje, where I often went late in the afternoon to spy from. There was a cave on one of the precipitous sides, where I saw some drawings done by natives with a dark-red ochre. The stuff would not rub off with the dry hand, and the few figures mostly represented animals, such as elephant and antelopes.

Another kopje some miles down the Tete road was

197

called by the natives " Chiperi." On the top of this kopje was a great rock in the shape of a rhinoceros horn.

Many of the hills in North-Eastern Rhodesia were like those seen in Mashonaland. By moonlight they often looked like ruined castles, with towers and battlements rising high in the air. Some of these hills were a solid mass of stone, or great boulders piled up in the most fantastic shapes, which gave a sense of wildness and primitiveness to the surroundings.

I can remember shooting two roan antelopes with one bullet, and not a solid one either. In an exchange I had got hold of a ·275 Westley Richards Mauser, which was quite a good weapon, being very accurate ; but the lot of soft-nose bullets I got with it did not open out sufficiently on contact. Several zebra, sable, and hartebeest I shot with it (I do not mention the smaller stuff like duiker and oribi, which are not much of a test) might as well have been hit with a solid bullet.

Coming on a herd of roan, I got in range and waited to see if I could bag two with one shot, and I did, for it was not difficult to wait until two were exactly in line, as they had not seen or winded me. The bullet stuck in the back one, and after some difficulty my natives found it. It had hardly expanded at all, though it had gone right through one animal and mostly through the other. A strange thing about this shot was that, though the two animals were dead in line and ought to have both been hit through the shoulder, where the first one got it, the back animal was hit behind, through one of its kidneys.

I lost this interesting bullet, as it slipped through a hole in the pocket of my shorts on the way home.

The action of bullets in game interested me greatly, so I kept several scores of them, and have them in a butterfly box with a glass top and partitions inside for the different game, such as elephant, buffalo, antelopes, and so on.

Any rifle is good enough for antelopes, but if I were able to go and hunt in Africa again, I think I would prefer a ·318 rifle. It was with rifles by Rigby, Gibbs, and Fraser that I did my best work; but the firm of Fraser is no longer in existence.

Often, when after elephant, one would see any number of antelopes of different kinds, and it was difficult to pass a good head which likely would never be seen again.

My best kudu head, only 57 inches on the curve, in comparison with a few I have seen and many I have heard of, is not an extremely large head, although I am quite pleased with it. I got it while marching from Fort Jameson to Tete in March 1905.

When walking along the broad path, commonly called the Tete road, I was winding through a short valley between hills, and heard the rush of a herd of game as they bolted amongst the rocks and trees. I took my rifle from the " boy " behind and followed in the direction, as we needed meat and I was prepared to shoot the first animal I saw.

Getting over the brow of the hill, I saw a fine herd of kudu on the opposite slope, with two bulls and about a dozen cows. The bulls were looking back, and I could not make out which had the best horns, as when game is in this position their horns slope to the rear, and it is impossible to know what they are like.

I took the easier shot of the two, and when I fired I noticed a bit of bark fly from a small tree in the line of fire. The kudu, however, stood upon his hind-legs and then fell, and never rose again. The herd then ran and were soon out of sight in the bush.

On going up to him, I noticed a hole the size of a 12-bore bullet in his left side right over the lungs, though I had fired with a ·303, using a soft-nose bullet. I went to the small sapling, which was only about 3 inches thick, and found that my bullet had hit

199

it and expanded before it took the kudu behind the shoulder.

This is one of the few animals I have seen hit in the lungs which fell and was almost instantaneously killed, as with a lung shot a beast usually runs some distance before falling dead. What accounted for its sudden demise was, of course, the great shock of the already expanded bullet making an extra large hole in its lungs.

With a ·256 or ·303 bullet I have found the exit hole in a small animal, which had been punctured right through, was often as large as a saucer—that is, when an expanding type of bullet was used, such as a soft-nose, hollow-point, or slit.

In thicker-bodied buck the bullet generally, though not always, stayed in, especially when the shoulder-bone was struck. If struck behind the shoulder, it often got through, but made a ghastly wound.

My favourite shot at antelope was on the point of the shoulder when they were a quarter facing, for if struck right, the bullet sent splintered bone inside which sometimes tore the heart and lungs to pulp.

As this is not an edifying subject to any except those interested in such details, I shall pass on.

Looking for elephant spoor near the Rukusi stream, in North-Eastern Rhodesia, in October 1908, I came on two fine kudu bulls and could not resist shooting them. One was standing up, and I fired at him and hit him hard. Suddenly another, which I had not at first noticed, jumped up and ran, and his horns looked very broad, so I fired at him, and after several shots, as I was tired with the heat and was not shooting well, I downed him. Before I could go up to him I had to sit down and remove one of my boots, as I had a bad festering sore under a toenail, caused by careless nail-cutting and much walking when it was inflamed.

I hobbled up to the grand creature, and sat down and had a smoke, and gloated over him, for he was a beauty. He was not so old as the first one shot, as one could tell from the formation of the horns at the base. When horns are still growing, it is possible, after much experience, to tell at once whether an animal is aged, as old horns have a more polished and firmer texture quite unmistakable.

When an antelope is old its horns begin to go back, and this is most noticeable in animals with fairly straight horns such as an old bull eland. By this I do not mean they shrink or grow smaller, but that the constant rubbing and wear are not replaced by new growth, therefore they decrease in length as time goes on. I have seen old eland with horns hardly longer than 20 inches, which were probably quite 28 inches when the animal had reached full maturity.

This fine kudu had horns measuring 49¾ inches from tip to tip, and 46½ inches on the straight. The curve length was only 54½ inches, and thus gives a difference of 8 inches more than the straight measurement, which is much less than the average difference, as it is usually from 12 to 16 inches. It was certainly an abnormal head in this respect.

The other bull had a fair head of 53¾ inches on the curve and 41½ inches on the straight, and from tip to tip 32⅛ inches.

A kudu head looks better on a wall than a sable's, unless the latter can be viewed from the side, when the sweep of the horns can be seen.

The puku, an antelope discovered by Dr. Livingstone and called by him *Cobus Vardoni*, after Major Frank Vardon, who travelled with Oswell and Dr. Livingstone in Southern Africa, is one of the prettiest of the medium-sized antelopes. It was not until I visited the Luangwa Valley, in North-Eastern Rhodesia, that I saw these well-shaped antelopes in any numbers. There they were very numerous. A few are found near Kongoni, on the Bua River in Nyasaland, and they are not very easy to find. Near the Luangwa River, however, they are extremely plentiful on the west side, and I shot as many as I wanted there.

The rams fight a good deal with each other, and I once found a large piece of horn embedded in the neck of one I killed, which had evidently been broken in by a sudden twist after he got the stab. As horn substance, and the core inside, are composed of tenacious matter, it must have needed much force to have caused such a breakage.

On hitting a ram with a bullet, I saw him go straight for another male close to him and strike him hard in the haunch, thinking that the bullet wound had been a butt. Just after making the attack he collapsed, and then the other one went for his body and gave it several hard prods, cutting the skin and making holes about ½ inch in depth. He seemed to hit as hard as he could, and I was surprised he did not do more damage, considering I had found the piece of horn quite 5 inches long in the neck of one I had shot a few days before.

Of course, horn points vary in sharpness, although the piece I found in the ram's neck was not particularly sharp, so it must have belonged to an exceptionally strong animal to have penetrated so deeply, especially through the neck, where the skins of all antelopes are almost twice as thick as the body-skin.

I saw a charming sight one morning close to a lagoon in the Luangwa not far from Chipofu's village. Early in the morning I had gone to the river to look for good puku heads. I took up a position on an anthill just after dawn, and sat entranced at the amount of game I saw coming to drink. There was a herd of eland feeding near the timber which bordered the marshy ground, and close to them two lots of waterbuck, one lot with a good horned bull; then a large herd of zebra came strolling along, and several troops of impala, besides various small companies of puku. Not far away some crested cranes were sitting in trees, making a sound like cats mewing loudly; and many other birds could be seen, including two ospreys fishing in the shallow water of the lagoon.

Suddenly I saw all the game begin to get suspicious, and then stand staring in one direction; and on looking to see what had attracted them, I saw two natives coming along to inspect some fish-traps they had laid at the mouth of the lagoon where it left the Luangwa.

Soon the game began to walk away from the disturbers of their peace, and later I followed them and got a couple of nice puku rams which I picked out of many I saw that morning. These two heads I have kept with many others, which remind me of past happy days in Africa.

The impalas found in this country grow much smaller horns than the East African species, which have splendid heads. I visited British East Africa for a short time in 1911, but did not see the impala country, and only got Grant's gazelle, Thomson's gazelle, and a few other species.

I did not fancy the type of shooting on the plains in British East Africa, and prefer a heavily bushed country where one can go in for tracking more, and where one meets with more surprises in a day's shooting. For those who like to fire long shots at game, the plains country is just the place, as the animals get more wary every year, and keep farther off. With the advance in flat trajectories they seem to be attaining an equivalent knowledge of ballistics.

There are certain species of antelopes which, when seen by the hunter or traveller, denote the presence of water; and if matters become urgent, the freshest spoor should be followed, and it will probably lead to a pool, small stream, or marshy hollow. The most water-loving antelopes are, of course, the situtunga and lechwe; but these are found where there is plenty of water, and I refer to the buck which in a dry country live close to it. These are puku, impala, and reedbuck, so if they are seen the hunter will find water within a mile or so. Waterbuck, on the other hand, sometimes go farther than six miles or so from water, and they are often found at this distance in stony, rocky hills running back from rivers.

If a river-bed is dry and green trees are seen on the banks, water is sure to be found by digging. A pool is often filthy and green with animals' droppings and urine, and the natives using paths bathe in the nearest pool, so this water should not be drunk. The thing to do is to make a hole a foot or two deep close to the water, but not joined to it, and let the water in the pool filter to its own level in the hole, when it will be cleaned by the earth or sand. This is simply a natural filter. The natives often do this, and I never drank direct from a pool, unless, which sometimes happened, it was in solid rock where one could not dig.

Once, when trekking to Tete, we had gone across country in frightfully hot weather, with the country as dry as a bone, and the trees that grey, lifeless colour which one sees in the drier parts of the African bush in what is called the dry season. Our water was finished by midday, and we had not found the pool some villagers had told us about. The carriers were just about beat, and I felt pretty bad, although I was not carrying a 45-lb. load on my shoulders or head, as these hardy fellows were doing.

About sundown matters became rather serious, as some of the men looked ghastly, with staring eyes and swollen lips. Personally I could hardly articulate, as my throat felt inflamed and sore.

I had walked over to a small kopje to have a look round, but before getting there I found the fresh spoor of a rhino which had passed not more than an hour before. It was impossible to say, of course, whether he was bound for or from water, and deduction had to be used. First, the spoor led straight and he was travelling and not feeding. Second, rhinos lie up during the heat, and only move about an hour or two before sunset, and often go first for water if the day is hot, and this one had been a scorcher. Third, the lie of the country tended to the water being in front of the rhino, as he had come from some stony hills about two miles away.

Telling the " boys " to make camp on the path, I collected gourds, kettles, and anything which would hold water, and sent three of the men off on the spoor. I knew they were good men on their legs, as one soon finds out the tough men amongst the carriers. The beginner in this country, when he picks his carriers, usually goes for the heavy, tall, muscular men, but after he has done much hard foot-trekking, he will go for the short, wiry fellows with thin shanks, as these are the more enduring under hard conditions.

Going off on the rhino spoor, the men were back in a little over an hour, as they said they had seen some birds rising from a hole in a rock, where they found some water, so, of course, left the rhino spoor. This hole may have been filled by a small shower which had fallen lately.

Two of the " boys " were really in a bad state, as they lay gasping under bushes, and I never felt so thirsty in my life, and could hardly whisper. When the water arrived the " boys " got it first, and it was horrible, stinking stuff, fouled by birds, lizards, and animals, but it was water.

Next morning, on waking, I heard my " boy " saying " Oogwe " outside the tent, so asked him what was wrong. He said a rhino had come behind the tent in the night when walking down the sandy path. His spoor was within 4 feet of my head, and he must have almost touched the canvas with his nose.

Every hill and kopje usually holds a few klipspringers, one of the most sporting of the small antelopes, and I used to like hunting them, as the cooler air of the hills was refreshing and invigorating after the stuffiness of the plains and bush. They have tiny feet and walk on their toes just like goats, and their hair is stiff, and stands out of the skins like pins in a pin-cushion. The Boers in South Africa used the hair for stuffing saddles, as they believed it did not form lumps like other materials.

Sometimes, after a shot, a cloud of hair would fly from the animal. The hair, if rubbed hard with a stroke of the hand, would often come out easily. I think this happened more at some times than others, possibly when the animal was shedding its coat.

Klipspringer meat is excellent eating, being like tender mutton, and I liked it better than anything except eland flesh. Many is the lonely kopje far in the bush which I have climbed to hunt klipspringers, and the sport must be rather like chamois-shooting in Europe.

When one or more of these buck run, they almost invariably stop to look back. This habit has caused many of their deaths.

The views from some of these rocky kopjes were simply grand, and it was in such places that I fully felt the romance of the African wilds.

Comparisons are popularly supposed to be odious, but I could not help comparing such pictures to the awful things called art one sometimes saw in galleries at home, often being gazed at in rapture by admiring crowds of chattering human monkeys, who often smelt horribly of cheap scent.

One of the antelopes I was very keen to shoot was an inyala, but I never got a shot at one.

When after buffalo in the Chiromo Marsh, I intended starting off for the Muanza, which flows into the Shire

206

River, to try to get one of these beautiful creatures ; but I got a bad attack of fever and had to make for higher levels, as the heat in the Marsh in October is terrific. I have only seen two places where it is so intense, and these spots are the Zambezi and Luangwa Valleys at the same season.

I have often had to take off my boots to cool my feet, and to touch any metal was impossible without burning the hands. The natives, notwithstanding their hard feet, on which the skin is usually quite $\frac{1}{4}$ inch thick, cannot walk without sandals, and the tin and steel boxes have to have pads of cloth or grass between them and the natives' heads and shoulders. At such times water is scarce, too, as evaporation takes place more rapidly, so hard tramping in the sun from September to the end of November (when the rains break) is strenuous work indeed.

One of the most sporting antelopes is the bushbuck, which is numerous in most places where there is plenty of bush. They have a habit of barking at night, if disturbed by a leopard or some nocturnal prowler, and the sound is not unlike a dog's sharp bark.

I liked stalking bushbuck, as they are usually wary creatures, especially a ram which has been much hunted. Having shot a good number of them, it is difficult to pick out my most interesting experience.

There was a ram I had seen several times on the top of the Zomba plateau which I got one morning when I had gone to find him early. A fairly long shot laid him low, and then, as I looked at his beautiful brown skin, with white spots dappled here and there, I felt sorry for a space ; and then I remembered finding one not long before which had been killed and eaten by a leopard, and it struck me that the victim of the bullet was the luckier animal.

This species is found either singly or in pairs, seldom in lots of many animals. As they walk along through

207

the bush they tread daintily and softly, and seem to be
more awake than some of the other small antelopes.
They have a bare patch on the throat which does not
seem to be of any use to them ; possibly it is done by
rubbing. The younger animals are often bluish-
coloured, and only the males bear horns. They seem
to vary in length of hair, as I have seen some old rams
quite profusely covered with brownish hair, whereas
others have shorter coats.

In South Africa they often shoot them with heavy
shot, and I hardly think this is very sporting, as the
bushbuck offers quite a good mark for a rifle if properly
stalked. I read in a South African paper many years
ago of a white man being killed by a ram he had
peppered, which attacked him and punctured him
in the stomach. Several I have approached closely
when wounded have jumped up and put down their
heads as I attempted to grab them, so I always finished
such animals with another shot. Near my hut at
Mzazas, on the Luangwa, I had quite a tussle with
one I had gone up to, after laying my rifle against a
tree some yards away. He was lying flat, and it has
been my almost invariable experience that such an
animal is dead, or on the point of death. This was
an exception, for as soon as I had grabbed one of his
horns, he began to struggle hard and almost threw me
off my feet. I knew if I let go his horns I should probably get them into my stomach, so I hung on, and
twisted him over until I got my foot on the horn nearest
the ground. Then I easily killed him. Now this
beast was hard hit through the lungs, and had he
happened to have been only very slightly wounded,
I am sure I could not have held him. All animals have
great power in their necks, so such strong beasts as
roan and sable antelopes should be treated with respect.

A wounded bull sable, when attacked by domesticated dogs, will lay them out rapidly with successive

quick sweeps of his scimitar-shaped horns; and I knew a native who went up to one which was sitting up (not lying flat) who stopped the point of the horn, getting it through a kidney, and died in a few minutes.

As the bushbuck I had a struggle with was bleeding profusely, I looked as if I had had a bath in blood when I had finished the tussle.

Talking about baths of blood: when a large animal such as an elephant or rhino is shot, especially the first of the trip, the natives, after disembowelling the beast, will get into the hole and throw blood all over their bodies. They don't wash it off—that is against their superstition—but allow it to dry on, until the sun's rays make it flake off. They smell a bit afterwards, but not worse than they usually do without the gore.

A lady coming to live in Central Africa for the first time was asked what was her strongest impression of the country. Without hesitation she said: " The strange odour of the blacks." She was right, but if she had known the language, she would have been surprised to find that that is the native's impression of the whites, as they say, when the European has fever, he smells " most awful vile."

When running along with a *machilla* (hammock on one or two poles), the natives naturally perspire profusely, as it is hard work in the hot sun. They used to carry sweat-scrapers made of soft iron with a flat, spear-shaped blade, but rounded at the point. These scrapers are decorated with beads, and sometimes hairs from elephant tails, and I have two nice ones which I got some years ago. In olden times ladies used back-scratchers when they wished to chase *Pulex irritans* (the common or ticklish flea), so " all the world is kin."

One of the most interesting of the smaller antelopes is Sharpe's steinbuck, and they are difficult to get shots at with a rifle (and I never cared to pot them with a shotgun). When disturbed they seldom stop to look back like the duiker, klipspringer, and others ; so, unless shot at quickly, one will need to try running shots. Their horns are very short, a good one measuring about 1½ inches. I once got a head measuring 1¾ inches, which is the second largest yet recorded.

I may say it is just as difficult to get a record of a small head as a large one ; possibly more difficult, as more small animals are shot than big ones.

It would not be very interesting to say much more about the smaller antelopes, so I shall pass on, and describe some of the other game.

I HAVE not said much about zebra, gnu, leopard, warthog, bushpig, baboon, crocodile, and hyena, so I might try to give a slight description of them in a short chapter, as they will be seen, or heard, at one time or another by the traveller in the wilds.

Zebras are very plentiful, particularly in hilly country covered with bush. They are beautiful creatures with what some naturalists would describe as protective coloration. When seen with the sunlight glancing through the interstices of the trees and bush they are difficult to see, except for the waving of their tails. No animal can be called protectively coloured which has a tail left to wag, as the constant movement quickly attracts attention.

If the sun is shining full on them they look white, and when the sun is behind them they then appear black. The stripes are not visible at a greater distance than about two hundred yards, unless with glasses.

The elephant-hunter detests zebras, for when disturbed they rush off, making a great clattering on stony ground, or on softer soil raising a great cloud of fine dust which will often be seen for several miles. Natives like the meat, although it does not appeal overmuch to the European, who naturally associates it with horseflesh. I have often eaten it when there was nothing better to be had, but I usually got my cook to put it through a small mincer—which I may say is a very useful culinary utensil to have in Africa, where most of the meat is tough and stringy. When handing a " boy " a mincer, it is best to show him how to use it, as he is likely to put his finger in the hole and slice a bit of it off ; which bit will probably be allowed to stay there and be served up with the dish.

Cooks are very careless in putting pieces of sharp fowl-bones in the soup, and I had a nasty experience in getting a sharp splinter at the back of my throat which it took me some time to get out. Before that happened I was nearly choked, as my face had gone partially black. This I noticed with the hand-mirror I was using to detect the splinter. In forcing it out with my finger, I lacerated the back of my throat so badly that I still feel a sympathetic irritation in it if I get a fish-bone into my mouth.

Zebra, like most game, usually feed up-wind, and I have noticed that, when zebra are moving along feeding they keep their heads all pointing in one direction. Other game, although they naturally feed against the wind, may face round the other way at times, and zebra may do so sometimes, but I have not often seen it.

The zebras in Nyasaland, Northern Rhodesia, and the adjoining territories are Burchell's, and are found in herds of up to thirty animals, although about half that number is the usual size of a herd.

Lions are extremely fond of zebras, and kill large numbers, and I have occasionally found remains in the bush, and seen several which had escaped from a lion after being badly mauled on the hindquarters. I came on one poor beast once, just dying, and the bullet I gave it was a merciful release, as the wounds had gone septic, and were numerous and deep.

When one looked on a tragedy of this kind, the idealist's idea of peace in the jungle seemed but a pleasant dream. There is no peace in wild nature as long as carnivora still exist, for the true law of the jungle is tooth and claw. Even were this not so, there is still the law of the strong when the males fight for the females.

The gnu or blue wildebeest is not very common where I have been, although I have shot a few. The Nyasaland variety has a white chevron on the face, which constitutes a variety, and I bagged one in the swamps of Lake Chiuta in 1903. Gnu like mixing with zebra and hartebeest, and seemed to agree well with both species when I have seen them feeding together. Hartebeest are more addicted to this friendliness than any other of the larger game, as I have seen them with almost all the antelopes occasionally. It is, of course, not what may be called a common habit for the species to mix, but it is not exceptional with regard to single gnu or hartebeest.

Leopards are very plentiful, but extemely difficult to find, and I have obtained few shots at them, although I have disturbed a good many in thick grass and bush, when they have gone off like a flash. I killed one near my camp on the Bua River which had a pretty skin, and there was not much excitement in shooting him.

They were very plentiful in the Mlanje range, and probably still are, where they are not killed off with set-guns. They are fond of hilly ground, and kill large numbers of bushbuck, bushpig, klipspringers, and other of the smaller antelopes ; and they must take a lot of fawns before they are old enough to escape. My friend Garden told me an interesting story of one which met his match in a drove of bushpig, which treed him several times, which shows how plucky these pigs are.

The warthog is plentiful, and his meat is quite good unless he is old. The natives hunt them with their dogs and spears, and kill great numbers. Being prolific, they are difficult to reduce. One I hit once was so dazed with the shock that he dashed into a tree and smashed one of his tusks to splinters with the blow. He then collapsed and died.

A big boar, with his dark-grey skin, is a very good mark for an enamel-faced or ivory foresight. Out of thirty-four I have shot, only two attempted to be nasty when closely approached, and they were both sows, although a boar once went for one of my natives. They are fairly easy to kill, except when hit too far back, when they carry on some way. Certain wounds, as I think I mentioned before, often cause a paralysis of the nerves, making an animal extremely tenacious of life ; but I need not dwell on this subject further.

It is amusing seeing a sow coming along with her large litter, all trotting along trying to keep up with her, and giving little squeals just like domestic pigs. When running off, warthog hold their tails straight up in the air, which gives them rather a ludicrous appearance. They are very ugly beasts with the warts on their faces, and it is a great insult for one native to call another a warthog. It is also opprobrious to use the native names for the hyena and baboon as terms of endearment. This shows that the natives have distinct ideas on the beauty attached to the expression of the sensations, so they may yet come to appreciate the wonders of impressionist and futurist art.

The bushpig seldom shows himself much in the open, and prefers to keep to thick bush and grass. Although his tusks are much smaller than a warthog's, he is a pluckier animal, and I have told how a drove of them put a leopard into a tree, and kept him there most of a night, as the ground was all trampled and marked round the tree with the pigs' spoor.

They go about in pairs as a rule, like warthog; but when the litter has grown up they may keep together for a time, until the young boars are driven off by the old ones, and have to fend for themselves. The bushpig is a better-looking creature than the warthog, as he lacks the warts. Along the ridge of the spine he has some whitish-coloured hair, not so bristly as the warthog's back hair.

Once, when I was looking for some meat for my Christmas dinner, I shot two near Luambali Hill, in North-Eastern Rhodesia, and the roast pork was quite good served up with banana instead of apple sauce.

Baboons are common in all hill country, and do some damage to the plantations of the natives and white men. At Mr. Garden's estate in Mlanje district they came and destroyed the plants, so I shot a fine old male, and hoped to keep his skull, but he had worn his teeth down to the gums.

People in South Africa sometimes assert that they are dangerous, although I never found them so; but then I never went about without a rifle when in the bush, and they know when a man is armed if they have ever been shot at before. I hardly ever fired, or found it necessary to fire, at them, and only killed two males.

When disturbed they are sometimes slow in moving away, and will sit and bark and chatter at one, hoping, I suppose, to drive one away. Should one advance instead of retire, they always go off, but should a movement be made of retiring, then they come along after one so as to keep the intruder in view. Animals are like some humans, and the incentive of seeing fear spurs them on, whereas an offensive action inspires fear and they retreat. Hunting-dogs, about which I have written before in this book, behave much the same as baboons, and retreat when faced with a rifle.

I remember, when I took part in some correspondence about them in *The Field*, there was a letter from a contributor in South Africa, who gave a case of a herd " boy " (native) who was killed and eaten by a pack of wild dogs. This is quite probable, for all animals differentiate between white men and natives, and they know that a native woman or child is less able to act on the offensive than an adult male. Native women are much afraid of baboons, as they say that the males will carry them off to the caves in the rocks, but this is, of course, absurd.

When out shooting near the Bua River on one occasion, I heard some women, who were working at their gardens under a large kopje, shouting, so two natives I had with me, and I, went to see what was wrong. We met the women on the native path, and they told us that a troop of baboons had come after them, so I went along and saw the animals on the hill-side, chattering and barking. When they caught sight of me (I had a beard) they started off over the rocks at their best pace, and the shot I sent at the posterior of a big fellow missed him, but sent some earth over him, which accelerated the pace of the troop wonderfully, as they were soon over the skyline and out of sight.

Women, when quarrelling, often tell each other that their father or mother was a baboon, and the retort usually is that the other's parents were hyenas or warthogs. I never heard a native say a good word for a baboon or a hyena. They have a good reason with the latter beast, as many a native has been injured with his terrible jaws.

Hyenas live on bones, and their jaw muscles must be tremendously strong, for they break the largest bones, and I have seen an elephant's thigh-bone severed by the animals, although this was done by gnawing, and not by a single bite. Near where I lived on the Bua there was an old woman who had lost the calf of her right leg some years before, and it was a ghastly wound. I have also seen a few men with bits out of their faces, seized when they were lying sleeping in the open. Instead of giving a clean bite, the hyena always gets his

SKINNING A HYENA, NORTH-EASTERN RHODESIA.
Odoriferous work !

A LARGE ANTHILL IN NORTH-EASTERN RHODESIA.

teeth in and tears the piece out by force, and he has such sneaking ways that it is safer not to sleep in the open without a good fire near.

Everywhere I have lived hyenas were numerous, and my most memorable experience with them was when my tent was pitched outside a fence I had made round a bull elephant. My natives were inside the palisade with good fires, but when I turned in, the small fire I had had in front of the tent went out. About 11 p.m. I was awakened by something hitting a tent-rope, which shook the tent. It was a black night, and I could not see anything when I looked through the slit in the tent-flap, so I lighted a candle and had a smoke.

By this time I heard hyenas parading between the fence and my tent, and the noise they made was most entertaining, and I wish I could have taken a record of it for future use. Of course, there was no danger, and I had my rifle, so I did not bother to call anyone to light the fire, for I like to listen to them.

They howled, cackled, champed their teeth, and moaned in rotation, and kept bumping into the rope which was fixed near the fence. This twanging annoyed me so much that I decided to go and lift the peg and fix the rope on one of the poles in the fence ; so I opened the tent slowly to see if I could get a shot first, but the cunning beasts heard me and rushed off, cackling with annoyance. The men inside the fence heard me come out and saw the lantern-light, as they were still sitting at their fires chewing elephant-meat. One or two of them helped me fix the rope high up, and then I went back to bed.

The noise went on all night, and the hyenas did not go until just before dawn ; but as the light came in they kept farther off, for I had got up early and hoped to put a bullet through one. When it was light enough to see I went to look round, and the beasts had made a

217

regular track all round the fence with their constant tramplings to and fro.

A calf died at my ranch on the Kapundi stream, and I buried it. Two nights afterwards a hyena came and partially dug it out, but was disturbed, so I sat up for him in the moonlight and shot him, or at least wounded him so badly that I spoored him up soon after dawn, and found him dying about fifty yards in the bush.

About this time I heard a duiker calling piteously one evening, and running into my hut for my rifle, I went out, as I thought something had got hold of it. When some way off I heard a rush, but the bush was too thick to see anything. However, on going on I found a duiker doe lying with deep wounds in the throat made by a leopard, which I had frightened off his prey.

When stalking some warthog near Mzazas, I was crawling up a large anthill to try to see the pig in the long and thick grass. The anthill had some small bushes and grass growing on it. As I looked over the top, a leopard jumped into the grass within a yard of me and disappeared at once. They are marvellously quick and cunning, and by far the most difficult animals I know to get a good shot at.

To revert to the hyena for a moment. They are wonderful walkers and cover a great extent of country in a night, often using the paths and going round villages looking for offal. At my camp on the Bua River there was an old hyena who passed my huts in his round every night, arriving punctually about 3 a.m., when he would give several of his melancholy howls, and then pass on towards some kopjes, where I think he lived. He was so regular that, after timing his visits several times, I knew, without striking a light and looking at my watch, what the time was.

The African jackals (two varieties) do not make nearly so much noise at night as do the Indian jackals. They are pretty little animals with nice coats in the cold

weather, and in South Africa their skins are much used
for making into karosses.

There are two varieties of hyena, the spotted and
the brown. The former is extremely numerous, but
the latter is very rare.

Crocodiles exist in most of the large rivers, and I
have shot a large number. If not killed instantaneously
a crocodile usually manages to get into the water, where
(if well hit) he probably dies and is eaten by the
others.

The largest crocodile I ever hit was from a steamer
on the Zambezi. He seemed paralysed after the shot,
but managed to slip off the bank and disappear. The
white skipper of the steamer, who had been on the
river for some years, and seen thousands of crocodiles,
told me he had never seen one approaching this
monster in size. He said, if I had killed it, that he
would have stopped the steamer and put me ashore so
as to measure it. I hit it with a soft-nose ·303, and
after the shot picked up my glasses to look at it, and
saw blood spouting out between its short neck and
shoulder. Just as I was preparing to give it another
shot, two Portuguese soldiers on the lower deck fired
at it with their Snider rifles, the bullets going over it and
hitting the sand, as I saw the dust fly. This seemed to
wake up the croc and, as I have said, he got into the
water and disappeared.

I never shot and recovered one over 14 feet, and the
monster I hit in the Zambezi looked half as long again.

The next biggest I saw was one I hit in the Luangwa
River, which was not nearly as large as the one I hit in
the Zambezi; but it was bigger than a 14-feet one
I killed and measured, shot close to Mzazas, on the
Luangwa.

On getting to a village, the natives told me a woman
had been taken that morning by a crocodile when
bathing in the river, so I asked them to show me the

place, and also asked whether the croc was still about. They said it was. Unfortunately, a whole troop of natives came along to see the fun, and it was through them that I did not recover the animal.

On getting near the place, I told the natives to wait, and went on with the headman's son. Approaching behind some reeds, we saw the crocodile lying on a large sandbank only about sixty yards off, so I felt sure he would die. I tried for the point of the shoulder, which is the spot for the heart, and probably the spine if a little high, and at my shot the croc stiffened at once, as they always do when well hit. Against my orders the villagers had crept up, and when they saw their enemy lying rigid, they gave vent to loud yells and rushed in a body along the sandbank, which reached out from the bank to where the croc was still lying motionless. I was watching him ready to put in another shot if he showed signs of recovery.

When the nearest natives, with their spears, got within a few paces, the animal began to wriggle, and lifted his tail up twice, bringing it down with a thump on the sand. It was quite impossible for me to risk another shot with all the natives in the line of fire, so I had to watch him gradually slip into the water, just as the nearest man gave him a jab with his spear, which glanced off the thick scales, the man nearly falling over the tail. He was well hit and died, for on asking the natives later whether he had come back, they told me he had never returned.

Crocodiles probably kill more natives than do lions annually in Central Africa ; and they are so dangerous in some places that the villagers make a stockade in the water, so that they can draw water and bathe in safety. They are loathsome creatures, and when I had nothing better to do when living near the Luangwa, I used to go out and put a bullet in any I saw, and that was a fair number.

When a crocodile is lying in the water watching, all one sees are the two knobs over his eyes, and sometimes a bit of his snout.

Selous, in his interesting book *African Nature Notes and Reminiscences*, gives some wonderful photographs of a large crocodile pulling a rhinoceros into a river. It must have been a large crocodile which was able to do this, and it shows their immense power and the tenacity of their jaws. Of course, in deep water a land animal has no chance, but in this case the rhino was not very deep when he was grabbed by a hindleg. The hindlegs being the driving power, so to speak, of all animals, I fancy the rhino might have escaped if he had been held by a front instead of a hind limb.

After my experience in the Bua stream, when I stood in the water up to my waist to shoot at a hippo, I took care not to go into deep water which was muddy.

The crocodile, when he gets hold of his prey, is supposed to drag it to a hole in the bank, or under a rock, and keep the body until it gets tender; but I do not believe this, as they are usually so hungry that they are likely to feed at once. If he stored the body, as some believe, the other crocodiles would soon come and take it, so this disposes of that supposition.

Many of the hippos I shot were scarred by crocodile teeth when they rose to the surface, although the wounds were never very deep, due to the difficulty of getting a good hold on such a bulky object.

In this book I have not given any snake stories, although I could have done so, as I have had several nasty experiences with poisonous snakes, such as puff-adders, mambas, and vipers. There is something about a snake story (like a fish story) which makes people suspicious of one's integrity, so I refrain.

Chapter IX SOME STRANGE INCIDENTS AND CONTRASTS

WHEN wandering about in a wild country one knocks up against some strange characters and hears many weird tales, which may, or may not, be true. Most of the people connected with these stories are gone ; but in case their relatives or friends may be living, I do not mention full names, but only give doubtful initials, as naturally I do not wish to hurt people's feelings.

B. was a strange fellow, a wild man of the woods, and a splendid elephant-hunter. He and another man were prospecting in Southern Rhodesia, and had come to a village in the evening, so they gave the headman a yard of calico for the loan of an empty hut for the night, as all the shelter they had with them was a canvas sheet which they used as a lean-to when on the veldt.

It happened at this time that the Rhodesian Police were looking for a man who had escaped from the Salisbury jail, and the headman of this small village had been warned to look out for him and another man who was believed to have joined him. Unfortunately, the headman had not been given a very close description of the man who had escaped, but he had been told there might be two, so when B. and his friend were in the hut, the headman gathered a few of his villagers round him and told them that he intended to catch the white men when they were asleep and hand them over to the police. So about midnight, when everything was quiet, he and some others managed to get into the hut

ELEPHANT BULL WITH A MALFORMED TUSK.
Shot in North-Eastern Rhodesia by the late Captain Martin Ryan.

222

and throw themselves on the strangers. B. and his friend had no rifles, but they each had a revolver, so when they suddenly found themselves attacked at the dead of night, they managed to grab their revolvers, which they had alongside them, and start shooting. They quickly laid out three, and the others bolted. The headman was one of the slain !

Then in a week or so they were chased and collared by the police and got several months in jail, for what was a pure mistake, as they were simply defending themselves from what they thought was intended murder by the natives. This rankled in B.'s mind, so he decided to escape at the first opportunity.

One day, when some prisoners were being led past the Salisbury Club, B. being amongst them, he saw a horse fixed to a rail, and whispered to the nearest man that here was his chance. He shook his head, so B. left the line and managed to free the rein and mount before the warder could do anything to stop him. As he went down the street, making for the veldt, a shot was fired which took the heel off his boot.

Being a good rider, he got clean away and rode many miles to the north, and then sent the horse back to the owner, whom he knew by name. He went on foot to the Zambezi, crossing it into Portuguese territory, where he spent some time. Then he went into North-Eastern Rhodesia, where he started to shoot elephants, an adventurous life which suited him. Later on he got enough capital to start a small farm, and he did well out of elephants, which he periodically hunted, mostly poaching them in Portuguese territory.

I believe the authorities in Southern Rhodesia heard in time where he was, but they decided to leave him alone, knowing that in the first instance he had been harshly treated with regard to the shooting affair in the village.

223

On one of his poaching trips in the country of the Portuguese, information had been sent to the officials that he was at a certain village with some good tusks, so a Portuguese official decided he would try to arrest him. He and his police surrounded his camp at night, and by stealth managed to get hold of him when asleep.

Next day the prisoner was put in a big dugout with the officer and several police, and the ivory and some of B.'s " boys " were packed in another similar canoe and they started down-stream. The right bank of the Luangwa in this part is British, and the left Portuguese. The river, of course, had many twists, and the current was sometimes best for travelling near the right bank. At one spot round a corner B. grabbed a rifle in one hand, and seized some reeds they were brushing past and pulled the dugout over until it gradually sank. When he had been captured, he had three ·400 cordite cartridges in the hip-pocket of his pants, and the rifle he had grabbed was his ·400, which the officer had foolishly placed between them at the stern of the canoe.

He got ashore quickly and loaded his rifle, and told the officer to keep quiet, which he was glad to do. Then when the second dugout appeared, as it had been some way behind, he held it up and made the black Portuguese police come to his side, helped by some of B.'s " boys," who were ready now to attempt a fight, although they were handcuffed. If the officer had known B. better, he would have been handcuffed too, but he had decently omitted this degradation, which says something for his good feeling.

B. now made the Portuguese take off the handcuffs from his men, and also made them help to pull the dugout, which was in about 4 feet of water, ashore and remove his kit, which was intact, but, of course, soaking wet.

Being in British territory, he knew the Portuguese

were now helpless, so he offered them some food when the officer had finished drying his clothes. B. did not bother to change, but dried in the sun. Then he wished the officer good-bye and better luck next time. There was a bit of a row by correspondence between the two Governments, but nothing more came of it, and B. made about £100 on the ivory he got on that trip.

Whether I have given the story exactly I do not know, but I believe my facts are mainly right.

When I was in North-Eastern Rhodesia B. left the country for Australia, as he suffered badly from fever, and I heard later he had died out there.

K. was another interesting character who loved to poach elephants in Portuguese territory, where he got many. The only fault I have to find with the elephant-poacher is that he shoots anything with a few pounds of ivory in its head, and he will take a cow or small beast whenever it offers if he cannot get a bull. In the course of time K. went north to hunt in the Congo, and entered into competition with the Arabs, who used to cross Lake Tanganyika in dhows to land parties in the Congo to poach elephants.

For some reason or other K. and an Arab had had a disagreement about something, and the Arab had threatened to have K. killed. As the Arab was a hard case, K. knew he meant it. This was enough for K., who believed in the adage :

"Thrice is he armed that hath his quarrel just,
But ten times he who gets his blow in fust "—

so he determined, the next time that the Arab's dhow appeared in the offing, that he would snooker his vindictive enemy, and he did ! This is the yarn as it was told me, and I believe it is true.

Some years ago (in 1912) various accounts appeared

225

in the newspapers of the death of an elephant-poacher in the Congo, one account being headed " Tragedy of the Congo : Elephant-poacher Trapped." His name was given in full, and the name of the British officer who so pluckily tracked him up, so there is no reason here for hiding the names.

About 1910 I was staying for a day or two with a friend named Greer, who had a cattle ranch and cotton plantation near Sasare Gold-mine, in North-Eastern Rhodesia. Another friend, Martin Ryan, was a partner of Greer's at one time, but " the call of the wild " was too much for him, and he later took to elephant-hunting.

While Greer and I were in his bungalow, some natives arrived and told Greer that there was a white man very ill with fever some miles down the Tete road, so he sent some of his " boys " out with a *machilla* to bring him in. He arrived in about six hours, and told us that his name was Rogers, and that he was a prospector who had been in all the gold-bearing regions of the world. After some days he got better through the kind attentions of Greer, and went on towards the north.

In 1912, as mentioned, I read in the newspapers about his end, which was as follows :

He had taken to elephant-poaching in the Congo and the locality round Lado, and the British officials had got on his tracks when they heard of his doings. A party of native police under Captain C. V. Fox (I think he was captured later in the Great War, and managed to escape from Germany) made after Rogers and his companions. The chase led through rough bush and swamps, and it was some time until Captain Fox's party got into contact with the poachers, but they were gradually overtaken. As it was the rainy season, great difficulty was found in crossing swollen rivers, and the poachers in their retreat broke the bridges, as they

226

had become aware through the natives that they were being followed.

For days the chase continued until Captain Fox heard that the poachers were near, so he pushed on with four of his native police, three of them being sent ahead. By this time the pursuers were hard put for grub, as they had only brought small supplies, thinking they would not have to go very far.

Then they came to a village where they heard that the poachers had shot a native, and that night Captain Fox pushed ahead in the dark, hearing the party was fairly near. In time he came to a large village which was being defended by a large number of the poacher's gang.

Captain Fox had not yet found the three men he had sent ahead, and it was difficult to know what to do with such a small party. Getting a guide, he was taken to a large hut at which the guide pointed, denoting that the white poachers were inside. Carrying his rifle, he pluckily knocked at the door, and a native came and told him his master was sick and wanted to see him. On hearing this he entered the hut, which was lighted by a flickering candle. At first he could not see anyone, but gradually made out a white man lying on a bed, with another European sitting near him. Nothing was said, and Fox thought he had been trapped, but he asked which was Rogers, and the man sitting by the bed said, "Rogers has been shot." It appears that the police Captain Fox had sent ahead had been attacked, and naturally returned the fire, and Rogers had got a bad wound from which he was slowly dying.

After some conversation Captain Fox left the hut, being told by Rogers that he would have shot him had he been able to move. Rogers also asserted that he was in Belgian, not Sudanese territory, and it turned out he was right, but he had only just got there, and

STRANGE INCIDENTS AND CONTRASTS

had been chased in British territory. Later in the night Captain Fox was called to see Rogers, who was just near his end, and they had a talk, in which Rogers asked that the white man with him, who, I believe, was a doctor, should not be interfered with, as he himself was the leader of the gang.

Captain Fox had to explain to the Belgian Commandant about the affair, as he happened to be across the border. It seems Rogers was hit in the lower part of the body, but was able to talk for some time, and he told Captain Fox that had the " boys " he sent ahead not arrived in the dark, they would all have been killed. Rogers had fired at them with a Mauser, and his white companion with a Winchester rifle, so after Rogers's death the Belgian Commandant took him and some of the natives to his station, where they had to stand their trial for their parts in the affair. The three " boys " sent ahead turned up later, as they (finding themselves outnumbered) had gone to find their officer, whom they missed in the dark.

Rogers, when I met him, looked a pretty hard case, but one met a good many in Northern Rhodesia, as white men used to wander up from the south to prospect, or look for jobs in a country where there was not any demand for casual labour, as natives are used for all the lower-grade work. I believe Rogers was an American who had been out in Alaska, and someone told me that he had been one of " Soapy " Smith's gang. " Soapy " was a desperado in the early days in Alaska who attempted to use the Yankee methods of " drawing first," and laying out anyone he objected to without giving them a chance. The Americans call them " bad-men," I think, and their deaths usually incur the death of the man who tackles them. The sheriff who laid out " Soapy " was killed himself, as they practically fired together. That sort of thing is not tolerated in British territory, and the only time

I saw firearms used was in a bar in Salisbury, when a drunken fellow began to shoot at bottles and always hit the wrong one.

When Alaska suffered from the gold rush and a lot of wild men went to the country, they found that in British territory the North-West Mounted Police under Colonel Steele were too much for them, so they kept quiet.

Two prospectors once arrived at my huts on the Kapundi stream with only a blanket, a few pots, and a worn-out ·303. One named C. told me he had been with B. when the natives were shot in attacking them at night, and I heard afterwards that this was correct.

These men had hardly a cent and their clothes and boots were worn to rags. I asked them what they intended doing, and they said they were going to poach elephants in Portuguese territory, so I asked them if they had ever seen an elephant, and they said they had not. Judging from the state of the rifling of their ·303, I would have backed the elephant every time.

After they had left, getting some food and socks, C. came back after he had gone about 100 yards, and said to me, " I suppose you have not a decent pair of boots you wouldn't miss " ; so I gave him an old pair about as bad as his own, as I did so much walking that my boots were usually in a state of disintegration.

Some of these old prospectors are very interesting men, and they seldom used to cadge for things, although one could see they needed them. They are usually " on the rocks " and live from hand to mouth, and they are not always honest with the natives, engaging " boys " to carry their few loads and then not paying them. In North-Eastern Rhodesia they used to be called " Distressed British Subjects," and the Government had to send quite a number back south and give them enough stores for the trip so as to prevent them robbing the natives.

In December 1905 I went to Tete from Fort Jameson, getting very ill on the road through fever added to a slight touch of the sun, which kept me to my tent for some days. It was sweltering hot, and being some way from a village, my cook could not get fowls to make soup. However, I gradually got better and reached Tete, where I arranged with a half-caste Portuguese for a houseboat to take me down the Zambezi.

When in Tete I stayed at the African Lakes Corporation house, as they usually had a couple of spare rooms for the use of travellers. A man named Bird was the manager, and he met with a strange end soon after I met him.

I heard afterwards that he had got orders from his company to take over their store at Feira, farther up the Zambezi. When he was on the journey, he had gone out shooting one day and wounded a small antelope, which ran down a hippo path leading to the river. He ran after it down the path. Suddenly his leg struck a native rope, which released a huge hippo spear-trap set over the path by the natives for a hippo. The spear hit him near the neck close to one of his shoulders, and penetrated deeply into the body, killing him on the spot.

I had a native servant afterwards who had been with him at the time, and who had helped to find the body after the accident happened, and he gave me these details.

It was an extraordinary accident, but one that might happen to anyone who did not spot the rope across the path in time. I once put my foot through a game-pit, but did not go through ; and another time a trap set for small buck, such as duiker, was sprung off when I touched it, the bent sapling and cord sending my felt hat off without touching my face. It was rather startling, as it twanged loudly.

230

Passing from humans to animals for a moment, my friend Captain J. Brander Dunbar, of Pitgaveny, brought out a fine bulldog to Nyasaland with him on a shooting trip in 1903. The natives had never seen anything like it ! When shooting in Central Angoniland he let the dog chase a hartebeest, which it brought to bay, but the hartebeest turned on the dog and horned it so badly that it died. If it had been a sable antelope I would not have mentioned this, but a hartebeest acting in this way was, I think, unusual, and shows the hunter that he may always get a fatal jab from any wounded antelope when he approaches it near enough.

A strange incident which caused the death of a very fine man was when D. D. Dobson, assistant magistrate, was killed by a rhino close to his station of Ngara, in Nyasaland. He had gone out for a walk in the evening to set some dry grass on fire, I suppose to induce the game to come to the ashes and fresh green grass which would spring up in a few weeks. A rhino suddenly rushed at him and struck him in the lower part of the body, the poor fellow dying next day from the wound.

I knew Dobson fairly well when I was living at my hunting camp on the Bua River, and liked him. When at Oxford he had been one of the best Rugby forwards of his time, as he was an exceptionally powerful fellow. He was fond of shooting, and was very plucky, for when the Administration wanted officials to go to the sleeping-sickness areas he was one of the first to volunteer for the dangerous work.

When Sir David Bruce's Sleeping Sickness Commission was working in the country to investigate this beastly disease, I collected some blood-slides of game for the Commission.

I have often been in districts where natives were dying of sleeping-sickness, and where several whites were inoculated with the disease, and consider myself very fortunate to have escaped getting it. One of the first signs is, I believe, a swelling and stiffness in the neck, so when anyone felt stiffness there, it was amusing to see him feeling his neck in a suspicious way, all the time looking very serious.

When the Sleeping Sickness Commission came out, finding that hunting and collecting did not pay well at the time, my friend Dr. Barclay tried to help me get a job with the Commission to shoot game for them. Sir David Bruce evidently did not think the risks worth more than a few pounds a month, so they did without me, although I agreed to send them some slides for nothing. When my friend the doctor heard what they were willing to pay, his language (mine too) was very sulphurous.

The doctor was a very fine fellow, and when suffering from lumbago, to which he was a martyr, he used to walk up and down his verandah saying in sonorous tones, " Damned country !—damned country ! " This used to tickle me greatly, but now I too suffer from rheumatism in this rotten east coast climate in Scotland, and when I get up in the morning I also say, " Damned country !—damned country ! " for we have not seen the sun for almost two months and every day has been dismal and damp.

One of the finest fellows I knew in Africa was the late Major (then Captain) C. H. Stigand, who was killed in November 1919, when he was leading a punitive expedition against the Aliab,[1] a section of the Dinka tribe in the Southern Sudan. He and a Major White were walking ahead of the column in heavy grass, and were ambushed by a crowd of Dinkas

[1] My friend Norman B. Smith (" Mannlicher " of *The Field*) came in contact with the Aliab on one of his shooting trips, and found them a treacherous and cunning race. I have heard that others found them a nasty type of savages to deal with, as they were thoroughly untrustworthy.

and killed. I heard from a friend, who was shooting in the Sudan at the time, that Stigand killed six of the enemy before he fell. At that time he was Governor of Mongalla Province, and his death was a real loss to the Empire, for he was an ideal Administrator in a new country, as he liked the wilds and the natives.

He had the most marvellous escapes from wild animals of any man I ever heard of; he was knocked down by an elephant in North-Eastern Rhodesia, and severely damaged by a rhino near Fort Manning, in Nyasaland, soon after walking a distance of 240 miles with his battalion when it moved south. Then, when going along the Uganda railway, he heard of lions at Simba and sat up, shooting three. One was wounded and he followed it at night and was badly mauled after a great fight with it. Luckily one of his shots had broken the jaw, and to this, I believe, he owed his life.

He managed to get to Nairobi and recover in time, although he had a stiff arm for years. Then he was knocked down by an elephant, which put a tusk through his leg, and he had to come home for treatment.

He was made Governor of Mongalla Province, in which country he met his death, as I have before mentioned. One of his best books is *Hunting the Elephant in Africa* (published by Macmillan & Co.), in which he mentions many of his adventures, and I advise keen big-game men to read this work, as it is one of the best I know on African shooting and adventure.

Regarding Stigand's mauling from the rhino, I have often wondered if the beast which killed Dobson was the same animal that went for Stigand. I think it possible that it was, as the black rhino in Nyasaland and North-Eastern Rhodesia is not addicted to charging, when unwounded, in this way.

I heard a very amusing story when in North-Eastern Rhodesia as follows : A young man who had come out to a billet in the postal service found, after a few months, that he did not care for the country, so he decided to wangle his retirement, with passage and expenses paid.

This was a difficult plan to work, and it took some thinking out if it was to prove successful. At last he struck on the idea of shamming mad, and called up the headman of a village and told him to collect a *machilla* team of native women, quite an unusual thing to do. Then, when they had arrived, he stripped naked and got into the *machilla*, and set off for the magistrate's house not far away. The magistrate was astounded to see such an apparition arrive, and he at once came to the natural conclusion that the poor fellow was " off his chump." Dismissing the village maidens, he took him in, and prepared to look after him in his spare room.

This masquerading was difficult to keep up, so the " madman " had to keep thinking out new devices. After the magistrate had turned in that night, he heard someone come into his room and grope about near where he kept his rifles, so he jumped out of bed and had a struggle with the midnight robber, who had managed to get hold of a weapon, which he prepared to use as a club, not having any cartridges. Then he had to be locked up in his room, which he smashed up so much that the scraps had to be removed next day.

He never would wear clothes, but as the climate is not a rigorous one during the day, he was quite comfortable, taking good care at night, however, to use the blankets on the bed.

The Administrator had been expected for some days on one of his periodical visits of inspection, and this was part of the young man's plan, for to gain his desire of a cheap retirement the authority of the Administrator was, of course, essential.

When the Administrator came along in due course, the magistrate told him the whole details of the sad story, and the Administrator agreed it was a case of sunstroke—the " damned sun," as he put it. He said, " Let me have a look at the poor devil," and they went off to the room, which was locked, of course. When the door was opened, the Administrator walked in and saw a naked youth on his back on the floor with his legs upon the wall, and was greeted with a violent shout and, " Go away, I'm a fly ; go away, I'm a fly." They retreated with remarks such as " Poor chap ! " " Poor devil ! " and so on ; and the result was most satisfactory, for the " madman " was sent home " carriage paid," and news came out in about six months that he had made a most remarkable recovery for such a seemingly hopeless case.

When living on the Luangwa River in 1905, I knew a man named Watkins, who met with a sad end. For a time he was managing the Luangwa Cotton Plantations, but he left there and went off to hunt in what was then German East Africa. After a time he began to suffer from constant attacks of fever, as hunters often do when in the bush, and he got weaker and weaker until he could not hunt. He was far from villages and could not buy fowls or grain, so was in a tight hole.

Struggling on slowly, he had at last to stop, so his " boys " made a shelter of boughs and grass for him to lie under, as the sun was intensely hot in the daytime. Here he lay for some days, until at last he died, so his " boys " left him, taking his rifles and the few odd things he had with him, including a short diary of his trip and a message to his people.

I remember Watkins telling me that he was a member

of Selous's troop of Colonials in the Matabele rebellion of 1896.

One of the interesting stories I heard in North-Eastern Rhodesia, which I never quite believed, though it may be true, was when a doctor put some incurables (natives) on an island in a large river so as to segregate them from other natives. These large African rivers, like rivers all over the world, soon get into spate with heavy rains. The doctor had been told that the rains were overdue and he had better remove the sick men, but he either was too lazy or he did not mind.

Anyhow, violent rainstorms broke out and the river, which had been very low all the dry season, rose by many feet in one night, completely covering the small island and carrying the invalids all away. Some people thought it was a good thing, as they had all been bad cases of their kind and would not be missed.

I may say to people who may feel shocked at such a story that life is held very cheaply in new countries, and things which are looked on with horror in Britain are all taken as a matter of course. In the tropics a man may be alive to-day and gone to-morrow, and people begin to look at such a common occurrence as death as simply the workings of an inexorable fate. The war made people think in the same way, and catastrophes which before the war would have been taken very seriously were hardly remembered more than a few days, because they were always being succeeded by others equally or more disastrous.

One of the men I liked best in North-Eastern Rhodesia was Martin Ryan. We had a lot in common, as he was very keen on shooting and wild camp life. He was a man who felt the true romance of the wilderness, and in the letters he often wrote me after I left the country there was a strange note of depression. This was partly due to the lonely and

236

MARTIN RYAN.
After a hunting trip.

FORT JAMESON, NORTH-EASTERN RHODESIA, 1905.

hard life he was living, and the difficulty of making both ends meet.

After he went to Southern Rhodesia with some cattle he wished to dispose of, he was kept in quarantine for many months owing to the regulations about imported cattle, so he spent most of his time in hunting. As there was often a difficulty in getting carriers, he did it on the " rough " and took only bare essentials.

In his spare time he used to lie on his " tummy," as he put it, and write me many pages about his experiences and about vital shots at game, which was one of my hobbies. Perhaps some day I may give some of the interesting letters I have received from big-game men. I have a big bundle of letters from Selous written from 1898 almost up to the time of his death, many interesting letters from J. G. Millais, Stigand, and others ; all containing splendid accounts of shooting experiences, trophies, and other game subjects.

When the war broke out Ryan came home to join up, and got into King Edward's Horse. Soon after he got a commission in the 25th Royal Fusiliers, the same regiment that Selous fought and died with, and I have often thought how much they would have to talk about, for they were both great hunters.

Ryan was killed on the 18th of October 1917, at Nakadi. He was in charge of 110 men of his battalion, who were sent to attack the German positions with some native troops on both sides of them. The Fusiliers for some reason were sent ahead, with the result that they were partially surrounded. After a desperate encounter they managed to fall back, having suffered some ninety casualties, amongst them being my old friend.

I can imagine Ryan in such a scrap, for he would glory in the excitement and risks, and I am sure, if he had time, some of the enemy died, for he was a cool shot. It is strange how many of the best go, but it was natural that men like Ryan should have been among the first to take a hand, for there never lived a pluckier or more patriotic fellow.

There is a vast contrast between life at home and life in the wilds, where one lives in a tent in the dry season, or a hut in the rains. The hut, if well made, should be watertight, although if new it is sure to leak. Then one will be awakened at night with small drippings over the bed and everywhere. The bath, basin, and pots and pans are collected to catch the water, but they are usually inadequate in a bad tropical storm to make much difference.

Contrast a weatherproof room at home, with comfortable bed, soft carpets, gas-fire in winter, with such an abode as a hut, and a bed made of buck-skin or a canvas folding-bed, and native mats or skins on the floor. To a person at home the contrast seems great, but I have been just as comfortable in the hut, for the climate is less rigorous. One can wash as well in a canvas or enamel basin as in a crockery one with nickel-plated taps, though I must admit getting water from a tap and pipe is easier than sending a nipper to the stream to get a bucketful. The tap-water is cleaner, too.

But at home one is bound with petty regulations and irksome restraints. Instead of being a free wild man of the woods, one has become a herd animal. One's individualism is less apparent because there is less scope for it. People do not understand that a wanderer returned views things from a different standpoint, as his life has been spent away in the vast spaces where simplicity is the rule, and not complexity. He feels lost even in great crowds, for nothing and no one seem in sympathy. The people he knows may be good fellows, but they do not understand him, and he does not understand them. Environment (a favourite word with parsons) is at fault, because it has become foreign to him, and he longs to get back to the bush, the hills, and the plains, where he spent some of the happiest days of his life, for there he felt an exaltation that no civilized land can possibly supply.

This, I may tell the reader, is a true picture of the feelings of a wanderer when he attempts to settle down in Britain after years of wild roving. There is only one thing that will still the longing to return, and that is for a man to marry the right woman. If he is lucky he will again be happy.

Talking of contrasts, the greatest one I ever experienced was the difference between the 1st of June 1914 and the 1st of June 1918. On the first date my wife and I were married. On the 1st of June 1918 I was with other members of the ambulance convoy (Croix Rouge Française) attached to the 45th Division of the French Army. The French and British had been retreating from the historical 21st of March 1918, and for many months afterwards. Our convoy had been engaged, on the date given above, removing many wounded from the Château of Gueux to get them back before the Germans drove on. An American convoy helped us later, and the place had been cleared just in time. A few of us were sitting in a shelter having some food within thirty yards of the château, when there was the rush of a 4·2 (some thought it was a 5·8) German shell, which carried over slightly, sending up the usual cloud of gravel and soil, which came pattering down on us. The man in charge gave us orders to go into a kind of underground passage which led to the kitchen quarters of the château.

A few hours before I had helped Rooper, one of our drivers, to fix a tyre on his car, and I noticed he looked highly strung. Perhaps it was two Hun aeroplanes which were buzzing overhead which bothered him. Another of our men, Lee, had shortly before been looking for a cup he had lost, and I remembered afterwards that he too seemed on edge. Like all the other members of the convoy, mostly composed of fairly young men with some physical trouble that prevented them serving in line regiments, Rooper and Lee were both very plucky fellows.   In fact I have seen many fine young men in my travels, and I never saw a braver lot than the members of our convoy.

The Huns, although they knew the château was used as a hospital, bombarded it with a number of H.V. shells, several hitting the roof, which sent down showers of stone, cement, and glass.   Another man and myself got a shower of the latter on the backs of our necks, but were not cut.   Then a shell hit outside, and we heard fearful screams from a man who was found to be our officer's chauffeur.   He afterwards lost his leg.   Another of our men got a small splinter in his calf, and a French driver of a horse ambulance wagon received a frightful head wound.   When he was carried in his brains were exposed, and he soon died. One of his horses was killed by the same shell and lay in the avenue.

When the shelling stopped, we were told to go to our cars and get back, and then it was found that Rooper and Lee were absent.   Their bodies were found close to Rooper's car, which they had gone to sit in instead of coming into the château.   Before leaving I picked up a pair of pliers on the avenue, which I think were blown out of Rooper's car.   Some of the cars[1] had got splinters through them, and the baggage car was hit in several places, various articles of kit having holes through them, including my roll of blankets.

[1] A large car with a Röntgen-ray apparatus was attached to our convoy, but we never saw it being used, as it was kept many miles behind the shelled areas, so the two men in charge had practically nothing to do and were never, or very seldom, in a danger zone.

There was a very steep hill called Bouloise which had to be crossed, and the Germans, knowing the gradient, peppered it hard at the steepest spot, so all the troops and cars on the road had to stop until the shelling abated. I saw two horses dead at the side of the road about here, poor mangled creatures, the victims of man's lust for slaughter. Why I do not know, but I always felt as sorry for a torn horse as I did for wounded humans; for after all it was not their quarrel, and one felt that fate had been cruel to them.

After we started the cars again, the Germans resumed firing and a good many splinters hit the road about us, Inglis getting eight small pieces in his car before we reached a more tranquil neighbourhood.

I have often wondered if Rooper and Lee had any premonition of their end, as on thinking about it afterwards, I remembered they had both been highly strung that morning.[1] Everyone was on edge with the strain of going along shelled roads, and particularly that awful night work without lights. The sight, too, of mangled humanity (and the ambulance men see the worst side of war) was torture to sensitive minds.

Another of our men, an Irishman named Malcomson, was killed a day or two after I had been with him on a lot of work to the shelled villages of Coulmell, Le Plessier, and Villers Tournelle. One day, as a shell burst close to the road, a splinter sent up a splash from the wet mud in front of the car, and Malcomson turned to me and said, " I don't think I will come through the war." This was a strange remark from a man of such a happy and optimistic temperament.

[1] There is what might be called a sixth sense in game animals, for I have sometimes noticed an animal suspicious and nervy when it could neither have smelled, seen, nor heard danger. Now that we have wireless telegraphy, it is possible that air waves may affect the senses of sensitive beings, although this is different from a premonition before the danger is actually present.

A few days after saying this he was at Le Plessier with Beaumont, his partner on the car, and was killed by a shell-splinter which hit him in the heart, killing him instantly. When I heard of his death his remark was remembered, and I have often wondered if man, in his subconscious mind, gets an occasional glimpse into futurity. It may be so. These two firsts of June, in 1914 and 1918, were indeed startling contrasts.

One more memory of France and these horrible days when the world was mad with blood-lust. On the 13th of April 1918 my cousin, Robert S. Low, and myself were sent to get a badly wounded man from a dugout under a house in the village of Rocquencourt.

Before going farther, I may say my cousin had a most marvellous escape from death in the New Zealand Alps. He was crossing the Alps alone on the 21st of February 1906, and slipped, dislocating an ankle and smashing his knee, and lay out for some days and nights before he was rescued by some New Zealand guides, who had great difficulties in bringing him away owing to the rough character of the mountains. At the time *The Times* said, in a short account published on the 9th of March 1906, that " Mr. Low's adventure in the New Zealand Alps constitutes a record of pluck and endurance probably unequalled in the annals of mountaineering, etc."

Well, to get back to France, and a night that will always be a lurid memory to me ! The Germans were shelling the village heavily, so when the French Red Cross men had carried the man on his stretcher and put him in the car, they ran back to their dugout, after helping us, by the light of a lantern, to get the car round. My cousin was driving, so when he was just starting, we found that we had not been told to which hospital in the rear we had to take this man. So I jumped out and ran through the gateway into the small courtyard and made for the dugout.

Just at that moment a shell burst close to the car and myself, the blazing flash almost blinding me. I was pushed hard into a wall, by the air-pressure of the burst, at a fairly good pace, but saved my face, when I landed against the wall, with my hands. There was a shower of grit and gravel, and a Burberry waterproof, which was wet with the rain, just afterwards felt like rough sand-paper, as the fine grit had been driven into the cloth. My cousin and I, almost at the same moment, shouted to each other to ask if all was right.

The Frenchmen, hearing the explosion, ran out of their dugout, and one of them got a hold of me to pull me into the hole, but I managed, though the breath was pretty well knocked out of me, to ask him where the man had to be taken. Then we got away.

The glass of the car screen had a hole through it by a splinter, which I believe hit the pin which held the flaps of my cousin's shirt-collar, as it was bent, we found, next day. It then went through the upholstery at the back of the seat I had just vacated, and lodged in the wood behind, where we afterwards found it. If I had been in my seat I would have got it in the chest.

We went on as quickly as possible, as the shelling was pretty bad, and Rocquencourt on that night looked and smelled unhealthy. Just about half a mile out of Rocquencourt we came on a large lorry which had been ditched, and was blocking the road, so we stopped, and the engine of the car choked. On trying to start it, the handle slipped and the beastly thing would not go. My cousin went off ahead to try to get to a telephone to ring up headquarters for another car to be sent to remove the wounded man, and I stayed with him.

The lorry driver thought he might try to find out what was wrong with our car, so I lighted one of the side-lamps, which up to this had not been lit. Whether it was this light, or the Germans were searching along the road in the ordinary way, I don't know, but I do know that as soon as the light was showing the shelling began to creep nearer, so we put it out.

Then two other big lorries arrived, and the drivers also had to stop as the first one blocked the road. They usually carried a steel cable for such emergencies, so they got it out and fixed it to the stuck lorry and pulled it aside. When they were doing this they heard the poor wounded Frenchman groaning, and one of them said he would give me a pull. The direction they were going was the same as my cousin had gone, so I very foolishly agreed.

Then I got in, and we started off, and I have never suffered such an inferno as the next fifteen minutes or so. It was pitch dark and raining ; and the wretched driver of the lorry put on pace, I suppose to get quickly away from what was an unhealthy neighbourhood at the moment. As the ambulance car swerved and bumped, the poor sufferer began to shriek in pain ; and I shouted until I was hoarse to try to make the driver hear me, so that he might stop. But it was no good, and all I could do was to steer the car and keep it from bumping into that bulky lorry in front, as it rattled and skidded on the greasy surface of the mud.

I believe he had been going for a good fifteen minutes before he heard my calls, and stopped when passing through a small village we had come to. My first thought was for the wounded man, whom I found in a dazed and semi-conscious condition, with his head and shoulders hanging off the seat. I then turned to the driver of the motor-lorry and swore at him in English, Hindustani, and Chinyanja, none of which languages he seemed to know.

Fortunately, after I had waited ten minutes or so,

one of our cars passed, it having been sent in answer
to my cousin's telephone call, so we got the sufferer
transferred and sent off to hospital. The poor
fellow had had a fearful time and was in a bad state
of collapse.

In about thirty minutes my cousin turned up. He
told me he had gone back to the place where we had
been stranded and, finding the car gone, had got a lift
and seen the car when passing through the village.

Eventually the starting-handle was fixed up and we
got back to headquarters, and were both glad of the
sleep which followed our exciting evening.

When I was being dragged along by the rumbling
lorry my mind naturally turned to other subjects, and
for some reason I thought of Barry in Assam, who had
a wonderful escape from a man-eating tiger. A
man-eater had killed two night-watchmen (*chowkidars*)
at Barry's bungalow, so the following night Barry, his
assistant, and another man decided to sit up on the
verandah of the bungalow and try to shoot the tiger
if he returned. Barry sat on a camp-stool at a corner
of the front verandah, his assistant lying down on a
mattress near him, and the other man sat on the back
verandah.

I may say that the assistant, not having a good
sporting rifle, was armed with a military Snider to which
he had attached the bayonet. The assistant was to
take up watch later on, so went to sleep, and Barry,
who was sitting close to him, got sleepy too after
waiting for some time without anything happening.

Possibly the assistant snored, which acted as a
soporific, for Barry went to sleep too, one hand hanging
free while the other was gripping the rifle on his lap.
He had a strange awakening, for he suddenly felt his
wrist grabbed as in a vice and was irresistibly drawn
to his feet, to find himself being dragged off by the
tiger, which had quietly come to the bungalow to search

245

for food, as he had been frightened off the watchmen he had killed the previous night.

A peculiar fact about this incident, which is quite true, is that the tiger did not run off and drag Barry off his feet. The animal simply went at a smart walk and Barry was able to keep on his legs.

Just after he was gripped he gave a shout, and with a foot kicked the assistant before he was pulled on by the tiger. Fortunately, the assistant (I have forgotten his name) was a very plucky fellow, so he seized the Snider and ran out into the moonlight after Barry. Barry, of course, was pulling back as hard as he could, and this retarded the pace slightly, so that the assistant soon got alongside. He plunged the bayonet into the tiger's side, at the same moment pulling the trigger, and the double wound made the man-eater open his mouth and release Barry and rush off into the jungle. Barry and his friend lost no time in getting back to the bungalow, the former with a mutilated wrist, although I believe the bone was not broken. I never met Barry in Assam, but people who knew him told me that his hair went white soon afterwards. I think I met Barry's brother, who was also a tea-planter, and he had white hair, so perhaps it was a family tendency to get white early in life.

Whether the shock of a bad experience can whiten the hair is doubtful, but it may be so. Anyhow, it was a beastly experience, but why I thought of it when I was being dragged helpless behind the motor-lorry I cannot say, except that my own experience aroused comparisons in my brain during that " nightmare " drive amongst the devastation of France.

Chapter X   SPORTING METHODS, RIFLES, TROPHIES,
CARRIERS, ETC.

THIS chapter is intended more for the young man
who has not yet done much shooting, and not
for the old hunter who has formed his own
opinions on the subjects in the above heading. The
only true teacher is experience.

When I was hunting in Africa, I got a good many
letters from men who intended to come out on a
shooting trip, and I invariably gave them the best
advice I could, and mentioned districts and places
where I had met with good sport. I know of others
who used to keep such information to themselves, as
they were jealous of others reaping the benefit of the
travel they had undertaken to find such places.

If a man seemed a good fellow, I helped him as much
as I could, and I advise others to do the same, as it
helps to consolidate that feeling of goodwill which
makes the person who asks for advice aid others when
he can do so.

Jealousy, of course, is the worst and principal
human failing, and all our troubles at home are
founded on that discreditable human trait. A
jealousy of endeavour may incite others to do better,
although it usually stops at that sublimity, and makes
men who are themselves incapable of attaining anything worth having still grudge their betters something
they have won by the efforts of intelligence and grit.
Instead of letting the weak drop out, which is Nature's
plan, we conserve the parasites, and consequently

dilute the bad with the good, to the deterioration of the whole race, for, of course, dilution means weakness.

However, as this is not a screed on the body politic, I shall get back to game subjects.

Personally, although I was always ready to tell a friend where to go, I preferred shooting by myself, as I was fond of solitude, and I found that when independent in one's movements one enjoyed the life better. Two men, when undergoing a certain amount of hardship, seldom agree for long. The matter may not develop so far as a quarrel, but there may be unpleasantness when one man wants to go one way and the other somewhere else. Besides, silence is the great thing in the game country, and a shot may be heard for many miles, and disturb the game, for animals are easily put on the *qui vive* and unsettled.

Therefore I advise big-game hunters, if they join a party, to arrange to camp at least ten miles apart, and meet occasionally to have a talk. Personally, I would prefer an African day's walk between camps, and that is a good twenty-five miles. Then the shots and movements of the one party will not disturb the other.

The more wary game do not like their haunts invaded by humans, and I believe the smell of a party of natives and the white man, who naturally wears boots or shoes, will cling to the place for a day or two, which is a message to wary animals that danger is near. Of course, natives are constantly moving about in search of something to eat, or for honey at certain seasons, and their paths pass through all the game haunts of Africa, for the whole of tropical Africa is a spider's web of native footpaths, so I fancy the scent of a white man is more alarming to animals than that of the natives, whose odour they must have smelt many times.

There are certain points the young hunter should

remember, as they may mean all the difference between success and failure :

1. Observation of the wind, as smell is by far the strongest sense in the game which inhabits bush country. On the plains sight is probably the sense which they use most.

2. Silence in movements and no loud talking.

3. Carry the weapon oneself, or chances will be lost.

4. Get as close as possible, especially to dangerous game, as nearness means better shooting.

5. Do not fire at another beast if one has gone off wounded, but follow and kill it first.

6. Never approach a wounded beast without a loaded and ready rifle, and always approach from behind if a dangerous animal.

7. When hunting, do not go too fast, or many important details may be missed.

8. Try to spot game before it sees one, as this, of course, helps one to get closer.

9. Climb a rise, anthill, or tree, or send a native to do so, for height is a great help in finding game.

10. Shoot with moderation, and put animals out of pain quickly. Do not grudge an extra cartridge in doing this.

I could go on for some time giving hints, but a plurality may draw attention from those which I have given. Certainly these clauses cover the most important points of game-shooting in a bush country in Africa, and a young man will not go far astray if he follows them.

The first thing to do, of course, is to learn enough of the native language to be able to understand them, and be understood.

As regards the necessary weapons, I have already said something on this subject ; but before going farther, I would warn beginners to treat with suspicion the theories of people who have had little or no big-game shooting. Such theories, formed after target experiments, are practically useless as a guide in the field, for an animal's body and a hard steel target are two different matters.

When the theorist advises the use of a rifle with the greatest velocity, I think he is labouring under a delusion, for weight in a certain bullet and the shape of the point is of more account than great velocity and a flat trajectory. For one shot which goes under a beast with any H.V. rifle of, say, about 2,000 foot-seconds velocity, two or more bullets will carry over and miss the animal.

For shooting in a bush country, the sighting should be correct at 100 yards, remembering to take a finer sight at closer distances. The front sight should be very small, not larger than a small steel pin-head, and white-faced with enamel or ivory. The distance between front and back sights should not be too far or it leads to a dimness in quick alignment. Both front and back sights should be screwed down to prevent a knock displacing them. Unless when hunting, a front-sight protector should be used, but it should be a pattern that can easily be slipped off.

For a magazine rifle 24 inches is the best length of barrel, as the magazine takes up some room. This enables the rifle to be moved more readily in thick stuff, and saves bumps on trees and branches.

Never carry a rifle in its cover, even when raining, when on the lookout for game.

Do not have an iron heel-plate on a rifle, but get the heel chequered. Metal gets so hot that it sometimes cannot be touched, and it is also very cold on sharp mornings.

Choose a rifle of a weight which does not exhaust one on a long day's tramp. Certainly nothing over 8 lb. is suitable. A heavy weapon drags a man to pieces under the hard conditions and hot sun, and it is

250

far better to use a small bore which is easy to handle than a more powerful and heavier rifle.

Do not believe in the idea of the second rifle, which is never at hand when most needed.

The practical hunter does not believe in expensive double rifles, which are more likely to jam than magazines, for a bit of grass or twig is enough to prevent the hinged barrels closing on the breech face. With a double one has two quick shots and then a long wait to get loaded again, just at the moment when a third or fourth shot may be vital. Doubles, being heavier than singles or magazines, are usually carried by gunbearers, and, as I have said, are seldom there when most wanted.

Fixing the weight which is comfortable to carry on a long day's tramp as nothing over 8 lb., we find some splendid rifles within this weight. There are three any one of which will kill anything in Africa just as well as the largest rifle made, and these are 7·9 mm. (·311), ·318 " Axite," and the ·350 either H.V. or " Magnum." I found all good, but if I were going back to Africa I should choose a ·318 made by Rigby, because I like the balance and sighting of his rifles and have always found them well made.

A sling is a useful accessory on a rifle, not only for carrying, but for shooting with. If not shooting from a rise or anthill, I always took a rest from a tree, taking care not to let the rifle touch the wood, as this, of course, causes the vibration termed " jump," which is likely to throw the bullet wide. Modern bullets with their high velocity are easily deflected, so care should be taken to shoot between twigs and even strong grass if in the line of fire.

Modern powders and nickel-covered bullets foul the rifling badly, so a funnel should be carried for pouring hot water through the barrel. There are various compounds for cleaning nitro rifles, and the

251

advice of the gunmaker should be taken on this point, as it depends largely on the type of powder used in the cartridges for the weapon. Nitro-cellulose powders give less trouble than do nitro-glycerine explosives, and personally I found cordite rather a bother compared with others I have used, as it not only fouls the bore, but it often corrodes the breech-chamber so badly that one suffered with jammed cartridges when using single falling-block rifles. That was my chief objection to falling-block rifles, for they are better balanced and nicer to handle than magazine-actioned weapons.

The first thing I always did after coming in from shooting, even when I was tired and a mixture between a sweep and a butcher with burnt ash and the blood when skinning and cutting-up game, was to clean my rifle carefully. After that came the bath and hot tea which replaced the plentiful moisture lost after long tramps in the tropical sun.

As regards other weapons, I never believed in revolvers, and preferred a ·220 rifle to a shotgun for shooting for the pot, as a shotgun is too noisy in a big-game country.

I always took three or four natives with me to carry the rifle and necessaries until I started to hunt. The gunbearer usually carried the cartridge-bag, camera, and glasses, and the others would have an axe and a native basket with a small kettle and some tea, sugar, and food. If it was unlikely we would find water, one or two gourds would be taken covered with leaves —banana or plantain leaves for preference—so as to keep the water cool. A canvas water-sack is useful, except that when the sun is very hot the evaporation which takes place is so great that in a few hours a sack will lose half its contents by evaporation, which is disappointing when everybody's tongue is sticking to the roof of the mouth.

People who have not hunted in a country like the Luangwa valley, in North-Eastern Rhodesia, have no conception of what real heat is, added to many miles through thick and often thorny bush and grass. Such work fairly frizzles one up unless in good tramping and physical condition, so the great thing is to dress as lightly as possible and go in bare legs, only wearing socks and light boots or shoes on the feet. I usually wore flat-soled, light brown boots with elk-hide soles with a few bars on them to prevent slipping on dry grass. Rubber is too hot for soles, and a few days of such work cuts it to pieces. The great heat often makes it get sticky, then it dries and cracks readily and soon goes to pieces. Rope-soled shoes in dry weather are fair, but useless if wet, and they also will not stand the strenuous wear and tear, so I advise flat elk-hide light boots for hard wear, although they are not so good in the rainy season, as the leather, being differently cured from ordinary leather, gets spongy and soft. Be sure to get bars put on, for when using such boots I once nearly went over a precipice, as my feet slipped on the dry grass, which was as slippery as ice. I recommend boots (but with light uppers) to shoes, because they will save one's ankles getting knocked about on rocks or stumps, and also present a surface for many thorns which may be struck when moving fast or carelessly.

People who have weak eyes or who feel sun-glare should take tinted eyeglasses. On rivers such as the Zambezi and Luangwa the glare is often painful, and one can also suffer from this in large stretches of light sandy country. I believe that eye strain can accentuate the effects of malaria to such an extent that, when the germ is in the blood, it can be roused to action by the sun-glare in the eyes.

I never believed in putting red cloth inside the shirt as a spine-pad, or in Africa wearing pith helmets, for

I found that a double " Terai " hat was quite sufficient as a protection for the head. What I often did in the hottest weather was to put a bit of wet plantain or banana leaf into the crown of my hat. These leaves are full of moisture and keep damp longer than any other leaves I know, and they certainly help to keep the head cool. If I could not get the leaves, I soaked a handkerchief and put it into my hat, and when it dried used a part of the water I kept as my equal share in rewetting the rag in preference to drinking the few spoonfuls required.

When out with the natives, I always divided the water fairly between all, and used mine for making tea in the small kettle I usually had with me in preference to drinking the tepid and often dirty fluid, which never satisfied me like the tea. I always found that hot tea was more refreshing than water, even when cold enough to be pleasant; and though this may sound paradoxical, it is a fact which others have noticed as well as myself when suffering from great tropical heat.

A most useful and interesting object to carry is a small pocket microscope, and one of its most necessary uses is for finding the ends of thorns which have broken off in the flesh. These are often driven some way in and very difficult to detect and extract with the naked eye. I always carried a small cartridge with permanganate of potash crystals, with which I made an antiseptic fluid to wash deep scratches or wounds on the natives and myself. Men I have known have often got bad veldt sores through leaving cuts or scratches untended, and natives often develop painful ulcers through inattention to wounds; but since I took to using these crystals I never suffered in this way, so it is clearly a case of " a stitch in time saves nine."

It is surprising the wounds which natives can endure without seeming to suffer extremely, for I have often seen a native knock one of his toenails off on a stump or rock, and sit down and proceed to wrap the injured member up with a bit of dirty rag from his cloth. Why they do not die oftener from septic blood-poisoning is a marvel, but they seem more impervious to poisonous germs than are Europeans. Nevertheless, when the thing goes too far they often lose their lives through gangrenous sores; and even when their lives might be saved by an operation, prefer to die than be operated on by a white surgeon.

When in my lonely camps in the bush, I have given them antiseptics to use, and have cured a good many who had not got to the incurable stage. At first they are very suspicious of help, and if a native is too far gone it is often a mistake to interfere, for if he dies his friends will likely say that his death was due to the treatment, which was meant for the best. I do not refer to drugs to be taken internally, of course, for unless one knows something of medicine, it is a mistake to give them anything except the simplest medicines.

Once a native woman brought her child to me when it was writhing in pain—something wrong with its digestive organs. I gave it half of a one-grain tabloid of opium, and she took it away, and came back from her village, which was about a mile away, in an hour or so, and said it was dying. Certainly it looked a serious case, for the child was absolutely still, with a dull look in its eyes, and its breathing was practically stopped. Instead of making further attempts in experiments, I called my cook and told him to hand the woman over to his wife in their hut near, and keep the child quiet. Fortunately, in about two hours, after I had paid several visits to look at the child, I discovered that it was slowly recovering animation, but it had a narrow shave. Later I read somewhere that children could not stand an opiate, and I was glad I had not administered the whole tabloid of a full grain, which would certainly have finished it.

The most amusing thing about this incident was the remark of my cook when I said that I was glad it recovered. He replied : " It was only a girl-baby and of no account ! " In his estimation, had it been a male infant it might have mattered more, as boys were considered more valuable.

As regards cameras, I always preferred Kodaks for films, as they are simple and no dark-room is necessary. I admit that plate cameras do better work, but spools of films are less liable to damage and take quite good pictures. In the heat and damp of the rainy season the films sometimes get spotted ; but as nearly all the game-hunting is done in the dry weather, this is of little account.

I always preferred ordinary field-glasses to the prism glasses so much used nowadays, as the former usually give a larger field of view and better definition. I had a small pair I used to carry in a breast-pocket of my khaki shirt, and they did all that was needed in picking the best head or pair of tusks in a herd. Telescopes were too much bother and took too long to focus for quick work in the bush.

Writing of telescopes reminds me that some people like a telescopic sight on a rifle. Personally I cannot stand them, and besides being bulky and in the way, a bad fall irretrievably spoils them. Peep-sights I also do not like, for the hole gets blocked with dust and a sharp knock may bend them. With a peep-sight (the Lyman is a well-known pattern) the distance between it and the front sight is too great, and as the bead has to be centred in the circle, this takes longer than the open V to get a quick alignment. I like the back-sight to have a fairly shallow, broad-cut V with a fine line in centre, or a cone of ivory or white metal in the middle.

The great thing with a rifle and its sighting is to get accustomed to the use of the weapon and then stick to the pattern. Constant changing is a mistake, as Selous told me after he began to try rifles with different actions and sighting, and I also found that a new thing was by no means necessarily better than an old one.

Most men who hunt big game wish to keep trophies, and they will be undecided whether to keep the head-skins, or masks, as they are often called. Unless a man is in a good enough financial position to house mounted heads and supply the necessary care they require, he would be better to decide against the expense of having his trophies set up. Mounted heads are very bulky, and the hairy skins are subject to the ravages of moths and other insects, so they need to be sprinkled with stuff such as turpentine, which when old has rather an offensive and rank smell. An untended mounted specimen, after a lot of the hair has fallen out, is an unsightly object, and unless the stuffing is done by a really capable taxidermist, the specimen is often a monstrosity to look at.

The horns on a fairly well cleaned skull take up less room, they are little trouble to dust, as there is no hair to catch the dust and encourage moths, and the shields cost a fraction of what the mounting of a skin costs ; so unless a man is in the position to keep mounted trophies properly housed and cared for, he should certainly only retain the horns and skulls of his game.

Skins, when kept in a place exposed to the sun's rays, get bleached and lose their colour, and the constant application of preservatives makes the hair dirty and sticky and they begin to smell offensively.

For a public museum it is necessary, of course, to have set-up specimens for the student and others, but few are able to afford the expense and room necessary for such a hobby.

Trophies, except to those who have shot them, possess little money value unless they are records or heads closely approaching the best, and many a man who has spent hundreds of pounds on the preservation of his specimens lives to regret the money he has paid for the work ; so a young man who is only fairly well off should think twice before he faces the great expense of mounting full specimens or head skins.

As to tents, the most comfortable are those by Edgington called double-roof ridge tents, fitted with a fly, and a two-men load, as they weigh over 100 lb. I always grudged the extra man, and did most of my travel with a single-load " Whymper " tent with the ground-sheet sewn in, but I had a meshed window fitted in the back. This pattern weighs about 40 lb., is 7 × 7 feet in size, and goes into a handy bag for carrying, with poles and ropes and pegs. If it was extremely hot, I used to get a grass shelter put over it, which is shown in one of my photographs. Such a tent of green rotproof canvas will last for several years with hard usage, and I had one which did me for over five years and with which I travelled thousands of miles.

I used an " X " pattern folding-bed, and a table of the same design, but for a chair preferred the ordinary " deck " pattern.

Rifles, cartridges, camp gear, and clothes should be bought at home, but nowadays all food required can be purchased in the townships throughout tropical Africa, and it is a mistake to burden oneself with boxes of provisions. Some years ago it was more necessary when the African stores were deficient, but now everything necessary in the food line can be got in Africa.

I never believed in carrying much liquor, as I found tea the best drink. I have always believed in the strengthening properties of plenty of sugar, as it seems to supply the wastage caused by hard physical exercise.

Regarding health, malarial fever is, of course, the most prevalent complaint. It is impossible to prevent getting it, and few men suffered more from it

HOT WEATHER IN THE PLAINS, NORTH-EASTERN RHODESIA.

than I did in India and Africa. The great strain of a hunter's life and the roughing-it he has to undergo are, of course, incentives, for the whites who have comfortable brick houses like the officials, missionaries, and storekeepers have at least a dry roof over their heads, and medical assistance and luxuries are close at hand, and in the larger townships good European hospitals with capable nurses and attendance.

I underwent many fevers when far in the bush and when living in a tent or leaky mud-hut.

A really bad attack of malaria (or blackwater, its culmination in some cases) produces such weakness and lassitude in its bad stages that one does not care whether one dies or not, although anyone with a spark of pluck will try his best to live as long as he is conscious. The long, dreary nights are the worst time, when everything is quiet except for the drip of the rain through the leaky roof and the sound of the night-prowlers, such as the hyena, which with his vocabulary of eerie noises seems to be singing a dismal dirge enough to inspire one with a premonition of death. Away in the distance, too, will be heard the beating of the native drums in some village where a beer-drink is in progress, and this, like the voice of the hyena, has a melancholy sound for an invalid. Then, as sometimes occurs, the native " boys," being without supervision owing to their master's illness, may decide to take the opportunity of bolting if they think they have a grievance. Once I was left like this when very ill with malaria, and I have not forgotten the hard time I had struggling up to get wood and water to make tea and boil a few eggs. These three " boys " were afterwards punished for their action, but this did not make up for the hardships they made me suffer before I was able to get about again.

Regarding native carriers, it is difficult to say which are the best. The best in North-Eastern Rhodesia are Awemba and Angoni, although Achewa and Achapeta are also quite good. In Nyasaland, Angoni and Yao are probably the best, although I never found the inferior races worse than the others, for it depends on whether they come from a wild district or whether they are the inhabitants of the villages near townships. Civilization does not improve them for rough work in the bush, and amongst them will be fewer men who are good at tracking and bush-lore.

Personally I dislike the native who wears a hat, coat, socks and boots, and he is never half so proficient as the more savage type who only wears a loincloth. The former may be able to sing " Rock of Ages " and read one's private letters, but he cannot spoor and withstand hardships like his wilder brother, and he will probably be for ever complaining and grousing about something.

I always got on well with my carriers, for they got lots of meat, which they love. The white man who can fill their bellies with *nyama* is usually more popular than the man who does not care to hunt game, and he is longer remembered.

After I left the country I got several letters asking me to come back again, as they were hungry for meat and fat, and I have little doubt that over the camp-fires I am not yet forgotten.

I have a great admiration for the fidelity, pluck, and toughness of these men, for I have travelled with them for many thousands of miles through rough bush, and slept out under the stars with them and discussed past and future sport. A good native has a natural politeness to the white man whom he respects, and one of the things I remember, because it so often happened, was how they used to clear a way through rough stuff, and hold branches or grass aside with their hands or spears so that I would not get my eyes and face damaged with springing twigs and obstacles. Then, if there was a hidden hole or rock, the man in front

260

used to smack his leg or side as a sign to look out, for I had taught them not to speak and shout for fear of disturbing game.

If they found honey, they would bring me the nicest and cleanest piece on a slab of bark, and one seldom came to a village in the old days without being offered native beer, which was quite refreshing when one was thirsty. A present of meat was usually given in return, and when fowls and flour were brought to the tent, a few yards of calico, a cup of salt, and some meat if one had shot anything lately.

I fancy, with the increase of travel past the villages near the main routes, this custom is dying down, but many years ago it was the rule, and probably still is in the wilder parts. As the natives become more accustomed to civilized ways they inevitably deteriorate, and it cannot be wondered at, for an influx of low-class whites is the worst thing for raw natives. These whites cheat the natives often, pat them on the back and treat them as familiars, quite forgetting that there is a white prestige to keep up when white deals with black. There is a vast gap between a reserved friendliness and familiarity, and the natives soon spot the difference and act accordingly.

I think I have already written that the great thing is not to break a promise given to a native, for although they do not think as we do on some subjects, they have a great respect for truth in the whites, although they may not practise it between themselves.

The game in Africa is being rapidly diminished [1] in some localities due to the coming of settlers, and it is bound to go unless the Government make adequate reserves for its preservation. I say "adequate," for

[1] Some people (despicably unsportsmanlike) have taken to hunting game in aeroplanes and motor-cars. Both methods demean the ethics of true sport, and should be prevented by the inauguration of the most stringent laws.—AUTHOR.

it is useless making a reserve in a district which is being rapidly opened up, and then expect the colonists to leave the game alone.

First of all, few of them are nature-lovers, and no one can expect a man who is trying to make a living by growing anything to put up with the depredations of heavy animals in his crops. Neither can we expect a rancher to tolerate his cattle or other stock being decimated by carnivorous beasts. I have always been against the poisoning of lions and leopards by farmers ; but not all of them care for hunting, and they look on these animals as the home poultry-farmer looks on the foxes or cats which kill his poultry. Some farmers would prefer following up a lion or leopard or sitting up for them, but these are the exceptions, and the ordinary settler is usually not a "sportsman" in the true sense of the word, or a man keen on hunting.

Game reserves cost money not only to make, but to staff with the requisite number of wardens and rangers. Ordinary fences will not keep out heavy game, but a ditch or *nullah* made on the reserve side of the fence will, as a rule, keep out anything. Elephants, rhinos, buffaloes, and elands would soon smash any fence down ; but if a ditch about 4 feet wide and the same depth was cut on the inside of such a fence, it would very seldom be broken, because heavy game could not step across it. As an extra safeguard the ditch could be filled with strong thorn-branches or tangled barbed wire, which would certainly prevent the egress of game from the reserve.

It is lamentable to think that rare and beautiful animals are on the verge of extinction through the lack of preservation and when there is still time for it to be done. Once gone, such animals can never be replaced, so it seems a scandalous proceeding to refrain from action when there is still time, particularly when so much money is spent on less worthy objects. We are simply trustees for the game, and it is a plain duty that our authorities should do their best to preserve it against extinction and to guard the rare species which are left. What a vast difference there is between a stretch of country inhabited by game and another where not a beast is visible! Of course, certain of the rarer animals live in bush country or in the depth of thick forests, and these, owing to their retiring habits, usually last much longer than the plains game.

I was amused, when in British East Africa (now Kenya Province) in 1911, at some of the white men I saw who went about in stiff riding-breeches and leggings, for on their knees, shoulders, and elbows were bright-coloured patches of leather, evidently to denote that they spent most of their lives crawling about on the veldt after game. The strange thing was that the leather always looked new and unscratched! Then round their waists would be a belt hung with various pouches, and a heavy hunting-knife in a sheath decorated with flashing metal. Usually a glittering wristlet watch was part of the stalking gear, and I wondered how it had escaped breakage.

The real white hunter wears shorts or pants made of khaki as a rule. On his belt may be a "Bushman's Friend" knife, because it is too large to go into a pocket in his pants. His khaki shirt never has leather patches, and neither do his knees and elbows, and he does not go about like a Christmas-tree.

The pot-house loafer at the bar of some frontier store who brags about the game he has shot is not the real thing, for he is usually a man who talks little except to others he knows as kindred spirits. Then he leaves blanks, which he knows will be properly filled by his listener who knows the game.

It is pleasant to look back to those happy days in the wilds, but impossible to help deploring the changed conditions, what with railways, motors, and ever-increasing settlement. Most people think that a complicated civilization is the best thing for such countries, but I am amongst the few who think that the old times were much better.

There is a poem by W. H. Ogilvie about the " Brumbies," the wild horses of Australia, from which I quote three verses, as they sound so true. I would like to give the whole poem, but do not think it fair to the author to quote him *in extenso*.

The three verses run :

> " For I know there are those in the world to-day
> Who are just such rebels at heart as they,
> Running uncurbed in the ' Brumby ' way.

> " Men who have never been bridle-bound,
> Bitted, or girthed to the servile round,
> Men of the wide-world's stamping-ground ;

> " Who have wheeled to the Dawn, have kept lone guard,
> When the soft bush nights crept golden-starred,
> Rebels that never the world shall yard."

INDEX

Accident, a rifle, 59
Aden, loss of P. & O. steam-
ship, 15
Africa, visit to British East, 203
— seasons in Central, 72
African Lakes Corporation, Ltd.,
51
Allport, fine elephant shot by, 141
Angoni, raids by, 86
Animals, strength in necks of, 208
Anthills, stalking game behind,
197
Ants, 65
Arab, a white man and an, 225
Asenga, 121

Baboons, 119, 215, 216
Baby, a drugged, 255
Baker, Sir Samuel, books by, 13
Balfour, Lord, quotation from book
by, 19
Barclay, Dr., 232
Barnshaw, record bushbuck found
by, 73
Barry, escape from tiger of, 245,
246
Bean, itch caused by wild, 75
Bees, fowls attacked by, 69
Bird, Mr., strange death of, 230
Bishop, Indian river-trip of a, 23,
24
Blantyre, arrive at, 59
Bradford, tea-planter named, 40
British Central Africa Co., 51
Brown, H. K., dogs kept by, 177
— Mr. Harry, 175
Bua River, 90, 91, 201
Buffalo, charging, 161, 163
— horn growth of, 161
— horns of, 85
— long chase after a bull, 159
— trip after Indian, 34, 39
Buffaloes, shoot four, 159, 160
— tsetse-flies and, 162
Bullets, actions of, 200

Bush, a night walk in the African,
193
Bushbuck, 207, 208
— a struggle with a ram, 208, 209
Bushpigs, leopard treed by, 213

Cachar, go to a tea-garden in, 15
Cameron, Catherine, grave of, 55
Carnivora, how game is killed by
the, 94
Cherra-Punji (India), heavy rain-
fall at, 32
" Chiggers " (burrowing fleas), 64
Chikala (Central Africa), 75
Chinde (East Africa), 51, 166, 169
— a strong smell in, 169, 170
" Chiperi," hill named, 198
Chiromo, marsh of, 206
Chiuta, Lake, 75
Cholera, deaths in India from, 32
Codrington, Mr., 88, 115
Coulmell (France), 241
Country, game-shooting in bad,
125
Crocodile, narrow escape from a,
90
— Selous' account of a rhino killed
by a, 221
Crocodiles, 219
— natives killed by, 220
Crood, hunter named, 131
Crozier, leopard shot in fowl-house
by, 41
Cumming, Gordon, book by, 13

Dedza (Nyasaland), 84, 85, 139
Digby, Captain Wingfield-, 63, 65,
66, 68
" Distressed British subjects,"
229
Dobson, D. D., rhino kills, 231
Dogs, mad, 80, 81
Dunbar, Captain J. Brander, 70,
76, 84, 231
Dust, whirls of, 110

265

INDEX